11-18-02

To Mrs. Joyce Hereford:

The writing of <u>Confronting the Odds</u> gave me the priceless opportunity to reconstruct African-American history, especially as it relates to entrepreneurship.

I do hope that you enjoy reading this book.

Sincerely yours,

Denie House-Swemekun

Confronting the Odds

African American Entrepreneurship
in Cleveland, Ohio

Bessie House-Soremekun

The Kent State University Press ▣ Kent & London

© 2002 by The Kent State University Press, Kent, Ohio 44242
All rights reserved
Library of Congress Catalog Card Number 2002003581
ISBN 0-87338-734-1
Manufactured in the United States of America

06   05   04   03   02   5   4   3   2   1

Library of Congress Cataloging-in-Publication Data
House-Soremekun, Bessie
Confronting the odds : African American entrepreneurship in Cleveland, Ohio /
Bessie House-Soremekun; foreword by Rev. Jesse L. Jackson, Sr.
p.   cm.
ISBN 0-87338-734-1
1. African American business enterprises—Ohio—Cleveland—History.
2. African American businesspeople—Ohio—Cleveland—History.
3. African Americans—Ohio—Cleveland—Economic conditions.
4. Entrepreneurship—Ohio—Cleveland—History.
I. Title.
HD2358.5.U62 C54 2002
338'.04'08996073077132—dc21
2002003581

British Library Cataloging-in-Publication data are available.

This book is dedicated to the most important women in my life: my mother, Jo Frances House; my grandmother, the late Bessie Annie Fannings, for whom I am named; my aunt, the late Willie James Chappell; my daughter, Adrianna Midamba; and my sister, Elois Jackson Meadows. Thanks for your unswerving support through the years.

Contents

Foreword

by Reverend Jesse L. Jackson, Sr.
President and Founder of the Rainbow/PUSH Coalition

While he is most often remembered for his "I Have a Dream" speech, Dr. Martin Luther King, Jr., was no idle dreamer. He was a practical man of action, focused on changing social, political, and economic policy in America for those who had been disenfranchised, a leader who understood that change required challenging the structure of entrenched arrangements. Dr. King was a visionary. Toward the end of his life, Dr. King became more and more convinced that the struggle for economic justice was central to the civil rights movement. He viewed the fundamental gap between America's potential and its reality as a resource gap (including an investment gap, a capital gap, a trade gap, and a historical legal gap) rather than just a race gap. The justice and prosperity that America seeks requires that these gaps be closed and that breaches are healed. Cultural blinders that limit growth, development, and market expansion must be removed.

Dr. King's last assignment to me was to expand Operation Breadbasket to Chicago, Illinois, and other northern cities such as Cleveland, Ohio. The mission of Breadbasket was to open up American business to the talent and potential offered by African Americans. Assisting Dr. King, and pivotal to the success of Breadbasket in Cleveland, was Dr. Otis Moss, Jr. We challenged the exclusion of African Americans from business and worked to open up franchises, loans, and investment for African American entrepreneurs.

In the tradition of Operation Breadbasket and in honor of Dr. King's legacy, the Rainbow/PUSH Coalition launched the Wall Street Project in 1997 to encourage Corporate America, and particularly the financial services industry, to embrace inclusion as a means of growth and to shine the spotlight on the fundamental missing ingredient in the formula for black business success—access to capital.

If I were to compose a four-movement *Freedom Symphony,* the first movement would be from slavery to emancipation—ending a traumatic period of trade in this country. The second movement would be the public accommodation laws and the struggle to end Jim Crow. The third movement would be the 1964 Voting Rights Act and the political empowerment that accompanied it, so well illustrated by the election of Carl Stokes to the Ohio legislature and, in 1967, to the mayoral office in Cleveland. The fourth and current movement—the most mature stage of our struggle—would be the democratization of capital.

I am convinced that the emergence of strong, vibrant, and competitive businesses owned and managed by people of color makes us all stronger. I am convinced that diversity in corporate America makes all of America better. I am convinced that when urban America is viewed as an emerging market with great economic potential, America prospers.

Yet, because of our cultural blinders, that which we might see were it located overseas is too often disregarded when it is located across the railroad tracks. Such blinders cause restraint of trade, and restraint of trade is the greatest sin against a growing economy.

Fly over the plains of Ohio today and you will observe clear demarcations of land, where some is green and some is scorched and brown. Some of it is irrigated, and some of it lacks the water to make rich soil grow. Good farmers know irrigation networks must be broad enough to ensure that water reaches the entire land. In modern economies, capital is to business growth what water is to fields. When we spread capital around, we expand the market and everyone benefits.

Take this concept a step further. Imagine two seeds of equal strength are planted and a wall is placed between them. One grows taller—not because of a defect in the seed that keeps it short or a special gene that makes the other seed grow tall. It's photosynthesis. Likewise in business, if we share the light, we all grow stronger and more productive. Inclusion is the key to growth.

There are great dangers in store if we are not inclusive. The danger to the continued economic success of our great country is ever-widening gaps in income and wealth. Increasingly, information is being released that people of color pay more for transportation, more for food, more for housing, more for mortgages and other loans. Indeed, the result of this is that more Americans live a substandard life, subjected to predatory practices on one hand and denied access to capital, industry, and technology on the other. This is the equivalent to a person having poor blood circulation and being denied a blood transfusion. Capital is to the economy as blood is to the human body. For either to be healthy, they must circulate and flow throughout the whole system. Just as a sick unhealthy body is a societal problem and not just an individual one, the suffering of business owners of color affect the entire economy not just an isolated few.

African Americans and Hispanics represent over $1 trillion in the consumer market. And that number continues to grow. In less than twenty years, these groups will constitute the majority population. Can America really compete using less than 30 percent of its talent (the percentage whites males will comprise of the population by 2020)? For the American economy to continue to grow,

African Americans, Hispanics, Asians, and women must continue to be educated and trained. They then must be afforded the opportunity to put their education and training to use. And Corporate America must increasingly view them not only as consumers but as trading partners.

For these reasons, *Confronting the Odds: African American Entrepreneurship in Cleveland, Ohio,* by Dr. Bessie House-Soremekun, is important as a historical background and as a policy manual for anyone seriously interested in African American business development and the critical role it must play not only in the American economy but in the future of America as a land where equal opportunity is real in theory and in practice. This study, while focused on Cleveland, Ohio, is a microcosm, offering insight into the challenges as well as potential remedies that face African American entrepreneurs nationally.

I often use the analogy involving baseball and business. In 1947, Jackie Robinson racially integrated Major League Baseball and was a subject of much discussion and debate. The uncomfortable feeling most of white America felt when Jackie first broke the baseball barrier is similar to the current phenomenon of Tiger Woods in golf and the Williams sisters in tennis. But just as America didn't know how good baseball, golf, or tennis could be until everyone could play, we won't know how good American business can be until everyone one can play.

Note

by George C. Fraser
CEO, Success Source, Unlimited
CEO, FraserNet

Confronting the Odds is not only a history lesson but a bold, in-your-face, multi-level system of strategies and tactics African Americans must engage in to begin the process of closing the income and wealth gap between blacks and whites in America. For those of you who have read my books or heard me speak, you know that Dr. Bessie House-Soremekun and I share a common vision and have reached many of the same conclusions in spite of the fact that my life experiences and perspectives have dictated using a slightly different approach and path. Nonetheless, both our paths provide black people with "options and choices"; they are compatible, and either will get you where you must go.

Dr. House-Soremekun has brought to light the African American history of business ownership in Cleveland, Ohio, and the impact it has had on the community. Cleveland serves as a great model (and that's not just because I operate my business here). Within the last four decades, Cleveland has played an important role in providing several examples of black empowerment. In doing so, the city has captured nationwide attention. Through firsthand accounts from black proprietors in Cleveland, Dr. House-Soremekun provides an analytic comparison and presents an accurate historic view. She gives the reader a peek into life as an entrepreneur, including the ugliness and the rewards. I must say that Dr. House-Soremekun's analysis of Cleveland's economy via the black community is both informative and inspiring. Her research illuminates the African American's continued rise in economic empowerment, the opportunities, and the plans that are now in action.

From my perspective there is no question that both history and new opportunities are moving people of African descent toward greatness once again, but we must meet opportunity halfway. As we gain greater knowledge of ourselves—of who we really are beyond our 350 years of oppression—there is no denying we will rise again. Our rise will take time and hard work . . . but it always has.

In my opinion, for each of us economic power is now our most important moral assignment and imperative, because as the individual grows stronger the community grows stronger; the stronger our community, the stronger the nation. I realize that one person alone cannot solve all of our economic ills, but if each of us succeeds personally, together, through group unity, we can change our condition in the twenty-first century. No one has ever accused me of being a pessimist!

When the goal is economic power, it makes sense to concentrate on jobs and businesses in which our best talent and most money are already invested. Which area you choose—and how you choose to work within it—depends on your personal strengths and interests. Let me suggest what I believe are some of the most promising areas of opportunities for black Americans today.

Education. This is $665 billion industry that needs more black educators and entrepreneurs. It also needs new and better schools as well as more preschool and after-school programs. Additionally, teaching our children how to apply technology to education is critical. All of this will develop significantly in the next twenty to thirty years thus making our schools more competitive with each other and more responsive to our long-term needs. In Milwaukee, Chicago, and Detroit blacks have started nearly one hundred charter and private schools for black children. These schools employ hundreds of black educators, support staff, and suppliers in addition to providing urban kids with a better education. Everybody wins!

Finance and banking. John Rogers, owner of Ariel Capital Management, a $2 billion black-owned fund management firm in Chicago, is helping blacks invest and multiply their money through selling mutual funds and other stock portfolios. Cleveland-based investment banker Eric Small recently created a mutual fund product of successful black businesses traded on the stock exchange. Other black bankers, financial advisers, insurance brokers, and stockbrokers are employing similar methods to help blacks more wisely invest, shed debt, and multiply their money. I believe blacks know the banking world; it's now time to expand into the late Reginald Lewis's world of high "corporate" finance.

Small business development. At nearly $600 billion in 2002, according to an economic forecast study from the University of Georgia, black buying power in America ranks among the world's richest economies, larger than the economy of the entire continent of Africa; yet less than 5 percent of this wealth recycles in our own communities. A recent survey of 125th Street in Harlem showed that other cultural groups owned 95 percent of all businesses, but blacks were still the customers.

There is tremendous opportunity, as well as a great need, to start and own our neighborhood businesses, both urban and suburban, retail and manufacturing. Where are the black theme restaurants? There are over 18,000 pizza stores in America producing $22 billion a year in revenue and employing more than one million people. Billions more are being made in Chinese and Japanese restaurants and Jewish delis. The opportunity to use our culture and business savvy to address the billion-dollar potential of theme restaurants and fast foods is just waiting for us.

Technology. The information superhighway and digital technology are providing new economic opportunities and distribution outlets for our products and services. This is a perfect arena in which to expand our tremendous creativity by developing new software and moving into positions where we can influence and control the content of the Internet and World Wide Web. "Black Planet," "Black Voices," and many other Afro-centric web sites and online services are good examples. Closing the home computer gap between blacks and whites is another major opportunity.

Publishing/Media. Only in the last five years has publishing discovered the financial power of black writers and reading audiences. Before that, black writers, particularly those who wrote nonfiction, were rarely published, based on three myths: black people don't read books; black people don't buy books; and white people don't buy books by black writers about black life. After *Emerge, Vibe,* and *Heart and Soul* magazines were successfully launched and books like *Waiting to Exhale, Jazz,* and *Possessing the Secret of Joy* hit the top ten on the *New York Times* best-seller list, the industry woke up. Today there are huge new opportunities in all publishing and media endeavors.

Urban redevelopment. Real estate and housing are prime business opportunities for African Americans. Land is limited, and survey after survey shows that proximity to downtown America is becoming desirable again for both housing and business. Technology and home-based businesses will increase the value of real estate. According to the Washington, D.C.–based Hamilton Securities Group, $2.6 trillion in multifamily and commercial real estate equity and debt will change hands over the next decade. Retro migration to the city is in. These are our neighborhoods, and we should be the prime developers and contractors of the regentrification of decaying urban America.

Health care. This very broad category is expected to increase twice as fast as the rest of the economy. An aging population (strengthened by medical advancements) is driving the need for health-related occupations. As long as insurance companies and hospitals mandate shorter hospital stays for patients, the demand for healthcare services and those who can provide them will continue to increase.

Once more, African Americans are ideally suited to meet these needs. All trends in health care point toward prevention, wellness, and holistic therapies that integrate mental, physical, and emotional well-being—the hallmarks of our healing traditions. Just as important, black doctors, dentists, scientists, researchers, and technologists will be in huge demand. The needs are great, the opportunities abundant.

Sports. By any economic standard, black sports stars are earning top money, but clearly we can't all be Michael Jordans. The opportunities in sports are not all "in the paint." Former NBA star Isaiah Thomas has for years been the only basketball player to invest his money in a team (the Toronto Raptors). That's just the beginning of a change, as a few big-money players are getting together in ways that can really pay off. Football legend Walter Payton, for example, led an investment group to purchase majority ownership in an expansion NFL franchise. With such ventures you can expect the front-office staff to become more inclusive of blacks, women, and other races and cultures; the possibilities all the way down the ladder are tremendous.

Entertainment. Like the sports industry, show business is another area in which we have a high profile and also spend a lot of time and money. But when it comes to controlling the product, we're just beginning to get our feet wet. Certain segments (and their offshoots) of the entertainment industry—specifically, film, television, and music—are becoming arenas of spectacular growth for African Americans looking to get involved behind the scenes in the many divisions and departments within this multi-billion-dollar industry.

Global commerce. Technology and instant global telecommunications are creating discontent among the 2.5 billion people still living under socialism and communism. People all over the world can now witness the "spoils" of democratic capitalism at work; hundreds of millions will want the myriad of choices enjoyed by the great democracies of the world. Opportunities to provide these products and services will be opening up all over Africa, Asia, Latin America, Eastern Europe, and the Caribbean.

These are the opportunities in the making; there are numerous examples and statistics to support them. But let's not just sit back and say, "Well, that's great, its good things are opening up." No. The idea is to get involved, to act, and to do. The fact that you are reading this book shows that you're one step ahead of the crowd already—you're curious, you want to be a contributor, someone who at the end of the day has made a difference for yourself and your community. Our history allows us no other course.

Our esteemed elder Dr. John Henrik Clarke reminded us repeatedly that "the role of history in the final analysis is to tell a people where they have been, where they are and what they are. Most importantly, the role of history is to tell a people where they must still go and what they must still be." For me another purpose of history is to use it as a guidepost for us to "do for self." Dr. House-Soremekun's *Confronting the Odds* shows us how!

Note

by George Forbes
Partner, Forbes, Fields and Associates Co., L.P.A.
President, Cleveland Chapter of NAACP

African Americans have a rich history in Cleveland's political and economic fabric. It is a history that embodies both triumph and failure. While many gains have been made, the road is long to achieving equality in both the political and economic arenas; yet the journey for such equality continues despite the road blocks to progress.

African American economic development in Cleveland does not exist in a vacuum. Rather, such development goes hand in hand with the political gains we have made. It was a historical landmark when Carl Stokes was elected mayor of Cleveland in 1967, the first African American mayor elected in a major city. Such election in Cleveland and, at various other times, the elections of African American mayors in virtually every important city, including New York, Los Angeles, Chicago, Detroit, Atlanta, and others, have provided opportunities for African Americans to become involved in the decision-making process that determines the fabric and quality of life in those communities. With that political involvement comes the opportunity to direct and/or to participate in the economic and business choices that are ultimately made.

I am a witness, firsthand, to this evolution. When I was first elected to Cleveland City Council in 1963, the power structure in Cleveland (and thus the political process) was devoid of African American decision makers. Once Carl Stokes was elected, this all changed. African Americans were appointed to key policy and decision-making positions in the city administration.

A metamorphosis occurred in the legislative branch of government as well. Louis Stokes became the first African American congressman from Ohio to serve in the United States House of Representatives. I became president of Cleveland City Council. In such a position, I was able to supervise and review all legislation that was considered in the City of Cleveland. As such, I was able to ensure minority participation in both the decision-making process and in the receipt of economic benefits that resulted from the projects that were undertaken at the time.

The African American community must strive to ensure that the political and economic gains achieved since the 1960s are not lost in the days and years ahead. Moreover, our community must recognize that the playing field has not yet been equalized.

The African American dream—and right—of equal participation in political and economic processes is under attack as never before in this modern era. Affirmative action initiatives, including minority set-aside programs, are under siege by the courts throughout this country. Indeed, the danger is real that our community will lose the hard-won successes we have obtained in the last thirty-plus years.

The African American community must reposition itself to continue to make gains as aspects of political and economic life change in Cleveland and across the country as a whole. Manufacturing jobs, many of which paid well without requiring much formal education, are disappearing, never to return. An additional danger exists as the country becomes more conservative following the September 11, 2001, attacks. Equality and other social issues are now taking a back seat to security and other national issues.

The potential exists for African American businesses in Cleveland to succeed as never before. African Americans own, manage, and provide employment opportunities in all areas of the economy, including real estate, construction, legal, retail, and manufacturing. Our community is also well represented by members in Cleveland's City Council (whose president is also African American), the Board of County Commissioners, and the Cleveland School District (whose CEO is African American).

African American entrepreneurship in Cleveland is not a utopia. It will continue to experience bumps in the road. Some of our businesses will fail, while others will succeed. We must, however, ensure that the future provides us equal opportunity to succeed or to fail because of the business skills we have and not as a result of the business opportunities we lack due to the color of our skin.

Acknowledgments

I would like to take this opportunity to thank a number of key individuals and organizations for their support during the preparation of this book. First, I would like to thank the Ohio Board of Regents for awarding me a two-year challenge grant of $64,000 for 1997–99 which provided the funding to perform the study. This economic support enabled me to go the step beyond to expand the parameters of the complex debate on economic development policy and its implications for African American entrepreneurs.

I am equally indebted to the Ohio Urban University Program for a grant award of $7,079 in 1995 that provided research funding for me to perform the initial pilot study that provided the cornerstone for the findings discussed in this study. In particular, I am grateful to Jim Tinnin, director of the Center for Public Administration and Public Policy at Kent State University (KSU) and Melinda Holmes, assistant director of the center, for their kind words of encouragement. Their faith in me and in this project have been truly meaningful.

I am especially grateful to the Cleveland Foundation for a three-year grant award of $153,358 for 1999–2002 that enabled me to implement the findings of this study by providing technical training and workshops to African American entrepreneurs in the greater Cleveland metropolitan area. In particular, I wish to thank Steven Minter, president/executive director of the Cleveland Foundation, members of their board of trustees, and Steve Rowan, former program officer for economic development. I also received a $2,500 grant from the Ohio Employee Ownership Faculty Associate Program in 1999 to perform research on broadening capital ownership in the black community as well as another grant from the Ohio Urban University Program for $7,493 in summer 2000 to perform more research on the impact of crime on black business success. Last, I received a grant award in summer 2000 from the Kent State University Research Council for $2,500. Altogether, I have received six grant awards for a total of $236,930 for research and technical training of African American entrepreneurs.

I want to thank John Hubbell, Director Emeritus of The Kent State University Press, who took a special interest in this project and worked closely with me to finalize the manuscript. I also appreciate the help of Joanna Hildebrand Craig, and the rest of the editorial staff at the Kent State University Press, and the reviewers of this manuscript. Their comments were insightful and greatly enhanced my work.

I would like to acknowledge the comments and suggestions of Don Williams (department of economics, KSU) and Ilan Alon, as well as John Logue and Caroline Tolbert (department of political science), on ways to strengthen this work. All these individuals gave of their time willingly in order to advance the status of this research project. Dr. Williams and Dr. Tolbert provided detailed comments and suggestions on ways to strengthen this manuscript, and I am deeply appreciative of their efforts. Dr. Alon took an ardent interest in my research proposal and volunteered a great deal of time to assist me with the statistical tests and analyses on the data from my pilot study. I also acknowledge assistance from historian Felix K. Ekechi and from David Belasco, who served as a statistical consultant on this project. I also want to thank my dear friend, Angela Neal-Barnett for her constant words of support.

I am equally grateful to Joe Danks, professor and dean of the college of arts and sciences at Kent State University, and Byron Lander, former chair of the Kent State political science department, under whose tenure I began my initial research on this subject. Dr. Lander was excited and energized about the potential of this project not only in terms of the important issues I was addressing and anticipated outcomes of the analysis, but also, more fundamentally, in terms of my ability to attract other extramural funding opportunities. I wish also to thank our current political science chair, Thomas Hensley, for his support.

I wish to thank my typists, Tanya Rogers, Judy Smith, and Madeleine Thomas, as well as my seven research assistants, Heidi Eichhorn, Keita Said, Kerry Macomber, Arie Goodman, Irene Barnett, Carolina Rubiano, and Neeraj Singhal, for their diligence on this project. I am also grateful to Julie Rice and Matthew Rollins for drawing the maps of Cleveland used in this work.

Some of the most important individuals involved in this research endeavor were, without a doubt, the African American business owners themselves who provided the primary data for this study. Without them, the project would not have been possible. I am also thankful for information provided by the following entrepreneurs for the biographical sketches in this book. They include George Fraser, businessman and author; Robert P. Madison, CEO of Robert P. Madison International; Leroy Ozanne, founder and CEO of Ozanne Construction Company; Dr. Oscar Saffold, CEO of Metropolitan Dermatology, Incorporated; Deborah Thigpen Waller, president of Thigpen and ADsociates, Incorporated; Brian Hall, CEO of Industrial Transport, Incorporated; and Shelton L. Moore, partner, The Nelson Group. They were willing participants, and I learned a great deal from them; I hope my work has also been of use to them. A special word of thanks goes to the following individuals who allowed me to interview them for this study. They include George Forbes, president of the Cleveland branch of the NAACP; Byron Mason, formerly affiliated with the Urban League of Greater Cleveland; Carol Hoover, former president of the Greater Cleveland Growth Association; Richard Andrews, former executive director of the Phillis Wheatley Association and of the Cleveland Business League; Shelley Shockley, former showtime editor of the *Call and Post Newspaper;* Ralph Johnson, executive, The Turner Corporation; John Bustamante, cofounder of First Bank and Trust, and the Honorable Judge George W. White, founder of First Club of Cleveland, Incorporated and president/director of the Cleveland Browns Foundation.

I am indebted to the Western Reserve Historical Society for allowing me to perform research on African American entrepreneurship during the earlier periods in Cleveland's history and to use photographs from the Allen E. Cole Photograph Collection. I wish to thank Samuel Black, former associate curator for African American History at the Western Reserve Historical Society, for allowing me to interview him for my study, and for assisting me with the selection of photographs for use in the book. These photographs have greatly enhanced the narrative presented in this study. I am particularly grateful for the opportunity to perform research in the African American Archives microfilm collection on Garrett Augustus Morgan and Charles Chesnutt.

My beautiful daughter, Adrianna Midamba, has continuously supported my activities throughout this project. Adrianna is in the ninth grade and was very cooperative on the numerous occasions when I had to cut short our story time together in order to get back to my computer. My dear mother, Jo Frances House, whom I love so dearly, has always been my friend and an anchor to me throughout life's journey. No matter what the situation has been, she has always encouraged me to be diligent and to work hard to achieve my career goals and aspirations. For this, I will always be grateful. I am thankful for the encouragement and support of my grandmother, the late Bessie Annie Fannings and my father, the late William Penn House Sr., who were great role models for me through the years. My brothers, William Penn House Jr. and Samuel House, and my sister, Elois Jackson Meadows, have consistently uttered uplifting words of encouragement. I would also like to thank my dear husband and soulmate, Maurice A. E. Soremekun, who occupies a very important space in my heart. In spite of his busy obstetrician/gynecologist's schedule, he has constantly encouraged me to be disciplined in each endeavor in which I participate, and he has become a dear and faithful friend.

Introduction

Over the past few decades, a growing number of academicians and public policy analysts have focused critical attention on the important role of African American businesses in economic development. Consequently, an important body of literature is now available on this subject.[1] While analyzing economic development from a variety of perspectives, many writers seem to agree that economic empowerment is one of the most critical problems facing the African American community today.[2]

Many studies of African American entrepreneurship have focused on economic development at the national level; few have examined this phenomenon at the local level.[3] This study complements the existing literature by providing an in-depth examination of African American businesses in Cleveland, Ohio, and its eastern suburbs. Cleveland was selected as the site of the study because it is a large urban center with a sizeable African American population, and hence it provided a good environment in which to examine some of the major issues selected for analysis.[4] In this study, African American entrepreneurship is analyzed in the nineteenth, twentieth, and twenty-first centuries, with emphasis on the contemporary period (1960–2002). The contemporary period is important because it includes the civil rights and post–civil rights periods, which were important in expanding the political and economic opportunities available to African Americans. It was also during this period that most of the businesses in this study were established. A critical question then becomes, to what extent have African Americans been able to use their expanded political opportunities to enhance their own economic well-being?

This book adopts the definition of small businesses that was formulated by the Small Business Administration (SBA). According to Section 3(a) of the Small Business Administration Act, "A small-business concern . . . shall be deemed to be one which is independently owned and operated and which is not dominant in its field of operation."[5] Small businesses are further distinguished in this study as those in which the owners utilized fairly small amounts of capital (usually less than ten thousand dollars) to start their enterprises; employed fewer than five hundred workers; and earned fairly moderate rates of profit. Although the entrepreneurs in the study reported a broad range of profitability, 68 percent earned less than one hundred thousand dollars per year. Of this group, about half earned less than forty thousand dollars. Nonetheless, small businesses continue to be an engine of economic growth. According to Timothy Bates, "A growing body of evidence suggests that in recent years the small business sector has yielded the bulk of all new jobs. The highly publicized research of economist David Birch proclaims that firms employing fewer than 20 workers 'have created about 88 percent of all net new jobs nationwide in the 1980s.' More credible studies have pegged the small business share of all new jobs at 51 to 56 percent."[6] Small businesses possess a tremendous amount of potential to expand and grow if the owners have access to appropriate business training and technical assistance. Most large black businesses in the United States today started out small because few blacks had the benefit of inherited wealth or access to loans and other sources of capital. This study seeks to answer four major questions: How successful are African American entrepreneurs? What are the predictors of success? What unique problems are faced by African American entrepreneurs? What role does gender play in the economic equation?

This study places African American entrepreneurs at the center of the analysis. Although my assistants and I interviewed some business owners over the phone, I also interviewed some of the owners in their actual business enterprises. This enabled me to make my research "user-friendly" in the African American community. As I have stated elsewhere, "The role of an academician at a university ultimately is to produce and disseminate knowledge which can be directed at real world problems."[7]

Although the main focus of this study is African American entrepreneurs, white entrepreneurs were also interviewed in order to more clearly understand racial differences between the samples. Hence, over the duration of this research project, I have visited businesses in the inner city, the eastern suburbs, and the corporate area of downtown Cleveland. I have seen the types of business enterprises in operation, the business neighborhoods, the level of economic development in various communities, the employees of black-owned firms, and sometimes, their customers. The entrepreneurs became more than mere statistics. I also interviewed some customers and employees in addition to entrepreneurs who attended my workshops and seminars. I was able to develop a significant data base on the characteristics and economic performance of the entrepreneurs. In the narrative portion of this work, special effort was made to replicate the language of the entrepreneurs.

This study includes a diverse group of African American– and white-owned businesses that are subsumed under the following categories: manufacturing, services, construction, and retail/trade. Businesses that were not included in these categories were placed in an "unclassified" group and included firms in the areas of real estate, distribution, and promotion (i.e., marketing and finance). Numerous types of businesses were included under the categories mentioned above, and a few of the entrepreneurs operated franchises that are linked to national chains.

This work is based on original field research. I developed my own research design, methodology, and questionnaire. Thus, the study not only presents quality data that provides detailed information on the business organizations themselves, it also includes pertinent information on the businesses' market area. Additionally, the study describes the social capital of the neighborhoods where the businesses are located, and information on the individual characteristics of the business owners.

I used a variety of research methods to collect data for the study. This included using the historical method as well as collecting primary data on contemporary entrepreneurs. To collect the historical data, I conducted research at the Western Reserve Historical Society in Cleveland and had the opportunity to interview Samuel Black, who is the former associate curator of the African American Archives. This study is also illustrated with numerous photographs that depict African American business enterprises in the nineteenth and twentieth centuries.

While each of the entrepreneurs in the study completed a detailed questionnaire, a few were selected for more in-depth interviews. This group included those who had both successful and unsuccessful business enterprises. I am especially grateful that entrepreneurs who had previous businesses that did not succeed shared their personal experiences with me. Their inclusion in this study greatly enhanced the quality of this work and helped me understand why some businesses succeed, while others do not. In some cases, these interview sessions lasted for several hours. These in-depth interviews afforded me the priceless opportunity to develop meaningful narratives based on the life experiences of the entrepreneurs. I found these sessions to be particularly rewarding, uniformly rich, and very informative.

While each individual business owner is different and should be examined on a case-by-case basis, it is possible to generalize commonalities among both categories of entrepreneurs (i.e., successful and failed). Although the failure rate for businesses in the United States is high, particularly during the first few years of operation, it is extremely high for African American entrepreneurs. National data indicates that only 69 percent of black-owned businesses in operation in 1992 were still in operation in 1996. Almost one-third failed within a four-year period. More recent information should be available when the 2000 census is finalized and statistical information is released.[8] Some unsuccessful entrepreneurs simply disappear from sight and never venture into the world of self-employment again. In other cases, the business owner may try again. Several successful entrepreneurs in this study previously had unsuccessful business experiences.

Black economic development has been affected both by cycles of economic growth and periods of fiscal decline at the national, state, and local levels. It would, indeed, be impossible to examine African American entrepreneurship without paying attention to these broader issues. The findings of this study, therefore, will be useful to academicians, public policy analysts, minority and female entrepreneurs, newly emerging and future entrepreneurs, minority institutions, financial lending institutions, community development organizations, and members of the general public. They will also be useful to politicians who develop and implement public policy in large urban environments.

Ownership and development of economic resources are seen as critical to providing economic empowerment for African Americans. In recent years, the number of small businesses in the United States has increased tremendously, and African American businesses have accounted for a significant portion of this growth.[9] There is an increasing sense of urgency on the part of African Americans to master the "art of entrepreneurship." They want to do it well. In 1969, there were only about 163,000 African American businesses in the United States, whereas by 1977, this number had increased to 231,203. By 1982, there were 339,239 African American enterprises.[10]

The greatest degree of growth occurred in the retail/trade and service industries as states such as Utah, Idaho, North Dakota, Alaska, and Maine experienced the largest proportional growth in the number of black-owned businesses.[11] About 424,165 black-owned firms were in operation in the United States by 1987. Between 1987 and 1992, this number had increased by 46.4 percent to 620,912. According to 1990 census data, California had the largest number of black-owned firms with 68,968, while New York ranked second with 51,312. There are approximately 26,970 African American businesses in the state of Ohio, of which about 3,474 are located in Cleveland.[12] When the eastern suburban communities are included, the figures increase to 6,987.[13]

According to the 1997 economic census, black-owned businesses were represented nationally in the major industry divisions in the following way: 7 percent were in construction; 1 percent in manufacturing; 9 percent in transportation, communications, and utilities; 3 percent in wholesale trade; 11 percent in retail/trade; 5 percent in finance, insurance, and real estate; 53 percent in services; 12 percent in industries that were not classified, and 2 percent in agricultural services, forestry, fishing, and mining.[14]

African American businesses are important because they are a critical component of national, state, and local economic development strategies that generally are aimed at facilitating greater self-reliance, employment opportunities, and capital expansion. A number of studies have demonstrated that black-owned businesses continue to be a critical source of employment. They are also vital actors in the creation of wealth and economic opportunities. In recent years, the public has become aware of the tremendous unrealized potential of the black-owned business sector.[15]

There is an inescapable symbiotic relationship between politics and economics. In some cases, political and economic activities at the national level mirror actions taken at the local level. Nationally, the civil rights movement, which started in the 1950s and continued into the 1960s, marked a time of tremendous change that affected every sphere of American society. Americans were forced to acknowledge the interrelationship between political activism and economic results.[16] As Lucius J. Barker and his colleagues have argued, "The century-long struggle for political access was based upon the premise that unfettered political participation would lead to social and economic equality. . . . Economic empowerment was the focal point of black political activity. Black politics during this period which is commonly referred to as the era of Black power, was conditioned by both nationalist and integrationist sentiments. Nationalist ideas were employed to lobby for public policies designed to help create a black entrepreneurial class and exhort black consumers to support black businesses. Integrationism was used to support the assimilation of black entrepreneurs into the American corporate elite."[17] The famous Supreme Court ruling in *Brown v. the Board of Education* in 1954 successfully decimated the foundation of the "separate versus equal principle" and ultimately served as an important catalyst for change during the civil rights period. The Civil Rights Act of 1964 and the Voting Rights Act of 1965 are particularly noteworthy.[18]

This book is organized into eight major chapters. Chapter 1 provides a brief overview of African American entrepreneurship at the national level. Chapter 2 provides an analysis of the development of the city of Cleveland and the African American community, with particular emphasis on black business development from 1795–1895. Chapter 3 examines black business development in Cleveland from 1895–1960. Chapter 4 shifts the focus to the modern period, 1960–2002, to analyze black economic and political development. Here, I examine numerous factors that influenced the contemporary development of African American businesses. This chapter also examines the important role of black political leaders in using their power and influence to enhance the condition of the black citizenry and the black entrepreneurial community.

Chapter 5 provides comparative data on black and white businesses in order to examine their similarities and differences to more clearly understand the various constraints experienced by African American entrepreneurs that are attributable to their race. Chapter 6 answers the central question that this study seeks to address: Why do some businesses succeed, while others fail? It also analyzes the role of gender in black business development by discussing the similarities and differences between black male and female business owners. Chapter 7 provides rich ethnographic information and brief biographies of successful and unsuccessful business owners.

Chapter 8 presents the conclusions as well as research and public policy recommendations. The conclusions from this study indicate that, although all black entrepreneurs share some characteristics in common, they also have important differences that are influenced by factors related to their individual life experiences. This study also challenged a number of stereotypes regarding black entrepreneurship that were advanced earlier in the literature, such as assertions that blacks have a low level of economic culture; that they do not have a strong work ethic; and that they do not give back to their communities once they become successful. On the contrary, this study has uncovered a strong tradition of black entrepreneurship that is manifested at the national and local levels of society. Moreover, black entrepreneurs cannot be viewed as a monolithic category. There was a great deal of variation between individual entrepreneurs.

CHAPTER ONE

African American Entrepreneurship at the National Level

In the past few decades, there has been a tremendous increase in the number of African Americans who are interested in entrepreneurial activities.[1] This interest includes an increasing sense of urgency on the part of African Americans to master the "art of entrepreneurship." They want to do it well. In March 2000, I made a presentation about important business issues and trends for northeast Ohio that emanated from my research to the Greater Cleveland Minority Technology Council. During the presentation, I used various charts and graphs to explain my research design, my overall approach, and specific implications of my work. About halfway through the presentation, one of the black entrepreneurs in the audience raised his hand and indicated that he was especially interested in knowing what factors lead to success and failure. He asked, "What is the bottom line?" This question was important because getting to the heart of the matter, or the bottom line, is the major purpose of my work. As I have stated elsewhere, "A study that examines the variables which enhance the long-term survival of African American [black] businesses is particularly germane at this point in time because during the past few decades, the number of businesses which are owned and operated by African-Americans has proliferated to a large degree. The increase in the number of African-Americans who are now 'self-employed' is attributable to the fact that economic development is seen by an increasingly larger number of African-Americans as a viable and practical avenue for long-term economic survival."[2]

Toward that end, numerous conferences and economic development summits have been held through the years to examine the economic conditionalities of African American people.[3] My own study emerges at a time when there is a need and interest on the part of African Americans to master what the Reverend Jesse Jackson refers to as the final frontier, i.e., the economic sphere. His Rainbow/PUSH Coalition Wall Street Project, launched on the birthday of Martin Luther King Jr. in 1997, has been instrumental in calling national attention to the needs of America's own underserved market, which he argues "contains more than sixty million people, about 25 percent of the American population" and "commands more than $600 billion in annual earnings."[4] This means that, when it is compared to the major economies of the world, it ranks fifteenth. This emerging market consists of the minority population of the United States, which is largely African American, Latino, and urban.[5]

Economic development and self-reliance have long preoccupied African Americans. Yet, the African American community has fallen far short in achieving its goal of attaining genuine self-sufficiency and wealth creation for the long term. The tremendous gains for African Americans in politics since the sixties are not matched in the economic arena.[6] As Melvin Oliver and Thomas Shapiro remind us, "Full equality, however, is still far from being achieved. Alongside the evidence of advancement in some areas and the concerted political mobilization for civil rights, the past two decades also saw an economic degeneration for millions of blacks, and this constitutes the crux of a troubling dilemma. Poor education, high joblessness, low incomes, and the subsequent hardships of poverty, family and community instability, and welfare dependency plague many African Americans. Most evident is the continuing large economic gap between blacks and whites. . . . Since the early 1970s, the economic status of blacks compared to that of whites has, on average, stagnated or deteriorated."[7]

More recent information from the Census Bureau indicates that the racial divide is not diminishing. Family inequality between blacks and whites is still high. In 1999, the median income of African American homes was $27,900, while the figure for whites was $44,400.[8] A growing body of data suggests that the economic position of the black family is still more a function of current income than it is of wealth accumulation over time, which is a better long-term barometer of a person's economic well-being. As Oliver and Shapiro have suggested,

> Middle-class blacks, for example, earn seventy cents for every dollar earned by middle-class whites but they possess only fifteen cents for every dollar of wealth held by middle-class whites. For the most part, the economic foundation of the black middle class lacks one of the pillars that provide stability and security to middle-class whites—assets. The black middle class position is precarious and fragile with insubstantial wealth resources. This analysis means it is extremely premature to celebrate the rise of the black middle class. The glass is both half empty and half full, because the wealth data reveal the paradoxical situation in which blacks' wealth has grown while at the same time falling further behind that of whites.[9]

Several noteworthy studies have provided analyses of blacks' historical struggle to achieve economic independence through their participation in entrepreneurial activities in the United States. Although numerous studies have been performed through the years, in this section I discuss a few that have particular significance for my work. Hence, this is not an exhaustive discussion of the entire literature.[10] John Sibley Butler and Juliet E. K. Walker have made significant contributions to our knowledge base regarding the extent of black business involvement in the American economy. Walker provides an extensive historical overview of the development of black businesses from the 1600s to the present and analyzes various areas of black business activity, which include participation in real estate, land development in urban and rural areas, building, and construction, as well as hair care, manufacturing, and international trade. Butler's study documents the tremendous tradition of black business activity and self-help that existed among black people and that he believes has been omitted by many contemporary scholars who conduct research on ethnicity, race, and economics.[11]

One of the most interesting contributions of Butler's book is his application of the "economic detour" theory to African American behavior. The idea behind the theory of the economic detour is that following the Civil War, in particular, African Americans were prevented by law from developing and operating their own indigenous enterprises in the open, competitive marketplace. Although other ethnic communities, such as the Japanese, were able to build up a clientele that was largely outside their own ethnic community, this was not true for most African American owners. When blacks were able to develop some sort of clientele outside their own ethnic enclave, they were apt to be more successful. Therefore, enormous differences emerged as European middlemen minorities had the opportunity to develop a market and other types of advantages, while African Americans became basically consumers, rather than producers. Governmental legislation had the end effect of circumscribing the development of African American businesses into very restricted markets or racially segregated areas.[12]

Timothy Bates identifies several key factors that are positively correlated with economic success for African American entrepreneurs. First, larger-scale firms have better chances to survive. Second, the age of a firm is important; survival chances increase with the age of the firm. Third, educational background is also important. Owners with lasting firms were usually those who had attended college for four or more years. Fourth, owners were also more likely to survive if they had invested sizeable amounts of financial capital into their firms. Fifth, firms that were purchased in buyouts have a greater likelihood of succeeding than those that started from scratch. He also pointed out that two other characteristics are important in firm survival: the owner's labor contribution in terms of the number of hours worked, and managerial expertise. Of the owner characteristics listed above, the gap between white and black owners was considered to be more fully explained by the difference in the owners' financial investment in their businesses.[13]

Bates posited that the three most important factors that continue to prevent entrepreneurial success by black owners are the difficulties they experience with regard to the acquisition of financial and equity capital, their business location, and increasing challenges to the constitutionality of assistance programs earmarked for minority-owned firms. Business location becomes a crucial factor, particularly for black businesses located in inner-city communities. In such areas, minority entrepreneurs must contend with the reality that these locations are frequently redlined by financial institutions, which significantly decreases the likelihood they will receive the appropriate amount of capital needed for their businesses to succeed. Additionally, the local clientele who reside in these economically disadvantaged communities often have little purchasing power. Consequently, some entrepreneurs decide to move to other areas.[14]

A number of scholars have pointed out that one of the most important variables with a direct bearing on the economic outcomes of business owners is their social capital. Social capital can be defined as resources one acquires from kinship networks, peers, members of one's own family or community, business entities, or other groups that provide various types of help to the business owner. These may include the provision of entrepreneurial role models, informal training in various community activities, financial support that one may acquire outside the umbrella or network of formal commercial lending institutions, the development of labor resources (i.e., employees), customers, and business clients.[15]

Gavin Chen and John Cole found that Asian and Hispanic firms are similar to nonminority businesses in the sources that they rely upon for capital, in the cost they pay for their capital, their total capital investment, and their access to capital. One of the most interesting findings of their study was that black firms have faced discriminatory barriers in their acquisition of all sources of capital, which greatly impeded their access to capital resources, increased its cost, and ultimately affected the overall profitability levels of their firms. This led to a situation in which black firms tended to have a lower level of capital composition, both at the time of the start-up of the firm and later on during the operational phase of their businesses. The only exception to this general pattern occurred in instances where both minority and nonminority financial institutions avidly competed for the patronage of black businesses, which led to a situation where the cost of borrowing funds was reduced and the availability of funds increased.[16]

Asian entrepreneurs received more economic support from their friends, family members, and the community at large than their business counterparts in other minority groups. For example, the authors found that the Asian community provides about 18 percent of the investment debt capital for its business sector, compared to 9 percent for nonminorities. The figures are 13 percent for Hispanics and 8 percent for blacks. Furthermore, Asian owners were also able to get financial assistance from the previous owners of their firms more than any other groups in the study (i.e, black, Hispanic, and nonminority owners). This phenomenon could be attributed to a number of factors, which may include the fact that the Asian owners in the study were more open or willing to buy out risky firms, or that the former owners of the companies may have had a positive opinion of the ability of the Asian entrepreneurs to become successful because of a perceived impression that they are hardworking and diligent. Whatever the case, a number of scholars have suggested that having strong social capital networks is a positive factor in attaining economic success. Hence, this factor has undoubtedly aided in the tremendous economic success that some Asian entrepreneurs have experienced, thus far.[17]

Frank Fratoe utilized data from a 1982 Characteristics of Business Owners (CBO) Survey to compare and contrast the use of social capital by black entrepreneurs and other ethnic groups, such as Asians, Hispanics, and nonminorities. One major strength of this study is that national and subnational level data were used to examine the issue of social capital. These issues had been examined in a much less systematic manner in the past. The CBO data base included information on 125,000 people who owned businesses in 1982, and the sample was divided fairly equitably among the Hispanics, blacks, and other groups included in the study. It also included women and nonminority males. Although the data base included information about the entrepreneurs on a number of important issues such as marital status, educational attainment, previous business experience, and hours worked per week, Fratoe relied largely on selected variables that related more to the use of social capital.[18]

Fratoe's study makes an important contribution to the literature on minority businesses because several writers have previously asserted that one reason blacks have been less involved in entrepreneurship relative to other groups is that less support has been made available to them by the black community and black institutions. Fratoe's analysis of this issue allows him to delve more deeply into issues such as this in order to empirically assess to what extent these postulations are credible when using comparative national data on minority and nonminority businesses.

A small number of black business owners (about 21 percent) indicated that they had relatives who were also entrepreneurs. This was in stark contrast to nonminority male owners whose percentage of relatives who were self-employed was almost twice the level of the black owners in the study. Fewer black owners had attended college for four or more years (25 percent) as compared with that of the Asians (42 percent), and nonminority males (34 percent). Hispanics were the only group in the study who had a lower college attendance rate (19 percent) than the blacks. Some of the dilemmas black owners face in the area of self-employment are related to the fact that they have fewer role models in entrepreneurship, and they lack large numbers of close relatives in the area of business when compared with Asians, Hispanics, and nonminorities. Moreover, about 70 percent of the blacks indicated that they started their businesses with less than five thousand dollars. One-third of black owners did not have any capital with which to develop their business enterprises.[19]

Last, Fratoe found that minority owners rely more heavily on equity or non-borrowed capital than on debt capital. CBO data confirmed that 40 percent to 50 percent of minority vendors utilized equity capital to establish their businesses. Many also used funds from their own savings accounts and assistance from their family. Nevertheless, the data still indicated that blacks do not receive support from self-help networks (friends, family, community) to the same extent as Asians or other groups. Faith Ando has also analyzed the issue of financial and human capital, based upon a small nationwide survey of business owners with different ethnicities, such Asians, blacks, Hispanics, and nonminorities. Ando found that the blacks and Hispanics in her study generally had the same financial and human capital as their Asian counterparts. Consequently, black-owned and Hispanic-owned firms performed as well as Asian-owned and nonminority firms. However, blacks achieved lower success rates than nonminority owners in obtaining commercial bank loans, although the terms for the loans were similar for both groups. Blacks in the study had acquired similar levels of education (one form of human capital) as the nonminorities in the sample. This was surprising, given the fact that a number of earlier studies argued that blacks' relatively lower level of educational attainment affected their ability to acquire good jobs, which ultimately affected their ability to invest in business enterprises.[20]

Ando also found that friends or relatives of Asians, blacks, and Hispanics invested similar amounts of capital in their groups' firms. One caveat, however, was that while Asians did provide more funds overall, it was in the form of debt rather than equity capital. This means that Asian business owners were required to repay the principal amount that they borrowed as well as interest on the loan.[21]

Firms that exhibited high levels of performance were distinguished in the following manner: (1) Their owners were usually educated, very experienced, did not work in a second job, and worked long hours in their firms. In fact, there was a positive relationship between years of formal education and the performance of the firm. The findings of this study stressed the importance of financial capital. (2) The firms usually had the requisite amount of capital, most particularly equity capital when the firm was first established. (3) The firm could be described as "maturing" rather than being "old." (4) The older the firm, the more likely that it would perform well, until it reached the age of twenty.[22]

In several of Bates's other studies, he examined the contributions black-owned businesses make toward economic development in terms of whether they employ workers. He also examined what ethnic/racial backgrounds most of their employees represent. In these studies, Bates found that black-owned businesses do create jobs. Second, he found that black owners consistently hire minority workers. This stands in direct contrast to white owners of small businesses whom, he argues, continue to exclude minorities from the workplace. According to Bates, this phenomenon holds true regardless of where the firms are located. In other words, data indicates that white employers rely on a predominantly and sometimes exclusively white labor force even when their businesses are found in inner-city neighborhoods. In vivid contradistinction, black firms in these same communities employ a largely minority workforce.[23]

A number of explanations have been put forward to explain why black-owned businesses rely so heavily on minority employees to perform their work. Some of these reasons include political constituency issues; the labor skills available in the local populace; geographical closeness between the location of the firm and location of the worker pool; and the practical issues associated with a black firm relying on a majority white labor force instead of utilizing its own constituency group to fulfill its labor requirements.[24]

In "Market Structure and Minority Presence: Black-Owned Firms in Manufacturing," Arthur G. Woolf examined the participation of black-owned businesses in the manufacturing sectors of the American economy. He analyzed the effect of seven independent variables or determinants of "black business prevalence." These variables were: (1) industry growth rate, (2) capital intensity, (3) the degree to which vertical integration is reflective or characteristic of different manufacturing fields, (4) the degree to which lines of business are controlled by small firms, (5) the ratio of advertising to sales in certain lines of manufacturing, (6) the share of output sold to the government, and (7) consumer goods in comparison to producer goods orientation. Although only 2 percent of all black enterprises were concentrated in the area of manufacturing during the decade of the 1970s, they made a contribution of 7.5 percent to the total sales volume of all firms owned and operated by African Americans. However, the number of black-owned firms in manufacturing did grow during the period 1972–77, as did their contribution to the total sales volume of black-owned enterprises.[25]

Woolf found that a number of factors continue to limit African American participation in the area of manufacturing. These include the fact that these businesses usually focus in areas where advertising costs are fairly low; they are disproportionately represented in areas where they sell a large amount of their output to the household sector directly; and they are underrepresented in areas of manufacturing that are controlled to some degree by large sales (those that exceed $5 million). Finally, he argued that capital intensity, in and of itself, does not seem to be an effective barrier to black entrepreneurial participation in manufacturing.[26]

In "The Competitive Advantage of the Inner City," Michael Porter drew our attention to the pressing developmental problems of inner-city communities. Porter postulates that previous efforts to rejuvenate inner-city areas in the United States, many of which have been implemented under the umbrella of a top-down, governmental-interventionist approach, have clearly not succeeded. The main purpose of his paper was to develop a new model that will enhance economic development in inner-city areas. This model places an emphasis on "private, for profit initiatives and investment based on economic self-interest and true competitive advantages" rather than on "artificial inducements, charity, or government mandates." He believes that previous efforts made by developmental policymakers have provided relief to the inner city under the rubric of social need concerns, rather than attained genuine economic development. Consequently, adopting a new model of economic development will, of necessity, entail "rethinking" the inner city in economic rather than social terms.[27]

Porter's perspective led to considerable debate among academicians, urban policy scholars, and public policy analysts. Consequently, *The Review of Black Political Economy*, fall/winter 1996 volume provided a special double issue to allow various scholars and practitioners to respond to the implications of Porter's work. Susan Fainstein and Mia Gray, who wrote articles for the volume, believe that Porter's argument was based on a false premise, namely, his idea that the problems associated with revitalization programs for the inner city are attributable to the inability to nurture or support the private sector. On the contrary, they posit that Porter fails to acknowledge many large-scale projects, previously implemented under the umbrella of the Comprehensive Employment and Training Act (CETA), that were placed aside so that Private Industry Councils (PICS) could carry out the work. They do, however, agree with Porter that many development possibilities exist in the inner city. Several viable areas that could be targeted are warehousing, distribution, recycling, food processing, and automobile repair. On the other hand, John Sibley Butler was very supportive of Porter's thesis. He did, however, note that Porter's model should be further expanded by emphasizing the importance of inner-city residents to the overall development process.[28]

Patricia Cirillo, George Erickcek, Ilan Alon, and I have analyzed economic development from a local and regional context. We have focused particular attention on economic development issues in the Midwest. Cirillo, for example, performed an analysis on the characteristics of businesses that were owned and operated by Asians, Hispanics, African Americans, and Native Americans in Cleveland, and compared them with characteristics of white-owned businesses. In all, she interviewed the owners of 225 minority firms and 112 majority firms. One important thrust of her questionnaire, in addition to examining demographic data, was to determine whether the businesses were certified or not, and whether the certification process had helped or hindered their business success. Respondents also were questioned about whether they had participated in a minority set-aside program, its possible impact on their businesses, and their familiarity with and use of services offered by the Minority Business Enterprise and Small Business Enterprise in Cleveland, Ohio.[29]

In some of my previous work, I have focused attention on economic development processes in Cleveland, Ohio. In "African American Businesses, Economic Development, and the Puzzle of Success: A Pilot Study of Cleveland, Ohio," I analyzed what factors promote successful business outcomes for black entrepreneurs. The results of my study indicated that several factors, both internal and external to the owners, affected their success. Several theme areas were discussed, including the impact of individual-owner characteristics, economic culture, and external variables on black firm success. Select independent variables were examined under each category to determine if they were correlated to the dependent variable.[30]

The data for this study was collected from September 1995 to September 1996. The study was essentially a pilot study. Forty-eight entrepreneurs were interviewed (thirty-four black and fourteen white). Statistical regressions were used to test the relationship between the independent variables and the dependent variable. The results from the pilot study confirmed some of the earlier findings of Bates and Ando with respect to the importance of a number of human capital variables such as the age of the entrepreneur, hours worked per week in the firm by the owners, and organizational attributes such as the number of years the business had been in operation.[31]

Alon and I also coauthored an article entitled "An Exploratory Analysis of Factors Which Affect Black Business Success: A Pilot Study of Cleveland, Ohio." While drawing on the same data base discussed above, we examined the effect of seven independent variables on two dependent variables. The independent variables included the level of education, age, marital status, hours worked per week by the business owners, the price of their products, the quality of their products, and the number of years their businesses had been in operation. The dependent variables were the amount of sales earned in the businesses and the number of employees hired to work in the firms. The result of the statistical tests indicated that number of hours worked per week on the job by the owner was positively correlated to the success of the African American entrepreneurs.[32]

Last, George Erickcek performed a comparative study of small business owners (those who had fewer than one hundred employees) in Cleveland, Ohio, and

Kalamazoo, Michigan. He received 590 usable surveys from Cleveland owners and 763 from owners in Kalamazoo. He found that many of the small business owners tended to sell much of their merchandise to a local clientele in comparison to having a large customer base outside their immediate regional location. Because of this, he concluded that small business owners may not be making a large enough contribution toward expanding the economic base of the local development area, which is very critical in enhancing economic growth.[33]

In Cleveland, 63 percent of the owners sold most of their goods to customers in the multicounty northeast Ohio region in contradistinction to 74 percent of the Kalamazoo owners who sold most of their merchandise within the county limit. Erickcek also found that most small businesses stay small, rather than expand, and in both cities, businesses were usually owned by individuals who were fairly well educated and had a wealth of job experience. In the Kalamazoo sample, 51.28 percent of the owners had a bachelor's degree or beyond, while in Cleveland, 52.6 percent had a bachelor's degree or higher. Most owners in both cities indicated that they had previous experience in industry, which presumably would be considered a positive factor in enhancing their possibilities for success over time. While Erickcek's study helps illuminate the contributions of small business owners in Cleveland and Kalamazoo, it seems to undervalue somewhat the tremendous contribution these businesses continue to make toward economic development by providing employment opportunities for workers, by developing products to be marketed, and by enhancing the tax base of the communities in which they are located. Much of this undervaluation is due to what the author describes as the tendency by many of the business owners to sell many of their products locally rather than outside their immediate regional area.[34]

Through the years, a number of propositions or hypotheses have been advanced by various scholars in the literature regarding black businesses. Some of these are listed below.

1. Black firms tend to sell to minority customers and to hire minority employees.[35]
2. Black firm owners are likely to be married.[36]
3. Black owners have had less exposure to entrepreneurial role models and business training than nonminority male owners.[37]
4. Blacks do not use or rely on their relatives or friends to acquire capital to the same degree as do Asians and other groups.[38]
5. Black business success is positively correlated with (1) size of the firm, (2) age of the firm, (3) educational background of the business owners, (4) amount of financial capital invested in the firms, (5) owner's labor contribution on the job, and (6) owner's managerial expertise.[39]

There is currently an "emerging group of black businesses" that exhibit the following characteristics:

1. They serve a clientele that is more diverse in terms of ethnic inclusion than they have in previous years.
2. They are more apt now to sell goods to other companies as well as to the government.
3. The new "emerging" lines of businesses are focused in the areas of wholesale, construction, business services, and finance.
4. They are likely to have paid employees.
5. Their mean annual sales volume is higher than that of more "traditional firms."
6. They tend to sell their goods to other businesses, including corporations, and to the government.[40]
7. Black businesses provide employment opportunities and they consistently hire minorities to work in their firms.[41]
8. Black businesses are undercapitalized as they seek to acquire equity and debt capital.[42]
9. Black entrepreneurs tend to be educated.[43]

CHAPTER TWO

The Historical Development of the African American Community in Cleveland and the Black-Owned Business Sector, 1795–1895

Cleveland's central location at the mouth of the Cuyahoga River "gave the city potential both as the northern terminus of a water connection between the lake and the Ohio River and as a Great Lakes port."[1] This location also aided considerably in Cleveland's eventual development into a major industrial and manufacturing center.[2] In 1795, the land of the Western Reserve was placed on the market to acquire funds to enhance the state treasury of Connecticut. The land was purchased by the Connecticut Land Company for $1.2 million. Moses Cleaveland, a member of the board that was established to oversee the Connecticut Land Company, agreed to assist in developing the land deal. Additionally, he added more than thirty thousand dollars of his own money. Cleaveland, who was eventually persuaded to head the first survey team to the area in 1796, is credited with founding the city.[3]

The original mandate given to the Connecticut Land Company was not to settle the land or, for that matter, to develop it for commercial purposes. Rather, it was instructed to take necessary steps to prepare the land for a quick resale.[4] Thus, parcels of land were put up for sale in the land lotteries in 1798, and individuals purchased land of varying quality. Although the Connecticut Land Company did not actively support settlement of this new area, settlers began to gradually move in and, by the turn of the century, fifteen hundred residents lived in the area. Cleveland became the county seat for Cuyahoga County in 1809.[5] The first black person to arrive in the Cleveland area probably did so in March of 1806. He was a fugitive slave called Ben who survived the sinking of a boat on Lake Erie. He was discovered near Lakewood by two hunters who took him to meet Lorenzo Carter.[6]

Carter did not support slavery for moral reasons. Ben's two owners eventually caught up with him and tried to take him back. They traveled toward Pittsburgh, going over the Cleveland-Warren Road, and were overtaken by two hunters on the outskirts of Cleveland. The hunters allowed Ben to climb down from his horse and run away into the woods. The two slave catchers were sent on their way, but Ben remained in the area for a while before going to Canada.[7]

Although many Ohioans did not support the institution of slavery, in 1802 the Ohio general assembly passed a constitutional amendment that impeded the overall progress of blacks. This "black law" prevented African Americans from voting and marrying individuals from other racial groups. Blacks were also forbidden to serve as jurors, witnesses, or litigants.[8]

The first permanent African American inhabitants of Cleveland were George Peake and his family members. Peake had served in the British Army during the French and Indian War (1754–63). Peake traveled to Cleveland in April 1809 with his two sons and in 1811 purchased a farm in the area that is now known as Lakewood. Available evidence indicates that his wife possessed significant financial means according to the economic standards of that period. Other black families soon followed.[9]

During the decades of the 1820s and 1830s, Cleveland had a very small African American population, probably less than 1 percent of the number of inhabitants. Nevertheless, some blacks served as horse breeders, seamstresses, blacksmiths, masons, brick layers, farm owners, hair stylists, tailors, and manufacturers. Alfred Greenbriar was a noted cattle and horse breeder in 1827. He owned a farm that was located in the area that is now Bridge Avenue on the west side of Cleveland.[10]

During the 1830s, the black community developed a library, a school, and a lecture program. Attitudes toward racial issues changed drastically during the 1830s with the influx of settlers from northern New England who introduced a more liberal perspective on social issues. Some of them even supported the abolition movement as well as the Underground Railroad. Leading members of the black community embraced the abolition movement and helped slaves escape to freedom.[11]

From about 1827 through 1847, Cleveland operated as an important transshipment point, where agricultural products were collected from the interior to be shipped east, while manufactured goods from the East were sent south. In 1840, Cleveland's population had increased to slightly more than six thousand inhabitants, and it became the largest city in northeastern Ohio. By 1861, about eight hundred blacks resided in Cleveland, and their numbers increased to about thirteen hundred by 1870. Many had migrated from the South.[12]

From the 1830s through the 1850s, more black businesses were established in various types of skilled and service areas, and several of them were quite successful. George Peake owned one hundred acres of land and invented a hand-mill that enabled citizens to produce meal from grain in a much more efficient manner than had hitherto been possible.[13] According to Russell Davis, "Prior to his invention, the 'stump mortar and spring pestle,' a rather crude instrument based on an idea borrowed from the Indians, was used for producing meal from grain. Peake's hand-mill decreased the labor needed to produce the meal, and it increased the quality of the meal. Thus, the device was indeed a distinct contribution to the community."[14]

Madison Tilley was an outstanding black politician and entrepreneur who placed an emphasis on African Americans using their potential voting power to enhance their material condition. Although state laws in Ohio prevented African Americans from voting during the early 1800s, the Ohio Supreme Court was asked to rule on the issue of race and color in 1831.[15] In the case of *Poly Gray v. the State of Ohio,* "a man of a race nearer white than a mulatto should partake of the privileges of white."[16] Hence, mulattoes were given the right to vote.

Although Tilley was not a literate man, he did have a charismatic personality and the gift of public speaking, which enabled him to provide leadership for African Americans. Initially, he was a Whig and later became a Republican. Then, he became a Democrat. For a number of years, Tilley and other members of his family were the only African Americans in the Democratic Party in Cleveland. Because of his effective leadership, he helped Governor Salmon P. Chase gain the support of the Second Ward. He also developed patron-client networks with prominent whites that greatly assisted him in his business activities. He established a highly profitable business as an excavating contractor in which he employed an integrated labor force of about one hundred men. Having an integrated labor force was very progressive for an African American or anyone else during that era. He controlled property worth forty thousand dollars in the old Hay Market District, and he left between twenty-five and thirty thousand dollars to his sons upon his death.[17]

The first African American physician in Cleveland was Dr. Robert Boyd Leach, who established a medical practice three years before the onset of the Civil War (1858). Dr. Leach attended the Western Homeopathic College, which was located on Ohio Street, and in 1858, he was able to complete a two-year course of study. Like other entrepreneurs of the day, he was involved in economic development and political activism. For example, he tried to ameliorate the plight of African American people and was often cited in news stories that examined the challenges that black people faced in Cleveland and, more broadly, in Ohio, as they attempted to achieve the full benefits of citizenship. One of his most important accomplishments was the development of a remedy to treat cholera, a remedy that was much needed around the Great Lakes area.[18]

The wealthiest African American in Cleveland before the year 1870 was John Brown, who established a barbershop in the New England Hotel in 1847. His income was of sufficient size by the early 1830s for him to help establish a free school for African Americans. His patronage was also, to some degree, a form of philanthropy to the African American community. When he died in 1869, he owned forty thousand dollars in property.[19]

By 1850, most African Americans in Cleveland were men, and most black households were headed by men. The size of the black community, however, was still extremely small, less than 2 percent of the population before the Civil War.[20] As David Perry has articulated, "In the nineteenth century, Cleveland was at the forefront of national development, as break-bulk [goods distribution point] cities such as Cleveland exhibited structural entrepreneurship in the shift from a mercantile to an industrial economic base. This shift attracted legions of ethnic immigrants, as well as new migrants, both African American and Appalachian white, from the South. Twentieth-century Cleveland has been no less instructive as an example of urban change: the city has evidenced a long and storied period of racial and ethnic unrest and economic decline and restructuring."[21]

A nascent class structure was gradually emerging within the African American community. Although Cleveland was developing into a major urban center, racial barriers still existed that prevented blacks from entering into various industrial job categories. Moreover, many of the jobs in the mills and foundries were now being filled by European whites. Much of the menial work was left to African Americans. Thus, during the 1870s, more African Americans comprised the two lowest job categories than did any of the other ethnic groups. These categories were domestic service and unskilled labor. Trade unions were also racially exclusivist in their membership policies. Although some of the older craft unions were integrated, newer unions such as the American Federation of Labor, barred blacks from becoming members. Because of the extreme difficulties blacks experienced in penetrating skilled job categories, many ventured into service occupations.[22]

While arguing that gender was a much more salient variable than race in explaining the predominance of African American women in the capacity of domestic workers at this time, Kusmer points out that 65.7 percent of all employed women in Cleveland were working in this category.[23] In other words, "It was females per se, not Black females, whose occupational status was depressed at this time."[24] Available data and various other scholarly works on the condition of black women in America differ from this interpretation and argue instead that a tremendous difference existed between the situation of black women and white women all over the country. These studies emphasize the tremendous impact of race in mediating not only the outcomes and economic condition of black women, but also of black men. Angela Davis has demonstrated that race was much more salient than gender in influencing the role of African Americans. Moreover, as the data in chapter 3 demonstrate, white women had many more options available to them than black women. Also, many black women had to work out of necessity because of the precarious economic situations of their spouses. Davis argued that there was a big gap in terms of the extent of black female involvement in the domestic work category compared to white women's participation.[25] To quote Davis, "During the post-slavery period, most Black women workers who did not toil in the fields were compelled to become domestic servants. . . . While Black women worked as cooks, nursemaids, chambermaids, and all-purpose domestics, white women in the South unanimously rejected this line of work. Outside the South, white women who worked as domestics were generally European immigrants who, like their ex-slave sisters, were compelled to take whatever employment they could find."[26]

Only about one-third of all African American men were employed in the area of the skilled trades. Moreover, African Americans, in general, had much more difficulty than other groups in ascending into the higher level job classifications.[27] Their lack of economic mobility undoubtedly acted as an incentive for some blacks to become involved in entrepreneurial activities. "At the close of the Civil War, a large minority of Cleveland's Black population had an aura of middle-class respectability. As a result of their unusual educational and economic opportunities, a significant number of blacks in the forest city were able to accumulate property. . . . In 1850 eighteen Blacks (23.6 percent of all heads of households) owned $15,660 in real estate . . . . The total value of real property owned by Cuyahoga County Negroes increased dramatically to $237,400 in 1870, while the total number of property owners rose to 101, or 27.8 percent of the heads of households."[28]

The economic status of the African American community in Cleveland was probably somewhat higher than that of similar communities in other cities. The only American city that surpassed Cleveland was New Orleans, Louisiana, where blacks were able to amass significant amounts of property and participate in a variety of occupations. In public education, Cleveland was perhaps more progressive than some other northern and midwestern cities. For example, the Cleveland public schools had integrated in spite of the fact that before 1887, Ohio had developed no explicit strategy to deal with the education of African American children. In the mid-1830s, the African American community had been the beneficiary of economic support from some individuals to establish their own school and during the following decade had received support from the city council to establish a private school for African American youth. By the end of the 1840s, the public school system in Cleveland was integrated, and this situation continued on into the mid-twentieth century.[29]

By 1870, more than ninety-two thousand people resided in Cleveland, and the city was ranked fifteenth in total population in the United States. "It had become one of the nation's important iron-manufacturing centers, with some fourteen rolling mills producing four hundred tons of finished iron daily. Plants supplied sulfuric acid, hydrochloric acid, soda ash, and other chemicals to a rapidly growing petroleum industry. In 1870, the city processed two million barrels of petroleum, making it the premier refining capital of the country."[30]

While Cleveland in the 1870s was more progressive on race than most cities, new ideologies emerged that championed the cause of racial supremacy. This included the popularization of the ideas that African Americans were inferior to Europeans and not entitled to the full rights of American citizenship. Discrimination against African Americans encompassed most public facilities. African Americans also became increasing more segregated and concentrated in areas that had unusually high concentrations of poverty and inequality.[31]

From the 1880s forward, large numbers of the newer immigrants came from southern and eastern Europe to replace immigrants from western Europe. Many blacks had migrated as well from the southern states in search of a better way of life. In part, because of the expansion of the southern population northward, a more diversified group of black businesses was established in Cleveland in the late nineteenth and early twentieth centuries. Some entrepreneurs were able to become part of the economic and political elite in the African American community. Others served as leaders in various civic organizations. Another factor that facilitated the development of black-owned businesses was the fact that some of the southern migrants brought their own set of skills, which they soon put to good use. Some black entrepreneurs owned grocery stores, hotels, and real estate companies, while others owned restaurants, clothing stores, and later on, automotive dealerships. While some European immigrants came primarily in search of work and planned to return to their native lands, others clearly desired to stay. Although German neighborhoods sprang up on the west side of town to the south of Bridge Avenue, Irish communities were located on the west side of the river and at the foot of Franklin Boulevard, which was a very advantageous location. Blacks, on the other hand, were generally spread out in various locations throughout the city.[32]

CHAPTER THREE

Black Business Development in Cleveland, 1895–1960

Black-owned funeral homes were catering mainly to a largely black clientele in the late nineteenth century, and that is still true today. The first black-owned funeral home in Cleveland, the J. A. Rogers funeral home, was established by James A. Rogers in 1895. It is unclear who was taking care of the funeral needs of African Americans prior to this period. The owner and director of the House of Wills Funeral Home was J. Walter Wills. He started out in 1904 as a partner in the Gee and Wills Company, which at that time was located at 2323 Central Avenue. Wills and Gee dissolved their partnership, and Gee later lived in Columbus. Wills reorganized the J. W. Wills and Sons Company located at 2525 Central Avenue. The company moved its offices to 2340 East 55th Street and later to 2491 East 55th Street. By 1920, the business had become very successful and was at one time the city's leading black funeral company. Like several other entrepreneurs in this study, Wills was also actively engaged in civic and political life in Cleveland as he helped establish the NAACP Cleveland branch, the Phillis Wheatley Association, and the Urban League. The E. F. Boyd Funeral Home was also very successful.[1]

From the latter part of the nineteenth century through the early twentieth century, George Myers operated a highly successful barbershop inside the Hollenden Hotel in downtown Cleveland. In 1879, Myers moved to Cleveland, where he worked for nine years in the Weddell House Barber Shop, where he first met Mark Hanna. Then in 1888, Liberty E. Holden brought him to work in a new hotel that he owned called the Hollenden. Eventually, Myers became the owner of the Hollenden Barber Shop. He received financial assistance from Holden and other prominent citizens, including James Ford Rhodes.[2] To quote Samuel Black, "For George Myers, the Hollenden Hotel was probably the number one hotel in Cleveland in the nineteenth century and for a great deal of the twentieth century. And he ran the barbershop. So, the fact that black folk weren't really staying in that hotel. . . . You know you wouldn't have 'the barbershop' of 'the hotel' in the city of Cleveland and you catered to mostly black folk. It wasn't that way. His clientele was primarily white

House of Wills Funeral Home. *Western Reserve Historical Society, Cleveland*

and very, very influential white ... Marcus Hanna, William McKinley, you can't get more influential than that. That was his clientele."[3]

Myers's barbershop employed about thirty-five people, including at its high point "seventeen barbers, six manicurists, five porters, three hairdressers for women, two cashiers, and two podiatrists."[4] Although ownership of the Hollenden Hotel barbershop enabled Myers to live quite comfortably, one of the most advantageous benefits of his work was the opportunity to interact with many important business leaders, politicians, and dignitaries. "The Hollenden, an entirely 'modern' hostelry, complete with electric lights, a hundred private baths, a vast 'crystal' dining room, and the plushest of fittings, became the center of Cleveland's political life. Possessed of good food (it was at the Hollenden that 'Hanna hash' was first concocted) and the longest bar in town, it became 'a small-talk center for precinct workers' and the headquarters of the big-wig politicos."[5]

It was considered by some to be the most modern barbershop in the United

The Hollenden Barber Shop. *Western Reserve Historical Society*

States. Because his barbershop was so popular, Myers had the opportunity to shave at least eight American presidents, including Cleveland, McKinley, Hayes, Harrison, Theodore Roosevelt, Wilson, Taft, and Harding; numerous congressmen as well as other well-known individuals such as David Lloyd George and Mark Twain. He was also very politically astute. He was a delegate to the Republican National Convention in Minneapolis, Minnesota, in 1892. Myers was extremely helpful at the 1896 Republican National Convention, where McKinley was nominated for president. Myers was given credit for helping secure the single vote that led to Marcus Hanna becoming a United States senator in 1897. Interestingly, William H. Clifford, an African American from Cuyahoga County, cast the deciding vote for Hanna. Although various political appointments were offered to Myers through the years, he decided to focus on his business. Myers sold the Hollenden Hotel barbershop shortly before his death in 1930.[6]

Although the Hollenden Hotel was well known and successful at this time, it is important to note that black participation overall in the barber industry in Cleveland declined from 43 percent in 1870 to 18 percent by 1890. In fact, at the onset of the twentieth century, fewer than one out of every ten Cleveland barbers was black and many of those were now catering to a largely black clientele.[7] According to Kusmer:

> The declining importance of black waiters and barbers and the gradual disappearance of black businesses that catered to a predominantly white clientele were common to all Northern cities during the late 19th to early 20th

centuries. In smaller, less industrialized cities, the process occurred at a much slower pace than the big centers of population, however. In Columbus, Evansville, Indianapolis, Des Moines, and Kansas City, Missouri, blacks were able to maintain their hold on the barbering trade much longer than elsewhere, because these cities did not attract the large immigrant workforce that was responsible for driving blacks out of barbering in other cities. In the major urban centers the process occurred more rapidly and in most cases was virtually completed by 1915.[8]

Jacob E. Reed was another black entrepreneur who developed a business that in its early years catered largely to a white clientele. From the 1890s through the 1920s, Reed established a business with Mathius Reitz, a European immigrant. The name of the business was Reitz and Reed Fish and Oyster Business, and it was located in the Sheriff Street Market area. Available evidence indicates that the business was quite successful. Reed ran for office several times and was a member of several black organizations. He was also very philanthropic and was a member of several fraternal organizations. He was not as involved in politics as was Myers, even though he did run for political office.[9]

Different types of businesses catered to different types of clients. For example, the black funeral homes that existed during this period developed a largely black clientele. This was due primarily to racial discrimination and to cultural preferences. White funeral homes would not provide burial services and disposition of deceased blacks. Also, most African Americans felt more comfortable having someone who looked like them and who understood their value systems and beliefs to assist them during their time of bereavement. This phenomenon is true to some extent today. Although some African Americans utilize funeral home assistance from other ethnic or racial groups, the vast majority still prefer to have members of their own community do this work. It is really largely a matter of cultural preference. These factors enhanced the success of local black-owned funeral homes such as E. F. Boyd and Son and the House of Wills Funeral Home.[10]

Around 1900, an increasing hostility was directed at black entrepreneurs by whites who wished to decrease their patronage. This period also coincided with the development of more intense levels of racial hostility and the emergence of the black ghetto. According to Miller, racial discrimination in Cleveland became more noticeable. Hence, blacks were not allowed to utilize various restaurants, theaters, and hotels. Because of Jim Crow laws, African Americans were prevented from entering Luna Park on certain days and were prevented from using the bathing amenities. Some of this increasing racial antagonism was attributable in part to the increasing visibility and size of the African American community. Across the country, African Americans who had relied on an almost exclusively white clientele for their business success were being replaced by a new group of entrepreneurs who catered largely to the African American market. They included a diverse group of entrepreneurs who served as newspaper editors, insurance agents, grocers, bankers, and real estate owners.[11]

Another highly successful entrepreneur of this era was Charles Chesnutt, who established a stenography business in the late nineteenth century. He later retired from the stenography business to write novels. In fact, he was the first Negro novelist and short-story writer to be published widely by a noted white publisher in the United States, gaining that distinction prior to 1900.[12] Like many of the other successful black entrepreneurs of this period, he was a man of multiple talents. Some of his most famous publications include *Conjure Woman, The Biography of Frederick Douglass,* and *The Wife of His Youth,* which were published in 1899. Other works soon followed. While his novels achieved critical success, they did not provide the degree of economic support he would have perhaps desired. Hence, he returned to his stenography business. Ironically, his novels are achieving great popularity now as several have recently been republished. He was fluent in several languages, including French and German, which undoubtedly helped him interact with European immigrants who resided in the Cleveland area.[13] According to Russell Davis, "The work of Chesnutt brought the Negro into serious recognition on the basis of merit. His experiences in the South during the difficult period of Reconstruction furnished the inspiration and theme for his writings. The bitter heritage of slavery, the clash of races, the strivings of the disadvantaged created dramatic situations, and he depicted them with the pen of a master."[14]

Another creative and innovative entrepreneur of this period was Samuel Clayton Green, who developed several business enterprises both alone and in conjunction with Welcome T. Blue. He is credited with being among the first group of African American entrepreneurs who used the corporate model. During a fifteen-year period, he established a number of business enterprises, many of which were quite successful. For example, he developed a patent for a combination sofa and bed in 1902 which is believed to have been "the best of its kind on the market at that time."[15] In conjunction with sixteen other African American investors, he incorporated the Leonard Sofa Bed Company and set up his office and factory on Cedar Avenue. He also established a store on Prospect Avenue in the downtown area. Like several other black entrepreneurs during this period, he was involved in several business operations. Green and Blue helped develop the Mohawk Realty Company, a black-owned corporation established to build homes and develop and manage rental properties. That company managed the Leonard Sofa Bed Company, a house and apartment located on Cedar Avenue, as well as an apartment building that had six suites with six rooms each. The Mohawk Realty Company also built the Clayton Building on Central Avenue, which housed various stores, apartments, offices, and lodge rooms. He also developed the S. C. Green Coffee Company.[16]

Although the markets for the sofa bed and coffee company were diverse, Green was also involved in developing products and services specifically earmarked for the African American consumer. For example, he and Welcome T. Blue established the Eureka Laundry Company as well as a skating rink and dance hall on Cedar Avenue. He also established the first black-owned theater in Cleveland, which was located on Central Avenue. Here, they showed motion pictures and vaudeville shows to members of Cleveland's black community.[17]

At least two businesses owned by Green, the Clayton Drug Store and the People's Drug Store, developed in 1905, failed during their first five years in operation, largely because of the lack of patronage from the African American community.[18] Additionally, like several other black-owned businesses in the nineteenth and twentieth centuries, different entities took over the business operations after the owners died. In some cases, new owners continued to further develop the businesses using the ideas promulgated by the original founders. In other cases, they did not. In far too many instances, the black business was closed when the owner died. Because of this and other complex factors, there are few self-sustaining black-owned businesses in Cleveland's history. Few family-based, black-owned businesses were passed on from one generation to the next. This factor has had negative consequences for the African American business community, some of which are serious and far-reaching. It has prevented the development of a strong business culture with the end result that "the business model is not the dominant model in the Black community."[19] On the contrary, the African American community still lags far behind other ethnic groups in the extent of their involvement in entrepreneurial activities. As a result, most black entrepreneurs today must start their businesses with no resources. Few of them inherit their businesses from family members.[20]

By 1915, a number of blacks were participating in professional occupations: there were eight doctors, twelve attorneys, thirty schoolteachers, two professional nurses, and three dentists. The number of black attorneys in Cleveland was notable when one places their numbers in the context of the overall size of Cleveland's small black community. Philadelphia and St. Louis had larger black populations than Cleveland in 1910, but the same number of black attorneys. Almost all the black attorneys in Cleveland operated integrated facilities, as did some of the black medical doctors. However, black professionals were not afforded the same type of opportunity to develop their activities as were the black craftsmen. In other words, black doctors, lawyers, architects, and dentists enjoyed limited success in Cleveland as their clientele was very much restricted to the black community in comparison with black tradesmen who often conducted business with whites.[21]

Alonzo Wright's Sohio Service Station. *Western Reserve Historical Society*

Jesse Owens and Alonzo Wright. *Western Reserve Historical Society*

Alonzo Wright was one of the most successful black entrepreneurs in Cleveland's history. He was also the city's first African American millionaire. Wright migrated to Cleveland from Tennessee during the great migration period in 1917. Although he possessed only an eighth-grade education, he was immensely resourceful. After working as a parking attendant in a Cleveland garage, he made the acquaintance of an executive of the Standard Oil Company who later helped him obtain a Standard Oil Service Station franchise, the first one to be awarded in a predominantly black community. During the following ten-year period, as more Standard Oil franchises were established in other black communities, Wright acquired additional stations, and by the 1930s, he owned seven Standard service stations and employed more than one hundred people in his business enterprises. Wright was also part owner of the Majestic and Carnegie Hotels.[22] Wright was very philanthropic. He was a benefactor for Jesse Owens, the famous African American sprinter who won four gold medals at the Olympic games held in Germany in 1936. Wright gave Owens a job at one of his service stations on Cedar Avenue, mainly as a form of advertisement to attract more customers to the service stations.[23]

Few black entrepreneurs in Cleveland's history have been as innovative as Garrett Augustus Morgan. He was born on March 4, 1877, in Claysville, the black section of Paris, Kentucky. Armed only with a sixth-grade education, he moved to Cincinnati when he was sixteen years old and got a job as a handyman. In 1895, he moved to the Cleveland area and began to work for various companies in the textile and garment industries as a custodian and a machine adjuster. During this time, he invented various accessories for sewing machines, such as a belt fastener that contributed greatly to the machines' overall level of efficiency.[24]

He opened a sewing machine repair business inside his home in 1907. He also sold sewing machines. In 1909, he was the owner of a clothing manufacturing business that employed thirty-two people and made coats, suits, and dresses. His genius seemed to lie in developing a diverse array of practical products.[25]

Morgan invented a breathing apparatus in 1912, which he developed into a gas mask. He received a patent for the gas mask in 1914. In order to further develop and market his product, he developed alliances with influential businessmen in Cleveland, and together they established the National Safety Device Company. Gas masks were marketed primarily to fire departments and the military who could use them when rescuing people from fires in order to avoid inhaling smoke and unhealthy fumes.[26]

In 1913, Morgan founded the G. A. Morgan Hair Refining Company. Although he developed a number of hair products, one of his most interesting was a hair straightener that Morgan had invented while he was developing products to decrease the level of friction in sewing machines. The invention of the hair straightener came about quite by accident. While at his home, Morgan was preparing a

Garrett Morgan. *Western Reserve Historical Society*

chemical solution that could be used to prevent the scorching of the sewing machine needle used to sew woolens. He was called to dinner by his wife. He wiped his hands on a piece of fur cloth that was in the room. Some of the solution he was preparing for the sewing machine model was thus transferred to the piece of pony-fur cloth. Upon his return to the room later that evening, he observed that the fuzzy part of the cloth where he had wiped his hands, had become quite straight. He pondered this discovery and decided to experiment with this solution on his neighbor's Airedale dog. He applied the solution to the dog and the solution straightened his hair to such an extent that even the dog's owner did not recognize him later on. Morgan also used the solution on his own hair. Thus, the first hair straightener for humans was created.[27]

Although any ethnic community could use the product, it was probably intended for and used widely by African Americans. To market his products, according to Black, Morgan placed ads in various Cleveland newspapers, such as the *Cleveland Advocate* and the *Cleveland Gazette*. Morgan encouraged blacks to invest in his business enterprises. He held meetings at St. John's A.M.E. Church to inform the black citizenry of various investment opportunities. Sometimes, he was highly successful in getting other blacks to invest in his business activities,

Garrett Morgan's gas mask. *Western Reserve Historical Society*

while sometimes he was not. J. Walter Wills, of the Wills Funeral Home, was a good friend of Morgan's and invested money in some of his business enterprises.[28]

Morgan had the opportunity to test his safety helmet/gas mask during the tragic Waterworks crib explosion on July 25, 1916, in Cleveland. Morgan, his brother Frank, and two other volunteers used his safety helmets to go inside crib number five under Lake Erie, which was 250 feet beneath the surface. Before they arrived, two rescue parties had not been able to bring the injured men out of the crib. Even though Morgan and his helpers brought the survivors out, and used his safety helmets to do so, Morgan was not given appropriate credit for the rescue. Various newspapers, both national and local, reported the explosion, but Morgan was not necessarily viewed as the hero in these reports. On the contrary, in several newspapers, his name was mentioned only briefly, and the authors of some of the official versions of the story did not even acknowledge that he was involved in the rescue. In the *Cleveland Plain Dealer,* dated July 26, 1916, for example, several pages were devoted to an in-depth analysis of why the explosion occurred. In these stories,

Cleveland, Ohio.   Oct. 26, 1917.

Hon. Harry L. Davis,
Mayor of Cleveland,
Cleveland, Ohio.

Dear sir:-
    I have voted and worked for your election to public office each time you have been a candidate, and feel that some of my friends have supported you because of my effort. At this time I do not feel that I can conscientiously support or work for you or ask my friends to vote for you, as I have done before, because I believe you have caused me to be deprived of the rewards which my work has merited, in connection with the recent Lake Erie Tunnel disaster of July 24, 1916, in which 19 lives were lost.

    However, there is room for me to be mistaken in your intentions and I think it only fair to give you an opportunity to explain your reasons for having so acted in the matter.

    First: I am interested in knowing why it was that you and your Director of Law, Mr. Fitzgerald, would not permit me to testify at the investigation of the Lake Erie Tunnel disaster; when you knew and was an eye witness to the fact that I positively lead the first successful rescue party that entered the tunnel and came out alive, bringing with me dead and alive bodies, among them Supt. Van Dusen.

    Second: Why it was that you remained silent and allowed the Carnegie Hero Fund Commission to give awards to me who either followed me into the tunnel, or if they went in at all, went in after my return in your presence with dead and alive bodies? This, too, in face of the fact that when I returned you congratulated me and told me you would see that I was treated fairly and would be commended for my bravery. You also knew that the police, firemen and lifesavers had worked nearly all night without success and that they looked upon my effort as a last hope of saving the persons imprisoned in the tunnel.

    Third: Members of the Cleveland Association of Colored Men and others are interested in knowing why you ignored their committees until three committees had been sent to you and you waited for six months after the disaster to write a letter to the Carnegie Hero Fund Commission in my behalf, which letter did not fully state the facts to which you were a witness.

    The treatment accorded me in the particulars set out in the questions asked above is such as to make me and the members of my race feel that you will not give a colored man a square deal.

                    Respectfully yours,

                    G. A. Morgan

Letter from Garrett Morgan to Mayor Harry L. Davis. *Western Reserve Historical Society*

Tom Clancy, a white man, was clearly portrayed as the hero of the day. Moreover, in the July 29, 1916, edition of the *Cleveland Gazette,* the article about the explosion focused attention on the fifteen dead men and the sounding of the alarm for help. After the rescue attempt took place, there was an increased demand from various police departments, mining companies, and fire departments for the gas mask to be demonstrated. In some of the southern states, Morgan had to use a Caucasian male to demonstrate his invention, particularly after it became known that the gas mask had actually been invented by a black man.[29]

The greatest affront and insult came about when Morgan was not even presented with a medal by the Carnegie Hero Fund Commission for his bravery and courage during the rescue. Tom Clancy, one of the men who volunteered to help Morgan go inside the tunnel, received a medal from the Carnegie Hero Fund Commission for his efforts. This unfair treatment was the source of much disappointment for Morgan, and numerous other citizens and organizations later appealed to politicians to rectify this treatment.[30] Morgan wrote a letter to Mayor Harry L. Davis protesting his unfair treatment in this matter.

Morgan never received a medal from the Carnegie Hero Fund Commission for his tremendous heroism in rescuing the men who were trapped under Lake Erie in crib number five, nor was he regarded as a major inventor during his lifetime. He did, however, receive a medal from a citizens' group in Cleveland, which was led by Victor Sincere, as well as an award for bravery from the Association of Colored Men. He received the First Grand Prize for his safety helmet at the Second International Exposition of Safety and Sanitation and a gold medal from the International Association of Fire Engineers.[31]

Morgan is also revered because he founded the *Call,* a newspaper that later became the *Call and Post.* Although he did not have a high level of formal education, he did possess a powerful sense of self-esteem that enabled him to believe in himself. This helped him to think big. And, the reality is that before you can do big things, you have to think big thoughts. In the words of Samuel Black, Morgan probably was saying to himself, "I'm just as good as Thomas Edison."[32]

One of Morgan's most enduring inventions was the tri-colored traffic signal light. A more modern version of this traffic light is now used to control the flow of traffic in many countries of the world. The first traffic signal was located in Willoughby, while his second one was placed on East 9th Street and Euclid. In order to operate the traffic signal, someone had to physically turn the lever to get the different lights to come up. In 1923, he received a patent for the traffic signal, and eventually sold it to General Electric for $40,000, which is equivalent to $417,543 in 2001 dollars. In 1923, he also established the Wakeman Country Club in Lorain County, which catered largely to the social needs of the growing black professional and upper class. It was extremely progressive to have established the Wakeman

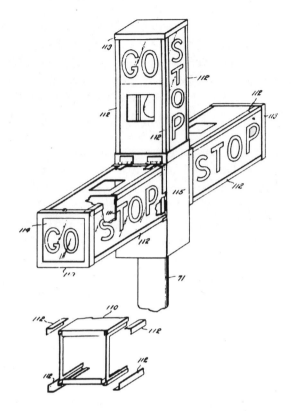

Morgan's traffic signal, patent illustration. *Western Reserve Historical Society*

Country Club for blacks.[33] Benny Mason also established a country club, circa 1930s, which was called Benny Mason's Farm. Mason owned a neighborhood grocery store and was essentially a racketeer. "But, he was a philanthropic racketeer as he made donations to several black churches in the Cleveland area."[34] He also gave money to black students to help them to pay their educational costs.

Morgan also served as the treasurer of the Cleveland Association of Colored Men. Members of the organization included people such as J. Walter Wills of the House of Wills Funeral Home; Tom Fleming, the only black city councilman between 1910–1930; physicians; and other entrepreneurs. The organization was a part of Booker T. Washington's National Negro Business League and emphasized promoting entrepreneurship and business activity in the black community. It also demonstrated a concern for civil rights and provided a professional network for black professional men.[35]

The African American press made notable contributions toward providing an outlet for the printed word. A number of these newspapers originated before World War I. For example, the *Journal* and the *Gazette* were viable black business

Benny Mason's farm. *Western Reserve Historical Society*

entities that competed with each other for a larger share of black patronage. The *Journal* closed down in 1912 as the *Cleveland Advocate* emerged on the scene. Morgan founded the *Call* in 1920, and the *Advocate* closed down in 1922. The *Post* was started by Herbert Chauncey and Norman McGhee. A few years later, *The Herald* was established and it closed down by the end of the 1920s. The *Call* and the *Post* merged to become the *Call and Post* newspaper, and it is today one of the few self-sustaining black-owned businesses in the Cleveland area.[36]

Cleveland's economy was also affected by the First World War (1914–18). At the onset of WWI, Cleveland was the sixth largest city in the United States. Her economy flourished from the manufacture of iron and steel products, machine shop goods, paint materials, and electrical machinery. Mayor Harry Davis appointed an advisory war committee to oversee the war activities of Cleveland. During the first few years of the war in which the United States exercised her neutrality, Clevelanders clearly benefited from contracts made for weapons, uniforms, cars, trucks, and chemicals used for explosive munitions. By 1918, Cleveland had provided about $750 million in munitions. When America entered the war on April 6, 1917, men were asked to defend their country, and by the end of the war, about forty-one thousand servicemen from Cleveland had enlisted in the armed forces. Because men were needed on the war front, women had to keep the economy moving in their absence. Another factor that necessitated the hiring of women to work in the factories was the fact that European immigration had seriously declined during the war period.[37] "Although Cleveland joined in the nation's desire to return to 'normalcy,' the war had left it changed in at least one major respect. It effectively blocked the flow of immigration from Europe to the nation's urban centers, a change that would be institutionalized in the restrictive immigration legislation

Call and Post newsboys. *Western Reserve Historical Society*

of the 1920s. To fill the resultant labor shortages, employers turned to the disaffected African American population of the south."[38]

As millions of Europeans migrated to the United States during the postwar period, some Americans were concerned about the overall prospects of assimilating so many diverse cultures. Inevitably, distinctions were made even among Europeans in terms of what groups were perceived to be more or less desirable. Some scholars and politicians believed that immigration should be restricted for inferior races coming from southern and eastern European countries. Quotas were put in place to reduce the number of immigrants from these locations, and Asians were not allowed in under the National Origins Act of 1924.[39]

As the European supply of immigrants decreased over time, employers in the Cleveland area began to cast their eyes toward the southern part of the United States for a steady supply of labor. Not only was labor more plentiful in the South, but it was also relatively cheap. Hence, because of the "great migration" northward, the African American population in Cleveland grew from about 10,000 inhabitants prior to WWI to 34,451 by 1920. Most African Americans who did acquire employment usually did so by working in service-related industries. This factor has exercised a significant impact on black business development because most black entrepreneurs in Cleveland own and operate businesses in the service-related industry today. This is a direct carryover from the historical past. Their involvement in service industries in the contemporary period has also been affected by economic restructuring processes that have been taking place in recent decades and is discussed in chapter 4. Although African Americans are clearly influenced by a number of factors when they decide on what area they wish to develop their business in, many tend to develop businesses in areas where they feel they have a talent or skill, or in an area that is similar to the one in which they accumulated their work or educational experience.[40]

The growth in Cleveland's black population was, in many respects, similar to the growth and development of the black community in Chicago, Detroit, or other midwestern communities during this time period. Moreover, numerous factors propelled African Americans northward, including their "collective disavowal of racial and economic oppression"; the search for better jobs and working conditions; and unbridled optimism for the future. More than one million African Americans migrated from the southern states from 1910–1930. Most settled in only a few midwestern and mid-Atlantic cities such as Pittsburgh, Cleveland, Detroit, New York City, and Chicago.[41] They also expanded their extended families and kinship ties, which they had developed earlier in the South in order to solidify the family life and structure of the African American community.[42] According to Kimberly Phillips, "Migrants' moves north established complex networks of kin and friends and infused the city with a highly visible southern African American culture. Intending to find better work and provide for families, they sought to reweave community by connecting traditions from the Deep south with the promises of the urban North. Rebuffed in neighborhoods, limited in job opportunities, and increasingly confined to segregated institutions, African Americans drew on a variety of cultural and organizational experiences and beliefs created in the South while also turning to new forms of individual and collective activism in workplaces and the city."[43]

There was a large increase in the size of the black-owned business sector from 1910 through 1930. Many of those businesses were small retail establishments, located in lower-income communities around Central, Woodland, and Cedar. Typical problems faced by entrepreneurs included inadequate capitalization, difficulty in being competitive against majority-owned firms, and having to rely largely on a lower-income clientele for their business development.[44] As Black has posited, "there are a number of black businesses that have expanded without the help of America's financial institutions. They were not given business loans. They'd have to take their profits and reinvest in their business and expand and that's something that a lot of white businesses haven't had a problem with."[45]

A number of entrepreneurs became successful by developing products and services that filled a need in the African American community. One such group of

Allen Cole in his photography studio. *Western Reserve Historical Society*

entrepreneurs were photographers who established studios in the black community. Some of these included Nelson Ellis, Bob Smith, and the Chesnutt Brothers (Louis and Andrew). The Chesnutt brothers operated their business as early as 1891.[46] One of the most noteworthy photographers was Allen Cole, who started his photography business during the 1920s. During the course of his lifetime, he took literally thousands of pictures of various aspects of life in Cleveland, most of which were of the black community—"its people, houses, businesses, schools, and churches. His photographs of weddings, Christmas pageants, church jubilees, family reunions, social clubs, sports figures, and entertainers reveal a thriving city within a city, its residents vigorously working to be—or become—middle class."[47] Although the vast majority of his clients were black, during the Great Depression, some of his customers could no longer afford to have their photos taken, and he began to get subcontracting work from various white studios in Cleveland.[48]

Cole attended Storer College in Harpers Ferry, Virginia, and graduated in 1905. Although some black entrepreneurs bought or leased buildings in various parts of the city for their business operations, other entrepreneurs, such as Cole, operated their businesses out of their homes. He became the only black professional photographer in Cleveland in the early 1920s and was the first photographer to develop tinted pictures. During this decade, the majority of the city's black busi-

Herbert Chauncey. *Western Reserve Historical Society*

nesses were located along Central Avenue, while some were moving out toward Cedar Avenue. During the 1920s, Cole shifted his studio to 9904 Cedar Avenue, which was fortuitous for him because this location was very close to the businesses and churches.[49]

Cole's simple marketing slogan was "Somebody, Somewhere, wants your photograph." Although he did not amass significant wealth during his lifetime, he did make a very important contribution to society, a permanent collection of photos that depicted the components and changing nature of black life in Cleveland. He was a member of the Future Outlook League, the Progressive Business Alliance, King Tut Lodge Number 11, and the Society of Professional Photographers. He also took photographs, at no charge, for the *Call and Post* during its early years.[50]

Some African Americans developed strategies to assist in the accumulation of wealth and capital resources. One such individual was Herbert S. Chauncey, perhaps best known for his efforts to bring together African American people to establish the Empire Savings and Loan Association, the first black-owned savings and loan in Cleveland's history. He received a charter to operate it in 1919 following the sale of capital stock in the company and opened an office on East 55th Street. The company prospered over time and finally, African Americans could acquire financing to purchase homes without being discriminated against because of their race. This was very important because homes and other forms of real estate could later be used by black entrepreneurs as collateral when they applied for loans to finance their business operations. A branch office was established in 1926 on Cedar Avenue close to East 90th Street.[51]

Chauncey also developed the People's Realty Company, which purchased and sold property and also established home site areas for African Americans. Last, he developed an insurance company that provided its members with accident, death, and sick benefits through the Crusaders Mutual Insurance Company and the Modern Crusaders of the World Company. "With the exception of Empire Savings, in which a few whites had savings accounts, all of Chauncey's projects were committed exclusively to the Negro market."[52] Unfortunately, Chauncey's business fortunes declined as a result of the depression, which lasted from 1929 to 1940. Like many other black business enterprises, his did not survive after his death in 1930.[53]

The African American community and many businesses, black and white, also felt the impact of the economic downturn in the economy during the Great Depression. According to Louise Freeman, "The Depression halted the progress blacks had made in the post-war period. Black businesses went bankrupt; several blacks in medicine and other professions were forced to accept jobs in the Works Progress Administration. . . . The prejudices of employers made themselves felt not only in the steel mills, foundries and trade unions, but in all other areas except from the most back-breaking labor and service. Even some black porters, shoeshine men and domestic workers lost their jobs to whites during the depression years."[54]

Several black institutions emerged to assist African Americans in adjusting to their new life, to become self-reliant and economically independent, as well as to facilitate the development of a working-class solidarity. For example, the Home for Aged Colored People, was developed by Eliza Bryant around 1896. It was located on Cedar Avenue for five decades and was then moved to Addison Road. The facility was renamed the Eliza Bryant Home in 1960. The Phillis Wheatley Association, founded in 1911 by Jane Edna Hunter, is still in operation today. Hunter believed firmly in the virtue of acquiring an education; she took classes at local colleges, attended law school, and later passed the state bar exam.[55]

The Phillis Wheatley Association provided a refuge or residence for unmarried black girls who moved to Cleveland on their own auspices or who had somehow been separated from their families. In 1917, Jane Hunter was able to raise enough capital to actually buy an apartment building at the intersection of East 40th Street and Central Avenue. This building provided lodging for seventy-five

Women of the Phillis Wheatley Association. *Western Reserve Historical Society*

girls. In 1925, the organization raised $550,000 for its building fund and used the money to erect a nine-story building that opened in 1927 on Cedar Avenue. The organization did experience opposition, however, from some members of the African American community who believed that it represented a movement in the direction of institutional segregation. When Hunter retired, she established the National Phillis Wheatley Foundation, which has raised thousands of dollars in scholarships to assist African American high school graduates attend college.[56]

The Future Outlook League (FOL) was established in 1935 by John O. Holly, who had also migrated from Alabama. It began by initiating a campaign to discourage African Americans from patronizing businesses that did not provide job opportunities for them; boycotts were put in effect against store owners in the central part of Cleveland who wanted blacks to patronize their businesses but refused to employ them. The boycotts were generally successful. However, in some instances, they became very confrontational and sometimes violent. Another important contribution of the FOL is that it helped fuel a working-class activism among African American people. By 1938, the FOL had ten thousand members, weekly newsletters, and offices in several other communities.[57]

Booker T. Washington is generally credited by African Americans who favored accommodation with providing the intellectual leadership for the development and expansion of the black-owned business sector. The National Negro Business League (NNBL) was actually established by Washington in 1900. That organization supported the idea of black entrepreneurial activities and emphasized the importance of racial support or solidarity as an important precondition for a successful business outcome. All members of the NNBL had to agree to patronize businesses owned by members of the African American community.[58] This idea was very progressive and should in fact be reanalyzed because it has a great utility for the current condition of the African American community today where a large portion of black wealth continues to flow outside the black community each month while little of it is spent in black-owned businesses and consequently does little to rejuvenate and expand economic growth in the black community. According to Claud Anderson, African Americans continue to transfer a large portion of their disposable income into white communities while holding on to only 5 percent of their total gross income.[59] "Of this 5 percent, approximately 3 percent is spent with non-black merchants, who take it out of black neighborhoods. Only 2 percent remains with black merchants. It is impossible for black communities to survive off of two percent of its annual income. . . . By spending their income with non-black businesses, blacks deprive their communities of a tax base for providing human services and jobs. In a capitalistic society, human worth is valued in terms of ownership and control of wealth, so blacks disempower themselves when they don't spend money with other blacks."[60]

Historically, blacks have been portrayed in a very negative way in the area of philanthropic activities. This stereotype is not supported by the data. Jacob Reed, George Myers, John P. Green, and Charles Chesnutt were all involved in the Men's Auxiliary of the Cleveland Home for Aged Colored People. They raised money for this institution and also utilized their business connections to assist them in achieving their goals. Alonzo Wright and other black entrepreneurs were also very generous. The reality is that African Americans, both today and in the past, were generous to and supportive of their communities. But, this philanthropy extended beyond making economic donations. Philanthropy has a long history in the African American community.[61] Samuel Black explains it thus: "I think what happens in the comments that people make about philanthropy and black businesses not investing or not being philanthropic is very stereotypical, and I think to the point that people are looking for black businesses to compete with a white corporation and not compete with those that are in the same economic bracket. You can't expect Madison International to compete with Turner Construction Company, as far as its philanthropy is concerned. They're on a different economic level."[62] The members of the Cleveland Association of Colored Men, many of whom were entrepreneurs, were quite philanthropic. On several occasions they held annual banquets and outings to raise money to provide scholarships for blacks.[63]

In examining the rather precarious position that African American women occupied in the economic sphere, it is useful to discuss the impacts of race, sex, and class on their economic advancement. A study written in 1938 on vocational opportunities for blacks in Cleveland made the following observations: "Although large numbers of Negroes are employed in the manufacturing and mechanical fields, and also in domestic and personal service, there are many other occupations which Negroes have entered in comparatively small numbers and in which they are successful. In the last three decades the number of Negroes in many occupations has increased, yet in relation to other groups the percentage of Negroes has decreased or remained the same."[64]

Although statistical data is scanty with regard to the actual number of black women in entrepreneurship during this time period, available data suggest that there was a tremendous gender gap in the nineteenth and twentieth centuries in Cleveland with regard to the participation rates of black males and females in business activities. Statistical data is more accessible, however, for various other categories of jobs in the wage economy. For example, according to a report on vocational opportunities for African Americans, 81.1 percent of black women who worked were employed as domestics in 1910, while 9.98 percent worked in manufacturing facilities, 0.69 percent in clerical jobs, 1.1 percent in trade, and 0.06 percent in transportation. Only 21.9 percent of white women were employed as domestics, while 14.54 percent were in clerical jobs, 7.12 percent in professional service, 10.17 percent in trade, and 25.26 percent manufacturing. In 1920, 77.7 percent of black women were still employed as domestics in comparison to only 17.8 percent of white women. By 1930, 86.65 percent of black women were domestics, compared to 20.9 percent of white women.[65]

Angela Davis's work has discussed in some detail the significant differences in the economic position of black and white women in America. Davis argues, for example, that white women would never consider domestic work unless they were sure they could find no higher level work, whereas black women had no choice until the beginning of World War II. Black women had few skills and little education and were subject to racial discrimination. Hence, several generations of black women have been involved in domestic work. Few black women were actually a part of the professional class. Some achieved this status through marriage while a few others were involved in professional occupations. Most of the black professional women were teachers, primarily elementary school teachers. It wasn't really until the 1930s and 1940s that black women taught in the high schools in Cleveland. Few owned their own businesses. Gender roles affected men's and women's work and perspectives. There was a cultural expectation that women would be primarily responsible for cooking, cleaning, and nurturing their husbands and their children. Men were expected to take a leadership role in their family and also within

Shauter's Drugstore. Mrs. Shauter is being presented an award in honor of having filled one million prescriptions, ca. 1952. *Western Reserve Historical Society*

the broader community.[66] When I asked Samuel Black whether he thought the role of women had changed through the years, he noted that

> Gender roles have changed a great deal. I think the change has come about be-
> cause of the effect the different generations have had on the outlook of Ameri-
> can society. Before World War II, I don't think many people or families sent their
> daughters to college to major in business administration or sent them to trade
> school to become managers. Most went to college to be social workers, teachers,
> or you just went to finishing school as they called it, but not to be a business
> owner. This was a very rare factor. Some women probably chose to go some-
> where beyond high school. [They thought] I'll go to Erma Lee's Beauty College,
> and then open up my place, and that's why we have so many of those places.[67]

Some women operated enterprises that were highly successful. One example is Shauter's Drugstore which was owned and operated by Frances Gray. It was originally established by Robert Shauter in 1935–36. After he died, his wife, Frances, operated the business. Later on, there were actually two Shauter drugstores in

Amanda Wicker's Clarke School of Dressmaking and Fashion Design. *Western Reserve Historical Society*

operation. One was located on East 93rd and Cedar and the other one was near 55th and Woodland. Frances later remarried and was able to manage a successful business enterprise.[68] According to Samuel Black, "if you talked to anyone who lived around Cedar Avenue during the 1940s and 1950s, they would tell you about Shauter Drug Store. It was like the hangout for young people. They had a good business. They operated a very professional drug store and pharmacy."[69]

Most female-owned businesses were located in the African American community and had a black clientele. They also tended to be family-oriented businesses. In general, women tended to become involved in business activities that linked them with their traditional roles. Hence, they often opened up beauty salons, beauty schools, or restaurants. Some of the beauty salons and beauty schools exist today. One of the most well known of the black female-owned institutions in Cleveland was Amanda Wicker's Clarke School of Dressmaking and Fashion Design, which existed for about fifty years. It lasted from the late 1920s to the early 1980s. Other female-owned businesses were established during this time period such as Erma Lee's Beauty Salon in 1934 and the Wilkins School of Cosmetology, established by Edith Wilkins in 1935. Many of these female-owned enterprises operated inside

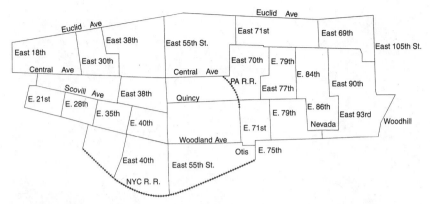

Central area of Cleveland, 1930–40. Source: Kimberly L Phillips, *Alabama North: African-American Migrants, Community, and Working-Class Activism in Cleveland, 1915–45* (University of Illinois Press, Chicago) 1999, p. 132.

the women's homes. This allowed them to take care of their children while they assisted their clients. Having home-based businesses afforded women many advantages, one of which was the fact they were cheaper to operate.[70]

By 1930, about 215 black-owned retail enterprises were noted in the census. Apparently, those enterprises employed 435 staff and reported an income of $1,156,859.[71] This figure does not include black-owned enterprises outside the retail industry. Many African Americans continued to reside on the east side of Cleveland. Some lived in the area around Central Avenue, bordered on the east by East 55th Street, with Euclid Avenue to the north and the New York Central Railroad tracks in the south. The downtown business area lay to the west.[72]

As stated earlier, during the Great Depression, the economic growth in the American economy declined sharply. As a result, black unemployment was on average about 50 percent, while in some black communities, it was about 90 percent. Yet, black-owned entities continued to develop. They included moving companies, manufacturing companies, insurance companies, restaurants, and grocery stores. Many of the moving companies operated out of their owners' homes. The photo of Lewis and Sons Moving Express dates to the 1920s. Although the business was owned by African Americans, it was located outside of Cuyahoga County. Crayton's Southern Sausage Company was started in 1932 by Leroy Crayton, and five years later, he started a manufacturing and distribution plant that was located around Quincy Avenue and East 90th Street.[73] The Dunbar Mutual Insurance Society was founded by M. C. Clarke in 1937. Two years later, he established the Bardun Mortgage and Investment Company. Slaughter's Grocery Store was established around 1937 and was located on Scovill. Bama's Barbeque existed in the 1930s, and Ulysses S. Dearing also established a restaurant in 1946.

Lewis and Sons Moving Express. *Western Reserve Historical Society*

Dearing had previously worked as a chef in various night clubs in the Cleveland area. His Glenville-based restaurant lasted for a number of years. While some restaurants were owned by men, some were also owned and operated by women.[74] According to Black, "entrepreneurs who owned restaurants were to some extent taking advantage of the southern culture and transporting it to Cleveland."[75]

America's involvement in World War II also had broad effects on the Cleveland economy. The United States entered World War II after the Japanese bombed Pearl Harbor on December 7, 1941. About 160,000 Clevelanders were asked to participate in the wartime effort. Although the city did experience a post-war decline, the demands of increasing wartime production led to an increase in employment levels in 1944, 34 percent more than their level in 1940. Most of this increase occurred in the manufacturing sector. Labor needs of the war economy also led to an increase of about 75 percent in the size of the African American population during the decade of the 1940s.[76]

Black entrepreneurs continued to develop business enterprises. For example, Elie Wrecking and Lumber Company was started in 1945 by Obie and George Elie with one thousand dollars in capital. Several decades later, they had gotten contracts from the government to perform work on the Central Armory as well as the Hopkins Airport.[77]

Slaughter's Grocery Store. *Western Reserve Historical Society*

R.F.W. Realty Company. *Western Reserve Historical Society*

Dearing's Restaurant. *Western Reserve Historical Society*

Two other notable entrepreneurs that emerged during the 1950s were Robert P. Madison and Leroy Ozanne. Madison founded Robert P. Madison International, an architectural firm, while Leroy Ozanne established Ozanne Construction Company. These two entrepreneurs will be discussed in greater detail in chapter 8 of this book, which provides biographical sketches of African American entrepreneurs. The decade of the 1950s is particularly noteworthy because it was during this period that the modern civil rights movement in the United States was born. The period is also momentous because it represented the beginning of the end of legalized segregation. This would have important consequences for African Americans and the black dollar which began to circulate in greater frequency outside of the African American community. The issue of getting blacks to patronize and support their own businesses would be a recurrent theme in the decades to come.[78]

CHAPTER FOUR

Black Economic and Political Development in the Contemporary Period, 1960–2002

The 1960s was one of the most memorable decades of the twentieth century. Several important laws were passed that provided better opportunities for disenfranchised Americans. The Civil Rights Act of 1964, for example, gave the Office of the Attorney General the right to guarantee that the Fourteenth Amendment to the Constitution was actually being enforced. Titles II and III of the 1964 law also gave the attorney general's office the right to implement *Brown v. the Board of Education* (1954), which prohibited segregation in public educational institutions and facilities.[1]

Executive Order 11246 (1965) gave the federal government the authority to challenge employment discrimination. This order, and its amendments, required recipients of federal contracts for more than $50,000 to develop affirmative action plans. Recipients also had to agree not to discriminate in employment and to utilize affirmative action principles in recruiting and hiring minorities and women.[2]

As political and economic opportunities increased for minorities, women, and the disabled, an increasing number of African American men and women entered the world of politics. Carl Stokes, who was elected as the first African American mayor in a major American city in 1967, was a representative of this new group. Stokes was also the first African American Democrat in Cleveland to win a seat in the Ohio legislature. His election as mayor was precipitated by a large mobilization of the black vote at the grassroots level of society.[3] According to William Nelson Jr., "Stokes viewed the outcome of the 1967 mayoral contest not as a personal victory but as a mandate fundamentally to alter the subordinate social, economic, and political posture of the black community. A native of Cleveland, Carl Stokes had been an active participant in the militant struggle for social justice waged in the city by civil rights activists in the 1960s. He represented a new breed of politician, consumed with visions of racial progress and committed to the proposition that creative social change could be achieved through the direct involvement of black administrators in local public policy making."[4]

While interpreting his victory as an important step in his quest to develop

Carl Stokes. *Western Reserve Historical Society*

permanent influence and power for the African American community in Cleveland, Stokes was also mindful of the need to establish a stable political organization that would be useful in putting his social reform agenda in place. This goal was accomplished in large measure during his first term by bringing together black democratic politicians in a separate black caucus unit which was called the Twenty-First District Democratic Caucus (TFDDC). To some extent, the development of the TFDDC provided an avenue through which Stokes and his followers could enhance the level of black influence in the Democratic Party. The refusal by the Cuyahoga County Democratic Party to allow this caucus to be involved in the selection of political candidates was reflective of the unease with which the new organization was greeted. In response to this, the members of the newly formed TFDDC pulled out of the Democratic Party as a group in order to develop their own organization.[5]

Eventually, the TFDDC became a very powerful political organization, similar to a political party. The organization used very formal rules which included screening and selecting candidates beyond party lines as well as putting forward an independent list of candidates for office. In this way, the caucus exercised influence over the black vote whether it was in the city, county, or congressional elections in the Twenty-First district. The caucus made important contributions in Cleveland's political development as it elected candidates from its slate to serve in public office while simultaneously soliciting black support for candidates from both the Democratic and Republican parties.[6] To quote William Nelson Jr., "The consolidation of political power in the office of the mayor, undergirded by the electoral strength of an independent black-controlled political machine, dramatically altered power relations between black and white communities in Cleveland. The existence of a cohesive political party base extending beyond the office of mayor opened the door to the prospect that black political control would become institutionalized in Cleveland. Through shrewd bargaining and careful political organizing, leaders of the caucus would be in a position to wring major concessions from both of the regular political parties."[7]

There is no doubt that Carl Stokes's election as mayor in 1967 served as a catalyst for the involvement of other African Americans in politics—Louis Stokes, Arnold Pinkney, Mike White, Stephanie Tubbs Jones, and others. In 1960, Cleveland's black community comprised about 40 percent of the city's population and yet, they were unable to elect a black representative to Congress because the Ohio legislature had created unacceptable districts. To solve this dilemma, the Cleveland branch of the NAACP put forward a lawsuit that challenged the legality of the procedures being used by the Ohio legislature. The Supreme Court ultimately vindicated the position of the NAACP in the courts as it provided guidelines and suggestions for the eventual development of the Twenty-First Congressional District. The creation of this district ultimately paved the way for the election of the first black congressman in the state of Ohio.[8]

Racial hostility intensified during the 1960s as the Cleveland Public Schools and poor communities were stretched beyond the limits of their capacity as new migrants moved in and needed educational and social services.[9] "Angered by continuing discrimination and segregation in the city schools, blacks picketed the Board of education; in response, whites staged a countermarch into black neighborhoods, overturning cars, breaking store windows, and beating black citizens; blacks then staged spontaneous sit-ins in school headquarters and buildings."[10]

In 1966, a riot broke out in the Hough neighborhood, precipitated by a disagreement between a white bartender and a black client in a bar. This disagreement set off four days and nights of violent activities between the white and black communities. In 1968, the Glenville community was the site of additional violent activities when black nationalists and local police officers clashed in the "Glenville shootout." These local riots were also affected by the increasing push for civil rights, equal opportunity, and economic parity with whites. Although Dr. Martin Luther King Jr. championed the path of nonviolent political change, other individuals supported more militant methods and some even condoned the use of violence. Some groups such as the Black Panthers, the United Black

Alliance, the United Black Student Alliance, and the Black Muslims even supported the black separatist approach.[11]

Carl Stokes served as mayor of Cleveland for two consecutive terms (1967–1971). The evidence indicates that blacks were able to improve their employment situation in various public agencies as well as in city, county, and federal governmental positions. Moreover, over the next few years, they also experienced gains in the Cuyahoga Metropolitan Housing Authority, the Regional Transit Authority (RTA), and the Cleveland Public Schools. On the whole, black politicians in several major cities such as Cleveland, Newark, Atlanta, and Detroit, began to use their power in office to try to effect a positive change in the economic condition of the African American community.[12] This included using a number of strategies such as appointing African Americans to head key city departments, appointing blacks to serve on municipal commissions and boards, as well as increasing their participation in the police forces. Black entrepreneurs benefited enormously under the leadership of Forbes and Stokes, as they literally received millions of dollars from their participation in minority set-aside programs to perform various types of services for the city.[13] According to William Nelson Jr., Carl Stokes was also instrumental in making city contracts available to black-owned businesses as well as helping to establish many profitable businesses. In the words of one of the participants in Nelson's study, "If you were to take the history of (Company X) you would not find any word that Carl founded that company. But he set these guys down in his office one day and said look, you five guys need to work together rather than apart so you can bid on a contract, not just in my administration, but in any administration. And that was the founding of (Company X). This is just one example. I could cite at least a dozen more. Chances are every time you see a large black company in Cleveland, it has some attachment to the Stokes administration."[14]

In *Promises of Power: A Political Autobiography,* Stokes discussed some of the major accomplishments of his administration with regard to the needs of the African American community. While in office, he appointed many African Americans to serve in key policy and decision-making positions in virtually all of the departments affiliated with city government, with the exception of the fire and police departments. (African Americans were hired, however, as police officers.) He also informed trade unions of his intentions to employ craftsmen to work for the city, especially black craftsmen who had historically been excluded by the unions.[15]

One of his major accomplishments was in the area of housing, where he oversaw the development of 5,496 units for low- and moderate-income individuals or families that was valued at more than $102 million. According to Stokes, no other American city could even compete with this record. He also went on the offensive to encourage Cleveland's banking community to be more flexible in developing criteria and standards for small business loans for African Americans. He met with the bankers and reminded them that sometimes black entrepreneurs may not possess the type of training and experience that bankers look for and that some do not have strong credit records and collateral. Nevertheless, Stokes argued that the stringent loan criteria used by the banks would prevent blacks from becoming self-employed. The bankers listened, but did not adjust their policies until Stokes decided to pull $50 million worth of money deposited by the City of Cleveland from the five large Cleveland banks and divide it up among smaller banks. Two days later, the bankers asked to have another meeting with Stokes. During the next thirty-month period, black entrepreneurs were provided with $6 million in loans from Cleveland banks.[16]

Stokes also helped black entrepreneurs by allowing them to supply goods and services to city hall. He "deliberately included the black businessmen in every aspect of the award and hiring process just as they had been deliberately excluded before. [His] actions drew reprisal. White concessionaires and suppliers who had enjoyed the former monopoly circulated rumors that blacks were getting jobs because they were paying off."[17] Stokes was also involved with Cleveland Now, a major fund-raising effort whose chief goal was to raise $177 million during an eighteen-month period. Presumably, the money was to be used to eradicate problems in health, welfare, and employment and for revitalizing Cleveland neighborhoods. Most of the money was earmarked for poor sections of the African American community. More than $5,567,000 was collected during the first part of the fund-raising campaign. Stokes hired more than 270 minorities for professional jobs in the city of Cleveland at a cost of more than $3 million. He also developed a policy to help black entrepreneurs to participate in competitive bidding opportunities for city contracts.[18]

Carl Stokes's two terms in office demonstrated that an African American could successfully serve as mayor of a major American city. But, like the administrations of many of his contemporaries, his was fraught with many frustrations, challenges, and contests over power. Stokes described the situation thusly:

> I have always understood the depth of this country's hostility and resistance when it comes to dealing with the basic functions of the nation. When you start dealing with real change you are talking about interfering with those who are in possession of something. Power never gives up without a struggle. You can get laws passed. You can get expressions and resolutions and even condolences in the proper cases on matters of human concern. But when you start dealing with the basic fundamentals of housing and schools and jobs, then you are talking about fundamental change and you are dealing with a resistance that is not going to yield peacefully. . . . I took the power of the

mayor's office and a solid constituency and went head on against those who didn't want the poor in their neighborhood, didn't want blacks in their neighborhood, were determined to exclude blacks from jobs and new economic opportunity.[19]

Although Stokes had his share of detractors, several black entrepreneurs had a very high regard for him. A number benefited personally from the leadership of Stokes, Forbes, or other black politicians and also participated in minority set-aside programs. Two of these entrepreneurs were Robert P. Madison, CEO of Robert Madison International, an architectural firm, and LeRoy Ozanne, founder and CEO of Ozanne Construction Company. To quote Robert Madison, "I was greatly supportive of Carl Stokes. As a matter of fact, when he was running for mayor the first time, I was with him at almost every debate and I wrote his positions on urban planning, architecture, and the city. And I wrote all of his speeches about that aspect. I was with him all the way and then when he was elected, I was appointed to what was called the Task Force for Community Development. One time they were considering me for the city planning director, but we just decided that I didn't want to do that job. Yes, I knew him very well. I was supportive of him and I was involved and influential in his election."[20]

Although in his autobiography Stokes did not mention having a personal relationship with Robert Madison, he did state that because of his efforts to use more black suppliers in city hall, qualified black entrepreneurs such as Robert and Julian Madison were able to participate in these programs. According to Stokes, because of various contracts received from the city, the Madisons were able to subsequently develop and expand their company from six employees to twenty-six and to open offices in New York and Washington.[21]

One of the most important contributions that Carl Stokes made was in demonstrating that a black man could govern. Stokes did not run again for reelection in 1971. Instead, he tried to help Arnold Pinkney, his chief aide, to be victorious in his bid for the position of mayor. Unfortunately, Pinkney was not successful and Ralph Perk, a Republican, became mayor in 1971. The conflicting relations that subsequently developed between George Forbes, Arnold Pinkney, and Congressman Louis Stokes subverted the possibility of the TFDDC achieving unity. One major point of disagreement arose over issues regarding organizational rules and procedures as well as how political rewards were to be allocated. After Forbes and Pinkney severed their ties with the caucus, other black officials soon followed them into the Democratic Party. Hence, white mayors controlled the city hall in Cleveland until Michael R. White was elected mayor in 1989. During this period of white ethnic control of the mayor's office, however, the city council continued to exercise significant political power and influence under the able leadership of

George Forbes. *Zarc Photo and Design*

George Forbes, who served as its president from 1974 to 1989. He served in this position for about fifteen years, which means that he was at the helm for the longest length of time of any city council president in the history of Cleveland.[22]

Most historians and political scholars seem to agree that "the most powerful black politician in Cleveland (some say the most powerful politician of the 1980s) was George Forbes."[23] His formal entre into politics actually preceded the election of Carl Stokes as mayor, as Forbes was elected to the Cleveland City Council in 1963 shortly after he received his law degree from the John Marshall College of Law. During the tenure of Carl Stokes as mayor, Forbes was considered to be very much a behind-the-scenes player, as he provided Stokes with both encouragement and support. When it became known that Stokes did not desire to seek reelection as mayor for a third time, Forbes's stature increased as he became one of the key negotiators to ameliorate the tension between the Democratic Party of Cuyahoga County and the Twenty-First District Democratic Caucus.[24]

Based on the early details of the agreement negotiated by the party members and the caucus, Forbes was going to serve as the cochair of the county party organization. However, things did not proceed according to the plan. Congressman Louis Stokes took the position and served in this capacity for more than one year. Party officials, however, made an agreement with Forbes that if he would not contest this development and step aside, he would be rewarded by receiving the support of the party officials if he were to run for the presidency of the Cleveland City Council. Subsequently, as agreed upon, Forbes became the president of the Cleveland City Council and also held the role of the county party cochair in 1974.[25]

Forbes became a very powerful political figure in Cleveland as he used both his position as the president of the Cleveland City Council and the cochair of the county party. He was able to skillfully use the new patron-client structures and resources that were at his disposal. Hence, he made innumerable contacts that allowed him to develop structures of support at both the city and county levels. Moreover, as president of the Cleveland City Council, he was able to further solidify and extend his power base "to become boss of the new Cleveland machine."[26] "The foundation of his power base was his ability to collect IOUs by determining the distribution of public and private patronage to members of the city council. A skilled administrator and politician, he parlayed his control over committee assignments and budgets into almost dictatorial control over the council."[27]

Forbes was also able to develop linkages with the business community of Cleveland, most particularly during the administration of Mayor Ralph J. Perk. Forbes actually worked with Perk to get the City Council to pass a redevelopment package designed to provide generous incentives and benefits to members of the business community. One of the main parts of the plan was the issue of tax abatement that would allow large corporations that were involved in doing construction projects to receive exemption for paying local taxes. It is unclear, however, how small businesses benefited from tax abatement initiatives. Forbes emerged during the Perk administration as a great friend of big business interests and he fought the efforts of Mayor Dennis Kucinich to eliminate tax benefits for large corporations.[28]

Forbes also fought for the rights and needs of black people in the city of Cleveland. His outspokenness on behalf of blacks, various unflattering remarks made on his radio show about whites, as well as the methods he utilized through the years, have alienated him from some sectors of the white community. That factor affected him when he ran for mayor in 1989 against Michael White. White received about 81 percent of the vote cast in white wards while Forbes only received 19 percent.[29] When I interviewed Mr. Forbes in 1999 and asked him about his political mission in Cleveland society, he was quite clear as he stated,

I had not forgotten that I was a black man. . . . I primarily represented black people, and I did represent some whites by the people who sent me. I knew that I was a black representative taking care of and representing those needs. I remember when Carl Stokes was the mayor. The snow was removed on the west side for white people faster than it was moved on the east side. Garbage was picked up on the west side faster than it was picked up on the east side, not because he [Carl Stokes] wanted it that way, but that was the way they had always done it. Bureaucracy was set in such a way. So, if you don't have black men and women in power saying no, it must be equal, I took the opposite approach. You are going to do it first for my people. If you did it for the whites before, all's fair in world politics, you take care of blacks first as far as I was concerned. I said that because I think that if young black men and women don't take care of the needs of black people, who else is going to take care of them? Martin Hoke? There is a tremendous need for development and a tremendous need for services in the black community. If you don't get it from your black representative, you're damn sure not going to get it from the whites. I feel very strongly about that.[30]

In spite of Forbes's efforts to improve the situation of African Americans, he was criticized by some African Americans for having too many links to the establishment in Cleveland and for not being connected to the real plight of the black poor.[31]

The Stokes and Forbes eras also coincided with the expansion of government programs that were specifically aimed at enhancing the growth and development of small and minority-owned business enterprises. Although the Small Business Administration (SBA) was created in 1953, its initial focus was not on minority businesses. Rather, it paid attention primarily to small businesses, most of which were owned by white entrepreneurs. A few years later in 1958, the status of the SBA grew as it became a permanent federal agency. At this time, one of the major focuses of the agency was to provide economic assistance in the form of loans to small businesses, as well as to assist them in receiving federal contract dollars.[32]

It was really during the presidency of Lyndon Johnson that the federal government first began to speak of affirmative action in Executive Order 10925 in 1965, which was signed by the president. Executive Order 11246, also passed in 1965, focused attention on providing more equality in the area of employment discrimination. In other words, this order, and its subsequent amendments mandated that any entitiy that received federal dollars for contracts in excess of $50,000 had to develop written affirmative action plans and utilize principles of affirmative action in their recruitment and hiring processes. All of these programs helped to lay the foundation and provide a climate that was conducive to establishing programs to assist African American entrepreneurs in the future.[33]

The Small Business Act of 1967 provided set-asides at the federal level for minority businesses that were eligible to participate. During the decade of the 1960s, however, members of Congress also expressed interest in supporting economically disadvantaged segments of the small business sector. Hence, the amendment to the Economic Opportunity Act of 1967 encouraged the SBA to focus on the needs of small businesses in urban or rural areas with high incidences of unemployment or people with low incomes as well as businesses owned by individuals with low incomes.[34] According to Timothy Bates, "The notion of focusing assistance specifically on minority entrepreneurs arose during the War on Poverty years of the mid-1960s. Since minority business set-asides were first formulated in the War on Poverty milieu, the program logically focused initially upon entrepreneurs with very low income. The language of 'socially or economically disadvantaged' entrepreneurs being eligible for 8(a) program assistance, however, opened the door to participation by minority entrepreneurs whose incomes actually exceeded those with a poverty level of existence."[35]

President Richard Nixon also supported the cause of minority business development when he issued Executive Order 11458 (1969), which laid the groundwork for the development of a national program which was designed to provide assistance to minority-owned firms. The secretary of commerce was given the task of establishing procedures and activities at all levels to enhance the survivability of minority businesses. Leaders of various federal departments were held responsible for developing reports for the commerce secretary who articulated the plan to promote success for minority businesses. The result of these efforts was the development of the Office of Minority Business Enterprise.[36]

Section 8(a) of the Small Business Act was particularly noteworthy because it provided an opportunity for the federal government to increase the number of minorities who participated in federal procurement efforts because the SBA was given the opportunity to establish contracts with federal agencies who subsequently awarded contract dollars to small businesses. In 1969, about $8.9 million was distributed to minority firms under the umbrella of the 8(a) program. In 1973, the value of the set-asides distributed to minorities had increased to $208 million, while between 1968 and 1977, $2.2 billion was awarded to minority businesses in federal dollars.[37] The Public Works Employment Act of 1977 as well as the Omnibus Small Business Act of 1978 developed goals for providing contracts for minority businesses. According to the above legislation, about 10 percent of all federal contracts that were awarded for local public works projects had to be given to minority business enterprises.[38]

Ohio's Minority Business Enterprise Act, House Bill 584, was passed by the state legislature in 1980. House Bill 584 was especially fortuitous for minority business development because it contained a number of important provisions that were designed to facilitate the growth and expansion of minority business enterprises. The bill "set aside 5 percent of the aggregate value of all state construction contracts and 15 percent of the aggregate value of state procurement contracts each fiscal year for bidding upon by minority business enterprises only." Furthermore, the law stipulated that construction contracts that were entered into by the state provide for about 7 percent of the overall value of the contract to be provided to minority subcontractors, service providers, and material men unless the Set-Aside Review Board modified or changed the requirement.[39]

Minority business enterprises were defined as business entities in which 51 percent of the company was "owned and controlled" by Ohioans who were from groups who were "economically disadvantaged." This included African Americans, Hispanics, Native Americans, and Asians. To participate in these state set-aside programs, the owner had to demonstrate that he/she owned the firm for at least one year before he/she applied for participation. The bill included many other benefits for minority firms including the creation of the Minority Business Development Division in the Department of Economic and Community Development as well as encouraging the Ohio Development Financing Commission to provide loans to minority businesses, community improvement corporations, and Ohio development corporations.[40]

Several of Cleveland's black political leaders have been supporters of affirmative action and set-aside programs. For example, George Forbes used the power of his office as city council president to develop affirmative action requirements for the city and he was also an outspoken advocate against racial inequities in the area of housing and law enforcement. In March of 1983, he demanded that airlines using Cleveland Hopkins International Airport implement Cleveland's Equal Employment Opportunity standards.[41] Forbes is also an entrepreneur himself. He is currently the managing partner of Forbes, Fields and Associates Co., L.P.A.[42]

A number of African American businesses in Cleveland participated in and benefited from minority set-aside programs. Nevertheless, these programs have increasingly come under attack in the wake of challenges to the basic principles of affirmative action. A number of cases against affirmative action were launched on the basis of "reverse discrimination" claims. The case of *Fullilove v. Klutznick* in 1977 is noteworthy because the Supreme Court reaffirmed its commitment to the federal set-aside program, which made it mandatory that state and local governments that applied for grants under the umbrella of the Public Works Employment Act of 1977 demonstrate that at least 10 percent of each grant would be used for contracts with minority businesses. As the Supreme Court upheld the 10 percent set-aside program, they emphasized the broad power of the Congress to try to overcome the impact of past discriminatory behavior.[43]

The famous Croson case, however, opened a floodgate of lawsuits against minority set-aside programs all over the United States. In many ways, the Supreme Court's decision in this case negated the progress that had been made in *Fullilove v. Klutznick.* The Croson case attacked the minority set-aside program that had been established by the city of Richmond, Virginia. This program allowed for the provision of 30 percent of contracts awarded by the city to be set aside for bids from minority contractors because of a record of past discrimination evidenced in Richmond in terms of the number of contracts that had been awarded to minorities. White contractors challenged the constitutionality of the program and received support from the Reagan administration that supported the utilization of a "strict scrutiny" test.[44]

> The majority decision, written by Justice O'Connor, made the critical constitutional determination that the strict scrutiny standard of review must be applied to state and local government set-aside programs. Under the strict scrutiny standard, [the] government must show that it is pursuing a compelling or overriding end, one whose value is so great that it justifies the limitation of fundamental constitutional values. Justice O'Connor observed that strict scrutiny was particularly appropriate in *Croson* because of the political power wielded by blacks in the city of Richmond, where 50 percent of the population was black and five of the nine city council seats were held by blacks. Further, the majority court was most concerned with the lack of showing prior discrimination by the City of Richmond.[45]

A number of set-aside programs were deemed "unconstitutional" by the courts using these "strict scrutiny" standards, including the programs in Atlanta and Cleveland. In the case of Atlanta, the Supreme Court in Georgia ruled that its set-aside programs were invalid and used the arguments advanced in the Croson decision to undergird its decision. The courts in Ohio have vacillated about the merits of using affirmative action and set-aside programs. In 1982, Judge Kinneary struck down House Bill 584, the Minority Business Enterprise Act, passed in 1980. In 1983, the court of appeals reversed this decision arguing that minorities had been affected by discriminatory behavior that existed in the procedures used in Ohio's purchasing and contract plans and policies.[46]

On March 28, 1996, Governor George V. Voinovich issued two executive orders in response to a detailed review of affirmative action programs in Ohio. The conclusions of the review indicated that Ohio's method of certifying minority businesses as well as its procedures for setting aside state funds for minority businesses, was not efficient in reaching the majority of minority businesses. Voinovich introduced a new program that used economic need and social disadvantage as criteria for participating in state set-aside programs.[47]

George Forbes is very concerned about introducing new groups (i.e., those socially disadvantaged groups) into the set-aside programs. Under these new provisions, economically disadvantaged whites would qualify. For Forbes, one major problem was that although new groups were being allowed to participate in the programs, the amount of money available for the contracts would not necessarily be expanded. This would lead to a situation where a larger group of people would be competing for a smaller piece of the pie. According to Forbes, "The courts are now restricting the set-asides but in order to preserve [them] in Ohio, [they are saying] I want to broaden it to Appalachia. I want to bring in Appalachian whites. I want to put it on an economic basis as well."[48]

In October 1996, State Magistrate Rita Bash Eaton ruled that Ohio should provide affirmative action awards using economic need as its criterion, rather than race. Hence, she argued that Ohio's Minority Business Set-Aside Program was unconstitutional when race-based criteria excluded individuals who experience economic disadvantage.[49] On April 7, 1999, the Ohio Supreme Court voted unanimously that a certain segment of Ohio's state set-aside programs for minority contractors was "constitutional." At present, then, set-asides for construction services are considered invalid, while programs for goods and services are still allowed. In 1999 alone, minorities and women received between $15 and $18 million in contracts from Cuyahoga County under the aegis of its Equal Economic Opportunity Program.[50]

In January 2000, the Equal Opportunity Program was formally repealed by the Cuyahoga County commissioners. This did away with a 1993 resolution that made it mandatory that both suppliers and contractors use minority subcontractors when they make their bids. One of the most noticeable effects of this repeal is that although women and minorities are still eligible for county bids, the previous requirement that majority-owned firms were compelled to do business with minority-owned firms, is no longer in place. In June of 2000, a federal appeals court rejected an Ohio program that committed millions of dollars in state construction contracts for minority-owned businesses. The 6th U.S. Circuit of Appeals, in a 3-0 vote, upheld a lower court's decision that found the law creating the program to be unconstitutional.[51]

The Associated General Contractors, the statewide contractors' organization that challenged the law, contends that forbidding non-minority contractors to bid on jobs set aside for minority contractors is illegal. The contractors were upset with minority-only bidding in the construction of the $10 million administration building that is part of a $50 million state prison being built near Toledo. A lawyer for the contractors' association argued that Ohio failed to justify the program by not providing evidence of historic discrimination against minorities who bid for state contracts.[52]

The end result of the various challenges to affirmative action programs has been an increase in the number of disparity studies that have been performed by state and local governments in the United States in recent years. These studies have been very costly. Disparity studies are also known as discrimination studies or predicate studies. One main function of a disparity study is to ascertain whether a local bias has developed against minorities with regard to economic and/or business discrimination. Several entities in the greater Cleveland area united their efforts to commission a disparity study. These groups include the Cleveland Municipal School District, Cuyahoga County, the city of Cleveland, the RTA, the Cleveland–Cuyahoga County Port Authority, Cuyahoga Community College, and the Cuyahoga Metropolitan Housing Authority. The state of Ohio has also commissioned a disparity study. In spite of all the controversy and uncertainty around minority set-aside programs, the statistical tests performed in my study demonstrate that they have a positive empirical impact on the success of African American entrepreneurs in Cleveland. Moreover, 67 percent of the entrepreneurs in my study felt that minority set-asides have had a positive impact on society.[53]

Over the past few decades, Cleveland, like many other American cities, has experienced significant economic change. One major shift has been the gradual movement away from an economy that was previously centered around manufacturing and durable goods to one that now incorporates a large number of service-related entities. Many changes also occurred with regard to employment opportunities in various industries in Cleveland. While employment in the goods-producing sector decreased by 22 percent, which was roughly equivalent to a loss of 69,000 jobs from 1979 to 1990, employment in the service-related areas experienced an increase of 16 percent or a net gain of 99,600 jobs.[54]

A second major change occurred in the shift of Cleveland's population. In 1900, Cleveland's population was 381,768. By 1950, the population had increased to 914,808. In 1990, the population had declined to 505,616, only "55 percent of its population in 1950."[55] About half of the population in Cleveland was African American in 1990.[56]

More recent reports released from the U.S. Census Bureau in October 2000 indicate that the current population trend discussed above is continuing as the exodus of people from large cities in Ohio to suburban areas is continuing. These statistics indicate that Akron, Canton, and Cleveland are experiencing population losses while areas like Twinsburg, Wadsworth, and Green are increasing in population size. According to the report, Cleveland's population had decreased to 501,662 by 1999. Cuyahoga County experienced a loss of 40,423 people from 1990–1999, which brought its population to just under 1.4 million.[57]

The economic situation in Cleveland continued to deteriorate to such a serious level that on December 15, 1978, Cleveland became the first American city to default on its loans since the Depression. Undoubtedly, the continual loss of jobs and the subsequent movement of people out of the city had severe long-term consequences for the city's ever-decreasing tax base. The roots of this contemporary crisis, however, can be traced back to the decade of the 1970s when voters refused to support the proposals that would have increased the income tax collected by the city. Consequently, by the time Carl Stokes completed his two terms in office as mayor, the city had accumulated a deficit of about $13 million. Ralph Perk, who succeeded Stokes as mayor, began to borrow money and to use bond funds to try to make up for the budgetary shortfall. He allegedly sold or leased several assets of the city. Thus, by the time Dennis Kucinich became mayor in 1978, little else could be done other than to default on the city's loans.[58]

African American businesses continued to develop during the 1970s as some of the entrepreneurs become more involved in owning franchises of national chains such as Burger King, McDonald's, and Popeye Restaurants. Several local entrepreneurs who were a part of this group included Narlie Roberts, Caesar Burkes, James Haynes, Dr. Oscar Saffold, Sam Tidmore, and Van McCoy. In the city of East Cleveland, Telecable Broadcasting of America was established under the leadership of Zakee Rashid, Ben Davis, Tom Darden, and Al Quarles in the 1970s and 1980s. Cheryle Wills, an African American female, also became chairman of the board of an integrated cable television franchise. James Taylor started an African American–owned radio station, WJTB, very close to Cleveland, while Hubert Payne helped to start WOIO (Channel 19).[59]

The 1970s were also memorable because another black-owned financial institution, the First Bank and Trust, was established in June 1974. According to John Bustamante, one of the bank's founders, it was developed primarily to provide economic resources to African American entrepreneurs and members of the African American community. Bustamante served as the chairman, chief executive officer, and president of the bank. The bank began its existence with $2.5 million in assets.[60]

The First Bank and Trust was a publicly held company and shares of stock were sold for $100 a share. About 80 percent of its stockholders were African Americans. Bustamante purchased 8,000 shares for a total of $800,000, making him one of the largest shareholders. Some of the other individuals who were instrumental in working with him to develop the bank included Leroy Ozanne, Harvey O. Mierke Jr., Timothy L. Stephens Jr., Wesley Toles, Carole F. Hoover, Fred M. Crosby, Dr. Esque Crawford, John James Carney, and Jacques L. Bossert.[61]

The bank was located in the downtown district at 232 Superior Avenue. By 1975, the assets of the bank had increased to $15.2 million, of which $90,366 was the net income. By 1976, the bank's name was changed to First Bank National

Association and through its acquisition of Community National Bank, its assets doubled in size. By May of 1982, the bank became the fourth largest African American–owned bank in the country. By this time, the bank employed 110 staff and had assets in excess of $68 million. In 1984, the bank was awarded the "Minority Bank of the Year Award" by the Minority Business Development Agency (MBDA) of the Department of Commerce. It also received the "Service Firm of the Year Award" in 1984 from the Chicago Region of the MBDA. By 1987, the unpaid loans of the bank led to a deficit of $3.2 million. Eventually the bank was unable to get more capital to cover its losses and was closed because of federal regulations in 1990.[62]

A critical question becomes, why did a highly capitalized, award-winning bank subsequently fail? In retrospect, several key factors contributed to the bank's eventual demise. First, the bank was established during the 1970s. During the administration of President Jimmy Carter, inflation and unemployment were very high as well as interest rates charged on loans by financial lending institutions. Bustamante actually advised some of the bank's loan customers to wait until the interest rates dropped before taking out loans. It was also during the 1970s that many savings and loan companies failed all over the United States. Second, many of the loans taken from the bank were never repaid. According to the bank's 1984 annual report, by the end of that year, it had a net loss of $861,000, which was largely attributable to significant charge-offs for unpaid commercial loans. Third, in 1984 First Bank became a holding bank when it purchased a banking facility located in Warrensville Heights. Although the assets of the bank initially increased, it is unclear whether this acquisition was beneficial to the bank's economic condition over the long term.[63]

Fourth, during the 1980s, First Bank and many other financial institutions became subject to excessive regulation by the federal government. In his 1984 annual report for the bank, Bustamante wrote, "The onslaught of deregulation, changes in regulatory policies, rules, objectives and procedures, the need to remain technologically advanced and non-bank competition, have all been difficult and costly during the past year." The following photograph of Bustamante seems to convey his own dismay at overregulation of financial lending institutions. The end result of this overregulation meant that the bank officers and other officials of First Bank had less time to work on the day-to-day operations of the bank because they had to produce so many materials for inspection by representatives of the federal government. These actions seriously hampered the overall effectiveness of the bank.[64]

Last, although Bustamante had a strong legal background, he did not possess extensive experience or education in the banking area. Nor did he have a business degree, which may have provided more management skills to him in his

John Bustamante shows concern about the overregulation of the First Bank. *John Bustamante.*

capacity of chief executive officer. Bustamante believes that certain individuals or entities probably wanted the bank to fail for various reasons. Although, most of the bank's customers were black, they also had clients from other racial groups as well.[65] According to Leroy Ozanne,

> The bank was never that profitable, but it maintained itself for that period of time until I guess we organized it to become a minority bank. I think what caused its demise was the fact that we thought we could become just a bank, and there's a word I will never forget. The people that spoke against us said that our "oligopolistic" attitudes with the other banks would not permit this bank to

From left: Judge George W. White, Kenneth L. White, and Bessie House-Soremekun at the golf course of First Club of Cleveland, Inc., Lodi, Ohio.

survive. And, of course, whether they intended it or not, the major banks did have better quality loans and degrees of deals on savings, investments, . . . We didn't have any great expertise in real estate and at that time it wasn't a very good spot to put dollars. Interest rates were really high. So, it failed.[66]

When the bank failed, all of the investors lost their money. The bank deposits, however, were backed up by the Federal Reserve Bank and were insured up to $100,000 per account.[67] When asked about what the possibilities are for another minority bank to be developed in Cleveland, Ozanne said, "I would see absolutely no possibility and the main reason I don't see a possibility is the fact of the acquisition of banks by other banks. Getting involved in the insurance business and securities business, which would eliminate, in my opinion, a struggling, small, capital-supplying bank. There are many other areas of business that you can get involved in rather than a bank, in my opinion."[68]

The 1980s also witnessed the development of an African American–owned country club outside of Cleveland in Lodi, Ohio. The country club is called First Club of Cleveland, Incorporated, and was established by Judge George W. White. The club is a nonprofit business entity that was created primarily to provide African Americans with the opportunity to do networking in a congenial environment. The club is located on 34.5 acres of land and has a par 3 golf course. Presently, there are about 60 members but additional members are welcome. Although most of the club's members are African Americans, other groups are also welcome to join.[69]

The African American community continued to face challenges in terms of economic and social mobility on into the latter decades of the twentieth century. By the latter part of the 1980s, almost half of all Cleveland households were either at or below the poverty line, and about half of the students in the public schools did not graduate from high school. Many parents who did not want to have their children bused in order to achieve integration, left the public school system and sent their children to private schools. One factor that precipitated the "white flight" from the city of Cleveland was a decision made by U.S. District Judge Frank Battisti that Cleveland and the state boards of education were to be held accountable for the racial segregation that permeated Cleveland's public schools. Hence, the school system was ordered to desegregate. Battisti's court decision came about as a result of a lawsuit filed by the Cleveland branch of the NAACP. The segregation that existed at this time in Cleveland's public school was to some degree a reflection of the deeply rooted segregation patterns that existed in its housing patterns, as well as in the society at large.[70]

Additionally, although some African American families moved into the middle-class category, many were still living in poverty. As a result of the economic restructuring process that was still underway in Cleveland, many businesses moved to the suburbs or to other states and countries where it was cheaper to operate. The resultant loss of jobs in the manufacturing sector hurt both blacks and whites. However, blacks were affected disproportionately. By 1990, Cleveland's black unemployment rate had reached 20 percent and discriminatory housing patterns continued to exist. The poverty rate in 1994 was exceedingly high at 42.2 percent. Wye has argued that Cleveland's black community was actually better off in 1970 than it was in 1990.[71]

Black political power declined somewhat during the 1980s, although George Forbes was still a major political figure. Congressman Louis Stokes still represented Ohio and continued to be an advocate for the disadvantaged groups in society. Nevertheless, he was never able to develop a formidable power base in the local political arena in Cleveland because he spent so much of his time in Washington. George Forbes ran against Michael White for mayor in 1989, and at first Forbes was believed to have better odds than White to be elected. Forbes had actually been very instrumental in enhancing White's earlier political career as he was helpful in working out the details of White's appointment to a seat which became open in the Ohio senate.[72]

Louis Stokes. *Western Reserve Historical Society*

White, who also had served on the Cleveland city council, became critical of Forbes, and during the mayoral campaign, articulated his vision of promoting better racial relations in Cleveland as well as enhancing economic growth and development. Michael White garnered 56 percent of the vote in the general election, and George Forbes received 44 percent. Although Michael White was controversial as mayor, he accomplished a great deal while in office. He spent a great deal of time in spearheading an effort to revitalize the downtown corporate section of the city of Cleveland. This included, among other things, the development of the Rock 'n' Roll Hall of Fame; enhancing Cleveland Hopkins Airport; the development of the Gateway Project, which included the construction of a baseball stadium for the Cleveland Indians and a basketball facility for the Cleveland Cavaliers (Gund Arena). He also focused attention on redeveloping inner-city communities. Under his leadership, Cleveland received several block grants that were used to develop new housing stock.[73]

Additionally, during Mayor White's tenure, the city of Cleveland became an active participant in the federal government's Empowerment Zone Program, an

Michael White. *Photo by Polk Photography*

initiative of the Department of Housing and Urban Development specifically developed to provide assistance to economically distressed urban centers. The geographic location of Cleveland's empowerment zones included Hough, Glenville, Fairfax, as well as the Midtown Corridor area, which includes portions of Hough, Central, and the Goodrich-Kirtland area. Over a ten-year period, the city of Cleveland received $87 million from Federal Economic Development Initiative grants; $87 million from Housing and Urban Development Section 108 loans; and about $3 million from grants accessed through Title 20 funding. To be considered for inclusion in empowerment zone areas, the communities had to be characterized as high poverty areas with high levels of unemployment and poor infrastructural capabilities. White created the Minority Business Council, which was designed to help minority contractors and businesses acquire city contracts. Additionally, U.S. District Judge George W. White decided to give control of the Cleveland Public Schools to Mayor Michael White and his appointed school board on September 9, 1998.[74]

Yet, not all black businesses benefited from economic projects that White has supported or received patronage from the mayor. For example, Leroy Ozanne stated that he had not been given the opportunity to participate in some of the major construction projects that took place during the White administration. There could be a number of reasons to explain this, one of which might be the fact that Ozanne was an ardent supporter of George Forbes rather than Michael White in the mayoral election of 1989. Madison, on the other hand, benefited from the political patronage of both Carl Stokes and Michael White as he has helped to develop several of the buildings in downtown Cleveland. When I asked Madison about his personal perceptions of White as mayor, he said:

> I think Mayor Mike White is one of the great mayors of our time. He has prob-lems, he's controversial, but in terms of being a mayor, and doing what a mayor's supposed to do, he has no equal. I didn't say that I go to dinner with him. I don't play cribbage with him. I said as a mayor, and what he was hired to do, he has no equal. He's a 24 hour a day, 7 days a week mayor. He's concerned about every aspect of it. I think he is also very concerned. He's proven that minorities do as good or better than anybody else, in his ability to see that people are getting support and I think more than anything, the fact that he took the Board of Education and decided to do everything he could for the school system because it was a shambles. But as chief executive officer of this city, he looked upon it as being his responsibility to see these children get a better education. All those things that they say about Mayor White, I won't even dignify it. But in terms of his mission, there's no doubt in my mind that he's great.[75]

CHAPTER FIVE

The Contemporary Condition of
Black-Owned Businesses in Cleveland

In this chapter, African American entrepreneurs are compared with white entrepreneurs in order to examine the unique challenges and constraints they face in the area of entrepreneurship. Local data on entrepreneurs in Cleveland is also compared with national data. The findings of this study demonstrate that African American entrepreneurs continue to make notable contributions to the local and national economy. These include, among other factors, providing important goods and services; providing employment to minority workers and other groups; paying taxes; assisting with the infrastructural needs of their communities; creating innovative products to be marketed and disseminated to consumers; engaging in philanthropy for various causes in the minority and majority communities; and serving as mentors and role models.

The vast majority of black businesses in this study operated using the corporation model, while fewer operated as sole proprietorships or partnerships. This was also true for the white entrepreneurs. Nationally, most black businesses are sole proprietorships. The largest group of both black owners and white owners owned a majority of the stock in their respective companies.

Fewer than one-third of the black owners indicated that their businesses were registered as certified minority business enterprises. A smaller percentage of the white businesses were certified. One of the major benefits of being certified was that entrepreneurs were eligible to participate in minority set-aside programs in the state of Ohio. In order to be certified as a minority business, at least 51 percent of the company had to be owned by an African American, Hispanic, Asian American, or Native American. Female-owned businesses also were eligible to participate in these programs. More recently, an "economically or socially disadvantaged category" has been added to the program, which means that other individuals are eligible to participate regardless of race. As stated in chapter 4, until 1999, Ohio set aside 5 percent of the aggregate value of contracts for state construction and 15 percent of the aggregate value of state procurement contracts for bids from businesses that were minority-owned. Seven percent of the overall value of the contracts was made available for minority subcontractors. In order to participate, businesses had to be certified.

Both black owners and white owners had generally high rates of involvement in the daily operations of their firms. Owners from both groups signed checks for their firms and were responsible for hiring their employees. More than half of the black owners were between the ages of forty-one and fifty, while the ages of white owners were spread more across several age categories. The majority of respondents in the black sample were male, while the largest group of white respondents were female. Most of the black owners and white owners were married, which is an important measure in this study of domestic stability.

Four major categories of businesses were included in this study. These were service, construction, retail/trade, and manufacturing. Most of the black businesses in this study (55 percent) were service-related entities. Fewer black entrepreneurs owned businesses in the areas of manufacturing, service, and construction. At the national level, most black businesses are also service-related entities. The largest number of white entrepreneurs (64 percent) also owned service-related businesses. Thus, both black and white business owners were overrepresented in the service category and underrepresented in construction and manufacturing, which typically have higher rates of profitability. This study focuses particular attention on African American businesses, however. A critical question becomes, why do African Americans gravitate toward service-related enterprises in such large proportion? One reason for the emphasis on service is historical in nature and can be traced back to the discrimination blacks experienced as they migrated from the South to find work in industries in the North, Midwest, and East. Many barriers existed with respect to equal opportunity in society and have been addressed in great detail in chapters 3 and 4. One important factor is that the few blacks who did secure employment in Cleveland usually did so in service-related industries. Hence, even today, data from this study indicate that African Americans in Cleveland usually decide to start businesses in areas in which they have prior experience or in which they believe they have a talent or skill. Additionally, many blacks may not possess the requisite skills or capital necessary to develop businesses in construction or manufacturing. Starting a construction or manufacturing business usually requires more start-up capital than many businesses in the area of service (particularly personal services) and retail/trade. Black and white involvement in the service-related industries is also related to economic restructuring processes that have been taking place at the national and local levels of society in the United States in recent decades.

Most black and white businesses in this study were first-generation enterprises, meaning that few were family-based businesses that had been passed down from

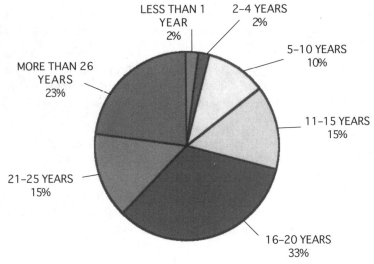

Fig. 1 Years of business operation, black respondents

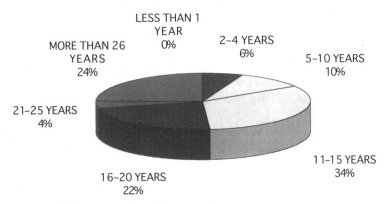

Fig. 2 Years of business operation, white respondents

generation to generation. Nevertheless, more white entrepreneurs inherited their businesses from family members. Fewer black businesses were self-sustaining across time.

Longevity is an important issue in assessing the overall success of the firms in this study. Almost one-fourth of both black businesses and white businesses had been in operation for more than twenty-six years. Fifteen percent of the black-owned businesses had been in existence for between twenty-one and twenty-five years compared to 4 percent of the white-owned businesses. Fifteen percent of the black firms had been in existence for between eleven and fifteen years in contrast to 34 percent of the white enterprises (see figures 1 and 2)

The data in this study corroborate two of Timothy Bates's arguments that black businesses do create jobs and that they hire predominantly black workers. Although there was a wide range with regard to the number of employees in their firms, only a few of either the black or white entrepreneurs had more than fifty employees. The majority of the employees hired by black firms were black, while most employees hired in the white firms were white. One of the most interesting findings of this study, which speaks to the increasing relevance of performing studies such as this, is that black business owners consistently hire minority workers. These data confirm an earlier argument made by Bates that while black owners tend to hire minority workers in their firms, this is in direct contrast to white owners who continue to exclude minorities from their workplace environments. According to Bates, this phenomenon holds true regardless of where the firms are located. In other words, white employers rely on a predominantly and sometimes exclusively white labor force even when their businesses are found in inner-city neighborhoods. In contrast, black firms in these same communities employ a largely minority workforce.[1]

The issue of education and business training is important in this study because knowledge is considered to be a form of human capital. As Frank Fratoe has argued, "The education and experience each individual brings to business ownership determines to a great extent how well that person performs. Human capital thus is our fourth critical factor for development. One of the soundest policies a community can adopt is to invest in high quality education systems that not only teach the basics well but help individuals recognize personal and economic opportunities. Secondary and post secondary education focused on developing latent business skills could produce many potential entrepreneurs."[2]

There was a wide disparity between the educational levels of the black and white business owners. Thirty-one percent of the African American entrepreneurs had received undergraduate degrees as their highest level of education while 16 percent had postgraduate degrees. This means that 47 percent of the black entrepreneurs had college degrees or better. This stands in stark contrast to 80 percent of the white entrepreneurs who had undegraduate degrees or higher (see figures 3 and 4). The data presented here on the educational attainment of black and white entrepreneurs are generally consistent with national data on education, which demonstrates that blacks still lag behind whites in attaining education at every level of the educational system. This local data should also be considered in conjunction with the fact that Cleveland's public schools have experienced a serious decline in terms of their ability to provide quality instruction not only for future entrepreneurs, but also for the future workforce. Additionally, many blacks who have MBA degrees decide to work for corporations and other types of entities rather than to be self-employed. Deciding to become an entrepreneur as well as receiving appropriate

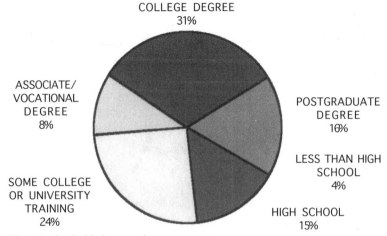

Fig. 3 Education levels, black respondents

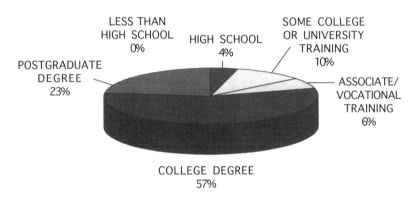

Fig. 4 Education levels, white respondents

levels of education and training also relate to the issue of economic culture in terms of whether self-employment is a value that is passed down in the family unit from generation to generation or whether a person was encouraged to work for someone else. National data again illustrates that blacks enter self-employment at a much lower rate than do whites. African Americans also experience difficulties in sustaining these businesses across time, as the discussion in chapter 3 indicated.

When black business owners were asked about various other types of training they had received through the years in the area of business management or accounting, they provided the following answers: 40 percent learned about business through college credits; 22 percent learned from company-generated materials; 5 percent learned from correspondence work; 14 percent had no training in business or accounting; 14 percent learned in other ways such as on-the-job training and SBA seminars. Among whites, 36 percent reported they learned about business from college credits; 33 percent learned from company-generated materials; 5 percent learned from high school courses; 15 percent learned from other sources such as seminars; and 11 percent had no training. While some black entrepreneurs use written business plans to guide the activities of their firms, many do not. Both groups of owners experience problems related to accounting or tax issues and also indicated that they sometimes have problems determining the appropriate pricing of their products or services in order to remain profitable.

Capitalization and equity are important issues because a number of previous studies have shown that access to capital and credit have proven to be major barriers that have affected the economic success of black entrepreneurs. Bates has argued that "the most serious constraint on the formation, growth, and diversification of black business has been rooted in problems of capitalization. Taken together, lack of personal wealth holdings and discriminatory treatment by commercial banks have produced an enormous obstacle to existing as well as potential black entrepreneurs."[3] Additionally, several studies have shown that some minority communities are redlined and that African Americans experience more difficulty than whites in acquiring assistance from banks and other financial lending institutions. The data from my study certainly substantiates these claims.

More than half of both black owners and white owners started their businesses with very little capital input (less than ten thousand dollars). This is consistent with national data, which demonstrates that most black owners started their business operations with relatively small resources. Butler has noted that in 1982, almost 70 percent of black owners started businesses without relying on borrowed funds. The majority of the owners started their businesses with less than five thousand dollars.[4] In my study, the majority of the black owners relied on their personal savings to start their businesses, while fewer received assistance from friends or relatives. A small minority relied on bank loans. Although more white owners in the sample started their businesses with bank loans than black owners, some white owners also used their personal savings to launch their businesses. The fact that a large group of the black entrepreneurs had to deplete their savings accounts in order to start their firms is also related to the fact that many of them reported that they had experienced difficulties in receiving assistance from formal lending institutions. Slightly more than one-third of the black owners reported that they never have problems when seeking financial backing for their businesses in stark contrast to more than half of the white owners who reported that they never have problems with seeking financial backing for their business operations. Even highly successful black business owners who operated profitable businesses that had been in operation for long periods of time indicated to me that they still experienced difficulty in acquiring bank loans.

Although there was some variation between the samples in terms of the level of business debt of both groups of business owners, most white owners owed less than ten thousand dollars in business debt. Having a low business debt is also linked to the fact that a large group of the black entrepreneurs started their businesses by exhausting their personal savings accounts. This meant that their level of business debt was initially low because they relied on their personal resources to launch their operations.

In an effort to gauge or assess the profitability of the individual firms, the owners were asked what their total profits were in United States dollars per year. By profit, I meant the amount the business owner makes after expenses are paid. Because of the sensitive nature of the question and because I was dependent on owners to disclose confidential information about themselves, it is at least possible that some respondents may have overinflated or underreported the actual amount they make per year in profit. However, I believe that most owners were probably candid on this question.

Almost half of the black owners (47 percent) and 41 percent of the white owners earn less than $40,000 per year in profits. Thirty-six percent of the black owners and 19 percent of the whites earned between $40,000 and $99,999 in profit. Three percent of the black owners earned between $750,000 and $1,000,000. More whites than blacks earned a profit that exceeded a million dollars each year (see figures 5 and 6).

I was particularly interested to know more about the black entrepreneurs in this study who earned less than $40,000 per year in profits. I performed cross tabulations on the data and found that 34 percent of these entrepreneurs had only been in business between one and five years while another 34 percent had been in operation for six to ten years. Twelve percent had been in operation for eleven to twenty years, 7 percent for twenty-one to twenty-five years and 7 percent for twenty-five to thirty years. Five percent had been in operation for less than one year. If one assumes that most entrepreneurs are operating on a learning curve, we can expect to see that if other variables are in place that significantly enhance entrepreneurship, some of these entrepreneurs will probably be more profitable in the future. However, the data indicate that a significant number of these entrepreneurs have been in business for more than six years and are still reporting marginal profits. Hence, other complex factors are affecting their ability to succeed. I wished to know more about whether some of these entrepreneurs at the lower end of profitability were operating their businesses part time rather than full time. Interestingly, more than 75 percent of these business owners spend more than thirty-six hours per week on the job.

Shelley Green and Paul Pryde define culture as belief systems that are transmitted socially and behavioral patterns that are prevalent in human communities.

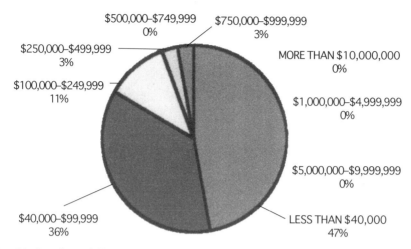

Fig. 5 Total profits, in dollars per year, black respondents

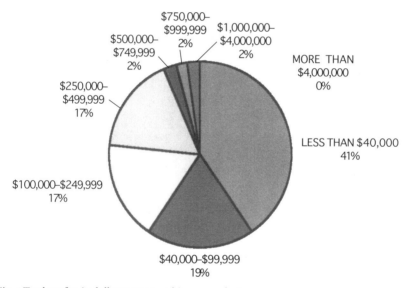

Fig. 6 Total profits, in dollars per year, white respondents

Economic culture refers to beliefs and behavioral patterns that relate to the production and distribution of wealth.[5] The variable of economic culture is an important concept in this study. In the following section, I provide information on the economic culture of the black and white entrepreneurs in the samples.

In much of the literature on economic culture, blacks have often been characterized as the ethnic/racial group with the most minimal level of success when utilizing entrepreneurship as a way of attaining economic and social mobility.

Their experiences have often been compared with those of the Japanese and the Jews who are regarded as "success" stories in the literature on self-employment. More recently, African Americans have also been compared with the Jamaicans, Koreans, and Cubans.[6] Oliver and Shapiro point out that comparisons such as these do not adequately take into consideration the tremendous role racism has played in militating against the successful incorporation of the black community in either the political or economic arenas in the United States. Moreover, they argue that no group in America has been as disadvantaged by the system as have African American people. From their perspective, "Ethnic comparisons that disadvantage blacks fail to adequately capture the harsh effects of the kind of hostility, unequaled in any other group, that African Americans have had to face in securing a foothold in self-employment. Racist state policy, Jim Crow segregation, discrimination, and violence have punctuated black entrepreneurial efforts of all kinds. Blacks have faced all levels of hardship in their pursuit of self-employment that have never been experienced as fully by or even applied as consistently to other ethnic groups, even other non-white ethnics."[7]

In this book, economic culture is defined as the values, orientations, and beliefs that African Americans hold that affect their economic choices and behaviors. This encompasses a broad range of factors such as their knowledge about the marketplace, entrepreneurial values and traditions, and general attitudes toward entrepreneurship. Very few of the black owners or white owners in this study actually inherited their businesses from their parents, which may be one indicator of whether entrepreneurship was a tradition that was passed on from one generation to the next. Although most of the white owners did not inherit their businesses, more white owners than black indicated that other members of their families owned businesses. Most black and white owners strongly agreed that they had received support from their families when their businesses were started, and this was a positive factor in enabling them to pursue self-employment. The support they received was economic, psychological, and physical, as some family members actually worked in the business enterprises.

More blacks than whites reported that they had business mentors who encouraged them or assisted them in pursuing self-employment as a career. When the owners were asked whether they felt that a business mentor would have a major impact on the success of any business, 88 percent of the black respondents agreed that they would, while 80 percent of white respondents agreed.

More black owners than white owners had ties to family members in terms of employing them in their businesses. For example, 57 percent of the black owners stated that they employ relatives to work for them in their businesses, while only 33 percent of the white owners reported the same. This finding may be related to the fact that in parts of the African American community, the extended family network is still very strong, and the family plays a very important role in the lives of the entrepreneurs. Historically, the nuclear family model has been much more dominant in the white community with perhaps less emphasis on maintaining close family ties past adulthood as many children move away to other communities. The issue of trust is also important. For many reasons, historical and contemporary, African Americans have learned that they have to be cautious in their dealings with the majority community. Therefore, blacks have hired members of their conjugal and extended family networks as well as members of their race to work in their business enterprises because they were able to trust them to a greater extent than outsiders. Of the black owners who indicated that they hired their relatives to work in their businesses, 77 percent hired one to two relatives; 15 percent hired three to five, while 8 percent hired six to ten. All of the white owners who indicated that they hired relatives to work in their firms reported hiring one to two workers.

Most black owners and white owners strongly agreed that being an entrepreneur is a rewarding profession. However, there was a noticeable difference between the groups regarding the importance of making a profit in relation to giving back to their communities. Most of the black owners strongly agreed that making a profit is important, but giving back to their communities was equally important. This is doubly ironic given the fact that blacks have been stereotyped in the literature as individuals who do not give back to their communities. Fewer than half of the white owners strongly agreed with this statement. When asked about the main reasons they became business owners, both groups indicated a number of different reasons, which included being their own bosses; work was unavailable at the time they started their enterprises; generating more income; advancing in the profession; having children; having flexible hours; pursuing their lifelong dreams; losing their jobs; and helping others. Both groups indicated that they give back to their communities in a number of ways, such as providing employment or accepting interns; donating or volunteering their time; sponsoring events, and donating money to worthwhile causes.

Gavin Chen defined social capital as the combination of a business owners' financial and nonfinancial assets, which include community investment, community patronage, and the community labor force that the entrepreneur's community agrees to invest in the minority-owned business.[8] Black owners tended to rely more heavily on their personal savings accounts than did whites, and a larger percentage of whites were able to secure bank loans from formal lending institutions. When both groups were asked if they had problems acquiring financial capital for their businesses, a big gap was apparent. Sixty-two percent of the white owners reported that they never had problems with financial backing for their firms compared to 36 percent of the blacks. In this section, I analyze the social capital of the neighborhoods where the businesses are located. I also discuss the issue of community investment and patronage as related to business success by looking at the composition of the firms' clientele as well as the characteristics of the economic environment where the business owners operate their firms. The data collected for this study indicate that black businesses were located to a large degree in predominantly black neighborhoods. Fewer of these firms were found in mixed or in predominantly white communities. Most white owners, on the other hand, did not operate in predominantly black neighborhoods, although some owners had businesses that were located in black communities. A critical question then becomes, do black owners and white owners operate within the same overall economic market or do they operate within the context of two segregated markets?

This is obviously an issue that will require additional research and analysis, but previous scholarship on minority businesses has indicated that group patronage of an entrepreneur's business by members of his or her own racial group may lead to a situation in which the owner develops the business enterprise by utilizing a sheltered consumer market network. According to Fratoe, in such a situation, neither the customers or the entrepreneurs are forced to operate outside the confines of their "ethnic enclave economy" in order to develop and maintain relationships between the buyers and the sellers. Proponents of the "ethnic enclave economy model" have posited that it is important for minority businesses to develop within such an environment in order to establish their own firm to a degree that might not be possible if they have to compete in the general economy.[9]

Critics have argued that operating in a segregated market ultimately constrains customer demand and prevents businesses from expanding because they do not operate fully within the larger market. It also limits their ability to generate higher levels of profit by selling products to a more racially diverse clientele. As Oliver and Shapiro have asserted, "The emphasis on owning and controlling business in the Black community recreates many of the negative features of the segregated market that characterized the economic detour discussed earlier. The purchase of small retail and service establishments within the Black community places Black entrepreneurs in unnecessary restrictive economic markets. The key to growth is to break out of segregated markets and into the urban economic mainstream. Second, a primary focus on traditional retail and service outlets may very well leave Blacks out of the most dynamic parts of the economy."[10]

Most black and white owners strongly agreed that the quality of their products and services were superior to that of similar types of businesses in the area. However, they did have slightly different perceptions regarding whether the price of their merchandise/services was higher than that of comparable businesses in the area. For example, only 7 percent of the black owners agreed that their prices were higher, in comparison with 21 percent of the white owners. Most of the African American owners operated in business environments at the national and neighborhood levels while white owners mainly operated their businesses at the city/county and regional levels. Few of either group operated at the international level.

There were marked differences between white owners and black owners with regard to how many steady customers they had. Almost 70 percent of the white owners responded that steady customers comprised more than 60 percent of their total client base. This was in stark contrast to only 36 percent of the black owners who indicated that steady customers make up more than 60 percent of their client base. This information suggests that the white owners in the study rely more heavily on a steady customer base that contributes substantially to their ability to get a larger amount of repeat business and ultimately promotes economic stability from one month to the next. Blacks, on the other hand, have to work harder to constantly attract more clients on a regular basis. This suggests that in some cases, black economic returns may be somewhat less predictable than those of whites. Some blacks in the sample, however, have been able to develop profitable business enterprises by constantly having a steady flow of new clients and contracts. This was particularly true for businesses whose major customers are other businesses, the government, or nonprofit organizations. The contracts may be few and unsteady, but may offer larger rates of profit than if the main customer base consisted of individual customers.

The data also demonstrated that marked differences existed between black owners and white owners regarding the distance customers travel in order to patronize their businesses. While 70 percent of the white owners stated that their customers come from more than twenty miles away to patronize their businesses, only 43 percent of the black owners indicated the same. Ten percent of the white owners stated that their clients came from sixteen to twenty miles in contrast with 6 percent of the black owners.

The issue of race is important in this study as well. Racism has permeated virtually every aspect of human endeavor in the United States since the slaves first landed in North America. American history is filled with numerous instances of racial hostility and intimidation that has traversed the economic, political, social, and cultural realms of society. As Sol Ahiarah has pointed out, "As black Americans contemplate the relationship of their business success to environmental factors, it would be unrealistic to think that racism, which continues to be the basis of a non-conducive environment, will disappear soon. Far from it. Racism enables some people to exercise power over black persons. Those who benefit from it will maintain it, or abandon it only if they have no other choice."[11]

As would be expected, there was a tremendous divergence between the two groups of owners in this study on the question of whether they had been discriminated against by a financial lending institution because of their race. More than half of the black owners (53 percent) answered in the affirmative on this question, while only 10 percent of the whites indicated the same. It is unclear on what basis the white owners felt they were discriminated against. While 38 percent of the black owners had either been a part of or benefited from a minority set-aside program, only 31 percent of the white owners had. Because only minorities, women, and, more recently, economically or socially disadvantaged individuals could participate in these programs, presumably the whites who answered yes to this question were from one or both of the latter two categories. Forty percent of the black owners strongly agreed that the impact of minority set-aside programs has been positive, in contrast to only 17 percent of the whites.

Nineteen percent of the black entrepreneurs strongly agreed that their racial identity plays a major role in their success as business owners. Only 13 percent of the whites strongly agreed that race plays a major role in their success as entrepreneurs. However, 43 percent of the blacks agreed that racial identity does play a major role in the problems they encounter in the world of business. Only 10 percent of the whites agreed that their racial identity is a major cause of the problems they have in business.

The data suggested interesting contrasts between the experiences of black and white business owners. First, white-owned businesses in the study tended to have a larger percentage of steady customers than did the black-owned businesses. Second, white-owned businesses tended to have more clients who came from a larger mile radius to patronize their businesses than did the black-owned businesses. Third, white-owned businesses tended to be at higher profitability levels than were black-owned businesses. And last, black business owners experienced more difficulty than did whites in securing loans from lending institutions.

CHAPTER SIX

The Continuum of Black Business Success: Why Some Firms Succeed While Others Fail

This chapter examines the major question this study seeks to address: Why do some African American businesses succeed, while others fail? The variable categories I examined were individual-owner characteristics, human capital, financial capital, social capital, economic culture, and race. Thirteen explanatory variables were examined in order to understand their effects on the economic success of African American entrepreneurs (see tables 1 and 2).[1]

Education
Years of experience in industry
Problem securing financial backing
Level of business debt
Percent of steady customers
Capital obtained from friends
Having a business mentor
Inheriting business from a family member
Receiving strong family support
Employing relatives in their business
Participating in and benefiting from minority set-aside programs
Age of the entrepreneur
Marital stability

Both quantitative and qualitative assessments were made on numerous variables that affect business success and failure. Two measures of success were used; these included the number of years the business had been in operation and profits. I selected the first of these as my main dependent variable model, however, because I found that more independent variables were positively correlated to this

Table 1. Factors Associated with Successful Black-Owned Businesses Using Pearson r Correlations

	Years in Operation	Profit per Year
Human Capital Variables		
Education	+	0
Years of experience in industry	+	+
Financial Capital Variables		
Problem seeking financial backing	0	0
Level of business debt	+	+
Social Capital Variables		
Percent of steady customers	+	+
Source of the majority of the capital entrepreneurs needed to start business	0	0
Economic Culture Variables		
Had a business mentor	0	+
Inherited Business from a family member	+	0
Received strong family support	0	0
Employed Relatives	+	0
Race Variables		
Participated in or benefitted from a minority set-aside program	+	0
Individual Owner Variables		
Age	+	0
Marital stability	+	+

*Years in operation is the main dependent model $*p<.05**p<.01***p<.001$
*0 means no correlation existed.

dependent variable than to the other measure of success used in this study. Fewer independent variables were associated with profits.

Pearson r Correlations were performed to determine which variables were correlated with economic success, using the variables included in the full model. The following independent variables were positively correlated with success and were significant when measured against the main dependent model used in this study, years in operation.

These variables included the age, marital stability, and education of the entrepreneur; years of experience in the industry; the level of business debt; employment of relatives; inheritance of the family business; having a high percentage of steady customers; and having been a part of or benefited from minority set-aside

Table 2. Full Model of Independent Variables Used

Explanatory Variables	Units of Measure
Human Capital Variables	
Education	6-point scale with 6=highest level of education
Years of experience in industry	0=1 year or less; 1=2–4 years; 2=5–10; 3=11–15; 4=16–20; 5=21–25; 6=more than 26
Financial Capital Variables	
Problem seeking financial backing	0=never; 1=seldom; 2=most of the time; 3=sometimes; 4=always
Level of business debt	9-point scale with 9=highest level of debt; 1=less than $10,000; 9=over $5,000,000
Social Capital Variables	
Percent of steady customers	1=0–20%; 2=21–30%; 3=31–50%; 4=51–60%; 5=over 60%
Source of majority of capital to start business	2=friends/relatives; 1=personal savings; 3=bank loan; 4=minority loan; 5=public agency
Economic Culture Variables	
Had a business mentor	1=yes; 2=no
Inherited business from family member	1=yes; 2=no
Received strong family support	1=strongly disagree; 2=disagree; 3=agree; 4=strongly agree; 5=don't know
Employed relatives in their business	1=yes; 2=no
Race Variables	
Participated in or benefited from a minority set-aside program	1=yes; 2=no
Individual Owner Variables (Demographic Variables)	
Age	1=20–30 years; 2=31–40; 3=41–50; 4=51–60; 5=61–70; 6=71–80; 7=over 80
Marital stability	1=single; 2=married; 3=separated; 4=divorced; 5=widowed

programs. These nine variables were all positively correlated to years in operation. Five variables were positively correlated with profits: marital stability; years of experience in industry; level of business debt; having a business mentor; and having a high percentage of steady customers.

The vast majority of the highly successful black entrepreneurs were married. Entrepreneurs received many things from marriage, including emotional support, physical support, and in some cases economic support, all of which enhanced the overall success and longevity of the firms. The overall stability generated from being with the same marital partner continuously also provides a sense of predictability in the entrepreneurs' lives. This predictability has positive benefits for their professional business lives as well.

Level of business debt also was positively correlated to the overall success of the firms. There is a positive correlation between having a high level of business debt and years in operation/level of profits per year. Many African American entrepreneurs had their relatives working in their firms. This occurred for many reasons: first, the entrepreneurs usually trusted their relatives, and trust is a very important variable in the African American community. Second, sometimes members of one's family unit will provide physical and mental labor for reduced costs or for no costs at all. This is particularly helpful to owners during the first few months or years of the firm's development when the costs of operating the business may exceed the revenues being generated. Third, because many African American businesses are one-person entities, it may be prohibitive in the early stages for the single-handed entrepreneur to go out and actively recruit the right quality of staff that he or she needs and have enough money to pay wages that accurately reflect the qualifications of their staff.

The independent variable of having problems seeking financial capital for the business was not correlated with success using either of the two measures of success, and hence was not included in ordinary least squares (OLS) regressions. Correlation coefficients measure the relationships between variables while regressions examine causation—in other words, what causes what?

The results of the regressions indicated the following results: Entrepreneurs who had high levels of education; had many years of experience in industry; and who inherited their businesses were more successful, when controlling for the other variables in the model (see table 3). When age was substituted for years of experience in industry, the following results became apparent: Entrepreneurs who were older in age; had higher levels of education; had a higher percentage of steady customers; and who inherited their businesses from family members were more successful, when controlling for the other variables in the model (see table 4).

The data from this study indicate that numerous factors have contributed to African American business failures in both the past and the present. Some of

Table 3. OLS Regression Presenting Full Model of Indicators of Business Success of Black-Owned Enterprises in Cleveland and Surrounding Metro Areas

Variables	Years in Operation	Total Profits per Year
Years of experience in industry	.468*** (.067)	.0909 (.075)
Highest level of education	.191** (.073)	.03937 (.085)
Business debt in dollars	.03489 (.185)	.147 (.465)
Percent of steady customers	.107 (.073)	.09854 (.084)
Capital obtained from friends/relatives	-.162 (.364)	.0998 (.446)
Inherited the business	.666* (.336)	.109 (.375)
Received strong support from family	.251 (.252)	.122 (.293)
Relatives work in business	.249 (.225)	-.01958 (.256)
Been part of or benefited from a minority set-aside program	.345 (.254)	-.06947 (.288)
Marital stability	.185 (.20)	.465* (.232)
Constant (a)	.03534	.643
Adjusted R^2	.455	.111
Standard error	1.1291	1.2567
F	10.522***	2.359**
n*	114	109

* Years in operation is the main dependent model *$p<.05$ **$p<.01$ ***$p<.001$
Note: Entries are unstandardized regression coefficients, and in parenthesis are the standard errors.
Source: Original telephone interview schedule, spring 1998–summer 2000
(N=130 for sample. However, some entrepreneurs did not report profits, which reduced the overall n for this regression analysis.)

Table 4. OLS Regression Presenting Full Model of Indicators of Business Success of Black-Owned Enterprises in Cleveland and Surrounding Metro Areas

Variables	Years in Operation	Total Profits per Year
Highest level of education	.194**	.03158
	(.074)	(.085)
Business debt in dollars	.04868	.161
	(.077)	(.088)
Percent of steady customers	.178**	.113
	(.073)	(.083)
Capital obtained from friends/relatives	.108	.151
	(.366)	(.448)
Inherited the business	1.223***	.191
	(.339)	(.378)
Received strong support from family	.110	.07335
	(.252)	(.292)
Relatives work in business	.157	.00326
	(.229)	(.260)
Been part of or benefited from a minority set-aside program	.292	-.08560
	(.255)	(.290)
Age of business owner	.681***	.05698
	(.101)	(.114)
Marital stability	-.02978	.474*
	(.212)	(.240)
Constant (a)	-.521	.761
Adjusted R^2	.455	.098
Standard error	1.1396	1.2660
F	10.137***	2.179**
n*	114	109

* Years in operation is the main dependent model *$p<.05$ **$p<.01$ ***$p<.001$
Note: Entries are unstandardized regression coefficients, and in parentheses are the standard errors.[1]
Source: Original telephone interview schedule, spring 1998–summer 2000
(N=130 for sample. However, some entrepreneurs did not report profits, which reduced the overall n for this regression analysis.)

these include inadequate capitalization of their businesses at both the front end (when the business first originates) and at the back end (as the business matures and expands); racist actions and barriers that prevent minorities from accessing the economic marketplace in the appropriate way; inadequate education and training by African Americans with regard to how to develop and operate a business; inadequate management experience about many of the intricate details regarding the day-to-day operations of the firm; and overemphasis on the "trial-and-error" method and an underemphasis on using well-established business strategies and procedures that have been tried and tested over time.

Additionally, many black-owned businesses fail because of lack of patronage of their businesses to the extent that they cannot remain profitable; lack of diversification of their client base to the extent that if one category of client disappears, the business is forced to close; selecting business areas of concentration without doing a market analysis first to determine whether the marketplace is currently oversaturated with a particular type of business; locating one's business in a geographical area where there is already an overabundance of that particular type of business and where the business cannot be supported economically in terms of the per capita expenditure for that particular community; locating one's business in an area that has a high level of crime, particularly violent crime; growing a business too fast; entering into business areas of concentration that have a very high risk associated with them without having the appropriate skills or training; not knowing where to go to get assistance before it is too late to save the business; the effects of external variables such as economic recessions or downturns in the economy; lack of written business plans that should be used to articulate in great detail the strategy to be used to help the business to expand and grow across time; and lack of a backup plan to be used in case the first plan of action is not successful. Although in some cases, a business may fail because of a single variable factor, in many cases, multiple causal agents interact and have a debilitating impact on the firm, leading to its subsequent failure.

The issue of gender is also important in this study because the data indicate that women and men access the economic marketplace in Cleveland in different ways. The vast majority of both men and women owned and operated businesses that are classified as service-related entities. This accounted for 57 percent of all businesses owned by the women and 65 percent of businesses owned by the men. More women (23 percent) than men (11 percent) were in retail, while only 6 percent of the women and 4 percent of the men were in manufacturing. Six percent of the women were in construction, while 9 percent of the men owned construction businesses. The other businesses, i.e., 8 percent for the women and 11 percent for the men were unclassified (see figures 7 and 8).

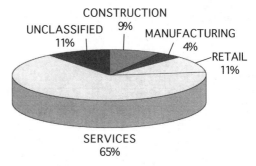

Fig. 7 Type of business, male respondents

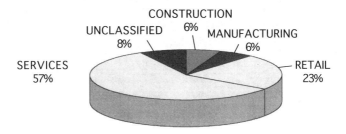

Fig. 8 Type of business, female respondents

In the area of educational training, the data indicates that male entrepreneurs had higher levels of educational training overall than did the women. For example, 31 percent of the women possessed undergraduate college degrees, in comparison with 34 percent of the men. Further, 57 percent of the men possessed college degrees or *higher,* while only 40 percent of the women possessed the same (see figures 9 and 10). A noticeable difference can also be observed when one examines the role of business mentors in entrepreneurial development. While 64 percent of the men said they had business mentors, only 39 percent of the women did (see figures 11 and 12). (Note: Data presented here is for the equalized samples.)

The area of profitability is very important and the data indicates while about 42–43 percent of both groups are fairly marginal enterprises that earn less than $40,000 per year in profits, a larger percentage (40%) of the female entrepreneurs reported earning $40,000–$99,000. Twenty percent of the men earned $100,000–$249,000 per year while only 11 percent of the women earned this amount. Twelve percent of the men earned $250,000–$499,000.00 per year. Only 3 percent of the women were in this profit category. A 1 percent difference existed between the male and female owners in the category of $500,000–$749,000. Here, 2 percent of the men earned this amount and 3 percent of the women (see figures 13 and 14). (This data does not include profit figures for the female entrepreneur included in the biographical chapter.)

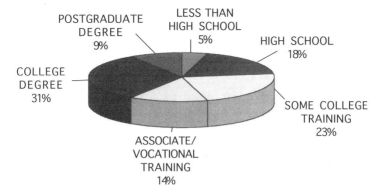

Fig. 9 Education levels, female respondents

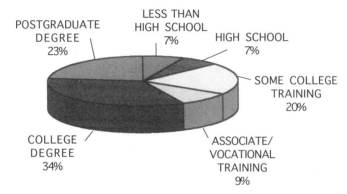

Fig. 10 Education levels, male respondents

Fig. 11 Percentage of male respondents with business mentors

Fig. 12 Percentage of female respondents with business mentors

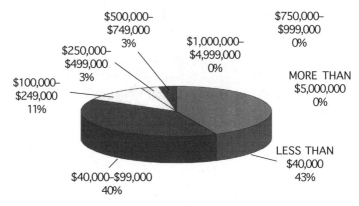

Fig. 13 Total profits, in dollars per year, female respondents

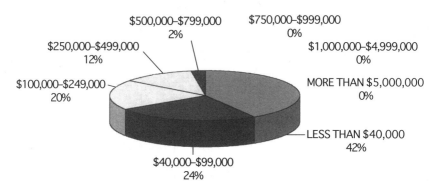

Fig. 14 Total profits, in dollars per year, male respondents

Note that the figures presented here comparing men and women are based on an equalized sample (see appendix for chapter 6). In other words, because more men were included in the study, for purposes of comparison, the two groups were equalized on the Statistical Program for Social Science using a random number list. Thus, while women in the equalized sample were represented more in the highest profit category by 1%, this is not true for the overall total sample. Here, the highest levels of profitability in the study were earned by male entrepreneurs.

Twenty-nine percent of the male-owned businesses had been in operation for twenty-six to thirty years while only 2 percent of the women had been in operation for this length of time. Fourteen percent of men had been in operation for twenty-one to twenty-five years compared to 5 percent of the women (see figures 15 and 16). Most of the female-owned (54 percent) and the male-owned businesses (60 percent) were located in the city of Cleveland rather than in the suburbs. The study suggested several interesting differences and similarities between male and female owners:

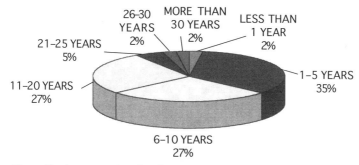

Fig. 15 Years of business operation, female respondents

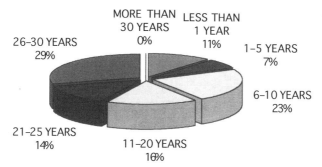

Fig. 16 Years of business operation, male respondents

1. More of the male owners were married than the female owners.
2. A larger percentage of male owners had achieved higher levels of education than had female owners.
3. Larger percentages of male owners had more years of experience in industry than their female counterparts.
4. The majority of both groups owned businesses that are classified under the category of service-related entities.
5. Sixty-four percent of the men had mentors, compared with only 39 percent of the women.
6. Both groups had about the same percentages of owners who earned less than $40,000 per year. However, 3% of female-owned businesses earned between $500,000–$749,000 per year, compared to 2% of male owned. Nevertheless, in the total sample the highest levels of profits were earned by African American male entrepreneurs.
7. A higher percentage of male-owned businesses than female-owned businesses reported having been in business for longer periods of time.
8. The majority of both groups owned businesses located in the city of Cleveland in comparison with the suburbs.

Several bivariate analyses were performed to further examine the relationship between gender and economic success. Gender was the independent variable in these analyses and was measured against the following dependent variables: marital status, highest level of education received; having a business mentor; years of experience in industry; profits; number of years the business had been in operation; geographical location; and type of business the owner operated (i.e., construction; manufacturing; retail/trade; and service). The results of the bivariate analyses indicated that three dependent variables were significant and positively related to gender. These were having a business mentor; years of experience in industry; and the number of years the business had been in operation. Variables that were significant and negatively related to gender were geographical location and owning a business in the retail/trade area.

CHAPTER SEVEN

Biographical Sketches of African American Entrepreneurs

In this chapter, life histories of seven successful and unsuccessful African American business owners in the greater Cleveland area are presented. The experiences of these entrepreneurs, George Fraser, best-selling author and entrepreneur; Robert P. Madison, nationally and internationally acclaimed architect; Deborah Thigpen Waller, owner of a marketing and public relations firm; Leroy Ozanne, CEO of Ozanne Construction Company; Brian Hall, owner of a freight company; Oscar Saffold, a physician in private practice specializing in dermatology; and Shelton Moore, a business partner in a computer company and former owner of several construction companies, are quite diverse.

Although there was obviously some variability among the successful entrepreneurs included here, all of them had several employees working in their business enterprises; provided important goods and services to their clients; were philanthropic in various ways; and earned profits in the six- or seven-figure range. Hence, all of the businesses made significant contributions in enhancing economic development in both northeast Ohio and the state of Ohio on a broader level.

Through their narratives, I examine more closely how and why they became entrepreneurs; their family backgrounds; obstacles they encountered through the years; strategies they used to overcome adversity; and their successes or failures along the way, as well as important lessons they learned. Each life history begins with a quotation by the entrepreneur that I believe encapsulates the essence of the person. The narratives end with an analysis of the factors that led to the success or failure of the business, using my model of success, which was discussed earlier in chapter 6.

GEORGE FRASER
Best-selling author, speaker, entrepreneur, CEO of Success Source, Unlimited

Well, I've always had a vision about my assignment. We spend our formative years in preparation to develop for the completion of that assignment. And that's why I've enjoyed every single job I've ever had, whether it was the first

From left: Lee Trotter, Bessie House-Soremekun, and George C. Fraser attending a *SuccessGuide*-sponsored reception in October 2000 at Landerhaven. *Photo by Rodney L. Brown*

job I ever had in a grocery store in the basement cleaning old pop bottles or mopping floors at La Guardia Airport or wrapping gifts in the basement of Halle Brothers. It didn't matter. I was there to learn, to grow. God had put me there for a reason and I extracted from it what I could at that moment in time and then moved to the next thing.[1]

George C. Fraser is the president of Success Source, Unlimited, located at 2940 Noble Road in Cleveland Heights, a suburb of Cleveland. This company is a sole proprietorship. Fraser is very warm, has a forceful personality, and is extremely charismatic. He is also a great communicator. All these things are important in understanding Fraser, the man, the best-selling author, and the successful entrepreneur. He was born in 1945 and raised in Brooklyn, New York. He was born into a family of eleven children. His father hailed from Guyana in the Caribbean and his mother was from Lupkin, Georgia. According to Fraser,

My father is blue black, and my mother is light gray, almost white. My sister and I look like mom, and all the rest of the family look like dad. Mom became deathly ill when I was five and we were put into orphanages and foster homes, and so I grew up on the streets of New York in foster homes. I graduated from high school and then went on to college [New York University] for a couple of years while I worked full time at LaGuardia Airport at night, mopping floors. I did that for a couple of years until I came to visit a sister in Cleveland, Ohio, because I'd never been out of New York, like most New Yorkers of that time. I thought that the streets were paved with gold.

Fraser and I talked at length about his early childhood in New York. Of particular interest was how the issue of self-esteem and love figured into his early development. His mother suffered from a psychological disorder and eventually died in a mental institution. Because of this, the children were sent to live in foster homes. Once he and his other siblings reached the age of eighteen, they were allowed to leave the foster homes and go back to their mother's house, where they lived together for a short while until they went out on their own. All of them returned home except those who were grown and married. To quote Fraser,

> My father, my blood father, never remarried. He was very loyal to my mother who was in a mental institution. He stayed very close to all of his children. So we saw him a lot in spite of the fact that we were in foster homes. He was an NYC cab driver where he worked fourteen hours a day. He could not take care of eight or nine children, so foster care was the only other alternative. But, we kept very closely tied and connected. As most West Indians, he was proud of who he was, and he had a deep sense of his own culture, his own blackness. He was a remarkable man, despite the fact that he was a cab driver. Everybody loved him. He had an incredible people sense. And he had a wonderful sense of humor.

Fraser has lived in Cleveland for about thirty-two years although many of his family members still live in New York. His first job in the Cleveland area was at the Cleveland Clinic where he washed surgical linens. He also worked as a "temp" at Halle Brothers, where he wrapped gifts. He then began to climb the work ladder as he acquired a position in the carpet department and the furniture department of this company. He left Halle Brothers when it was purchased by another company and sold Britannica books from March 1969 to July 1972 under the umbrella of a little business he started called Black Educational Development, Inc., that sold black historical books to various schools, colleges, and libraries.

In July 1972, he was recruited by an African American friend who owned Ran Associates, an employment agency. Ran was given an assignment by Procter and Gamble to encourage black people to go into their sales and marketing management program. Fraser interviewed for the position and was offered the job. According to Fraser, "I had created my path [as] one of the first blacks to be hired into a management program without a college degree." He worked with Procter and Gamble as a marketing manager from July 1972 to July 1984. Then, he was hired by the United Way because of Cheryle Wills, a friend who was chairing the United Way at the time. She was looking for someone with extensive public/private sector marketing experience. Fortunately, Fraser had both. He worked for United Way for three years, from 1984 to 1987 and was then recruited into the Ford Motor Company Minority Dealership Development Program. Fraser was the first African American Ford-Lincoln-Mercury dealer in Cleveland, Ohio. He participated in a two-year program (1987–89) and graduated at the top of his class. After realizing he did not want to sell cars, he decided to start his own company so he could teach what he had learned about the art and science of human relationships, more commonly referred to as "networking." Thus, in January 1988, he established Success Source, Incorporated. This was primarily a communications company, under whose umbrella Fraser could emphasize the importance of networking and other business skills.

This company was incorporated and was located at 1949 East 105th Street in an inner-city community. He decided to locate his business there because he wanted to be around African American people and black resources that were located in the downtown Cleveland area. In order to launch the business, he needed between $250,000 and $499,999. He acquired his start-up capital from a combination of sources, including personal savings, funds from friends and relatives, and a bank loan. The business was quite profitable even though its level of business debt was very high. Between six and ten people were employed to work in the company, some of whom were his own relatives.

Numerous variables have affected the economic outcomes of African American entrepreneurs. One of these variables has been their skin color. This variable has been examined primarily because many black entrepreneurs and black people, more broadly speaking, are still affected by it, in one way or another. Fraser is very fair and could probably pass for white. When asked if skin color affected his personal life, Fraser answered in this way:

> It had a significant role, because remember here you had my sister and I [who] were light/white looking kids, and a really large group of dark, very black-looking kids. Those were brothers and sisters. They all looked very black. They looked like my dad who was very dark and my mother was very light because she was from a different descent, but very southern. A southern light-skinned person. So yes, you had these two light-skinned people in the midst of this very dark skinned family. But no one in our family made any fun of it. We were teased about it a little bit, but only in jest and in a good way. We used to call ourselves the black sheep of the family, my sister and I, and my brothers made fun of that. But they never made us feel different, and they never treated us any different. And every member of the family embraced. We never felt any

better. We never felt any worse. We never felt we were different. It was really a great sense of brotherhood and sisterhood.

Although on various occasions, Fraser has been mistaken for a white person, he never felt white. In fact, on several occasions, he has been asked, "Why in the world would you choose to be black?" His answer: "Because I am black. When you talk about color, you're not really talking about color, you're talking about culture. And I grew up thinking black. For me not to be black would be to deny who I am." Fraser is saturated with black cultural values. For him, it's not just about skin color, it's also about who you identify with from a cultural perspective as well as the moral history that has been interwoven with the black church and black people. His racial identity has always been very clear. This is one reason that he begins his speeches by saying, "Yes, I am black."

I also wanted to know more clearly what impact his skin color had on his success in the business world. Was he accepted because of his skin color more than darker-skinned entrepreneurs and what role has it played in terms of helping him develop contacts and alliances with members of the white community? Does he have a special entrée into the white community because of his skin color? Fraser answered the question in this way:

Absolutely, there's no question that I have it, absolutely. Any light-skinned person with "good hair" and there are exceptions. But . . . there's no question about that because there still is a negative perception of dark-skinned people. And it'll take generations for that stupidity and narrowness of thinking among white people and even some blacks to get over that, by the way. We have dark-skinned people who have been so dehumanized and so the image has been so thwarted and tainted by the images of welfare and poverty and drugs we see so often that really hurt black people, in particular, dark skinned [blacks]. So yes, any fair-skinned entrepreneur is going to have an advantage, or it's going to be less of a hurt. The hurdle is a little bit lower.

The other side of the coin is how he relates to black people. In other words, do African Americans think he's black enough to represent their interests and perspectives, given his physical characteristics? According to Fraser, "It wouldn't take you long, listening to what I have to say and the way I say it to know that I am black. Because the way I speak, the things I say, the nuances and subtleties only a black person would make." Moreover, his books are really geared toward helping African Americans, although he also has many whites in his audiences because they are eager to learn about African American people. I also asked him what role race has played in his success or lack of success as an entrepreneur. In other words, if he had been white and was doing the same type of work that he is currently engaged in, would he have been more successful or less successful? He said,

> Race has helped me tremendously because my products and services are race-based. That's where I felt my strength was. So, I think that race can be a huge factor, but it's a double-edged sword. In my particular case, race has helped me because my products and services are essentially for black people, and I have profited from that, both financially and spiritually. I feel good about what I do, so it has been wonderful. I also serve white folks with my products as well, because they're interested in how to get one to understand better to learn about the nature and culture of people. So, through my products, through my talks, they're interested in knowing about race-based kinds of things.

Fraser has worked in a wide variety of jobs and feels he learned something important in every one of them that ultimately prepared him to become an entrepreneur. He reached an important point in his life after he worked with the Ford Motor Company because he was to have purchased one of their franchises in March 1987. Here, he had the chance to "dip his toe into the entrepreneurial bucket." In so doing, he learned a lot about running a business. However, he had to sell cars and sell them the way Ford Motor Company wanted them to be sold. He then decided that it was time to take a leap of faith and begin sharing what he learned from his many successes. Therefore, he founded Success Source, Incorporated, in January 1988, to teach black people how to succeed. Success Source, Incorporated, was a communications company. He started out by doing daily events because he was very adept at networking. At these events, he began to collect literally thousands of business cards that he organized and put into a directory for people. This collection of business cards represented a tremendous amount of human capital.

He published a paper in 1987 on the intellectual capital of African Americans. Thereafter, he created the first *SuccessGuide,* which was essentially a guide for black resources in Cleveland. His book *Success Runs in Our Race* became a national best-seller, and he was commanding huge fees to speak before audiences all over the world. I asked him why he felt he became so successful. He said:

> I found a need. Our people are looking for information and direction. I get twenty phone calls a day from folks who go to my web site [www.frasernet.com] and do networking and call me up and they're looking for information. . . . We're hungry to talk to people outside our immediate sphere of influence and social circle to those who have "succeeded" at some level, whether it's writing a book or speaking or authoring how to do business. We're hungry for infor-

mation, but beyond the information, when I give people the information, they are illuminated by it. But, the next thing is direction. Even as "accomplished" as I am, there's a 54-year-old black man really tired of what I do, speaking and writing best-selling books, [who had a] huge demand as a speaker; there are things, as I continue to evolve and grow that I need direction on. [So], I call people in my network [of friends and acquaintances], the majority of whom are black, who have been there for me. I call because I talk to them, ask questions about certain things, and I get direction from them.

Fraser has experienced both success and failure as an entrepreneur. While his original company, Success Source, Incorporated, was very successful initially, after a while, it failed. Several critical factors contributed to its demise. In its initial stages, the company was quite profitable. Fraser made six-figure profits very quickly. He employed six to ten staff members in his company. He was very high profile and served on a lot of boards. Then, he decided that if he could be so successful in Cleveland, it would be good to expand this idea. He grew his business very rapidly, which had negative consequences; he could not manage and control that much growth at such a fast rate. Even financially, he was unable to find the type of investors who shared his vision of how the business should be run and structured.

A second area of weakness was his lack of extensive experience in managing all the complex details of running a business. Although he had previously been trained to own a Ford Motor franchise, it was very different from launching his own corporation from scratch. He underestimated the importance of having a solid background in dealing with profit responsibilities. Although he had also worked at Procter and Gamble for twelve years and had been given sales and marketing responsibilities, he had not dealt with profit issues. He had also not been responsible for cash management issues. Because of this, he experienced his third major problem area, tax issues. In essence, he began to rob Peter to pay Paul. One of the products produced by his company was a networking guide book that listed names of important individuals and information about their careers. No one was required to pay to have their photographs and biographical sketches included. He continued to have custom photos taken for each volume even though his cash flow was weak and his quarterly tax payments were due to the IRS. His level of business debt was also very high in relation to his profitability level.

The fourth reason he failed is that he made bad people decisions. While he is the first to acknowledge that ideas are great, the reality is that they are very much driven by people. This area falls under the category of managerial skills. Another error was to allow people to take out ads in his *SuccessGuide,* some of whom never actually paid for their ads. This accelerated his cash flow problems. Last,

Fraser had expensive consumption practices. Although he was giving more than one hundred speeches each year and receiving several thousand dollars for each, his lifestyle was very expensive; he maintained a large house, wore expensive clothing, and drove a Mercedes Benz. It is unclear how much of his earnings were being reinvested in the business as opposed to maintaining his increasingly high standard of living.[2] The result of all of these bad decisions was that he declared bankruptcy.

He filed chapter 11 bankruptcy in March 1996 for his business. Fraser stated, "I found as I filed for corporate bankruptcy that my big creditors went after me personally, which put everything in jeopardy. So, the only protection against that is personal bankruptcy, which is really driven by corporate bankruptcy." Although all of the above factors led to the overall decline of Success Source, Incorporated, the major cause of failure was Fraser's inability to make the appropriate decisions at the right time. "It was me. It didn't succeed because of me, because I made all of the decisions. It was my lack of experience, my lack of training in small business. They're two different worlds. My lack of small business mentorship. I had big business mentorship. It was not because of the lack of business. I just did not make enough right choices. So, I closed. The business failed because of the choices I made, and I made those choices because of lack of choices and lack of knowledge."

I asked Fraser if he had any advice about how fast entrepreneurs should grow their businesses because it is one of the major reasons many businesses fail. He said that if you have a successful business today and a new concept, and you have articulated that business model and replicated the profitability of that business over several years and you have written your business model down, then grow it by one and grow it if humanly possible within a one hundred-mile radius. It is also advantageous to have it located somewhere that you can get to by car. He acknowledged that this is the model of Sam Walton, the owner of Walmart, the largest retail chain in America. That was his secret.

Several other factors are also important in examining the failure of Fraser's first business, based on the success model I developed in chapter 6 of this book. First, black entrepreneurs with higher levels of education were more successful. Hence, Fraser's educational level was not very high, meaning that he possessed less than a college degree, although later on he participated in several business training programs. Many of the highly successful entrepreneurs in this study possess high levels of education, and the educational training is often in the area that the business itself focuses on. Fraser had weaknesses in both these categories.

Entrepreneurs in the study who had more years experience in industry were also more successful. Although Fraser had worked in various capacities for different companies through the years, the knowledge and experience he gained did not necessarily prepare him to start a communications firm. It would have been more beneficial, for example, if he had worked for a communications firm where he could have gained knowledge about the area his business was based on. Also, although Fraser earned a sizable profit, the level of his business debt was very high.

Fraser started another business, Success Source, Unlimited, in 1996. This business is performing well, and Fraser has written a second best-seller entitled *Race for Success: The Ten Best Business Opportunities for Blacks in America* (New York: William Morrow, 1998). He is still making presentations and lectures to diverse audiences and still publishes his editions of *SuccessGuide* each year.

In addition to attending New York University, Fraser also completed business courses at the Amos Tuck School of Business at Dartmouth College in 1992 and 1996. He was awarded an honorary doctorate of humane letters from Jarvis Christian College in 1999. He has received numerous honors and accolades through the years that include, among others, the Distinguished Service Award from the Consortium for Graduate Study in Management, 1999; Distinguished Service Award from the 100 Black Men of America, 1998; Unity Award at the African American Male Empowerment Summit, New York, New York, 1998; Men of Courage Award from the Nestle Corporation, 1996; Black Achiever Award from the Voices of Cleveland, 1992; and Black Professional of the Year Award from the Black Professionals Association of Cleveland, 1992. He was listed as a top power broker in the United States in *Upscale Magazine* in August 1991 and was included in *Who's Who in the Midwest, Who's Who in America, Who's Who in Black America,* and *Who's Who in Business* from 1983–2000.

ROBERT P. MADISON
Architect, CEO of Robert P. Madison International

> Back in those days [the 1950s], there was no affirmative action, no MBE, none of that stuff. We just believed that we would make it. The reason I got all this training was to say nobody could ever say that I'm not qualified. I was the only architect in Cleveland, Ohio, at that time [the early 1950s] who had a Fulbright and a Harvard degree, but I was black.[3]

Robert Madison, who was born in 1923, is an accomplished man of enormous talent and capabilities. This was evident as I entered his office at his architectural firm, located at 2935 Euclid Avenue in Cleveland, Ohio. Numerous plaques, awards, college degrees, and photos of some of the buildings he has helped develop through the years as an architect adorned the walls of his office. He is also a man of experience, which is etched on the contours of his face.

Robert P. Madison. *Photo by W. A. Rogers*

Madison's father, Robert J. Madison, was born in Mobile, Alabama, and his mother, Nettie Madison, was born in Selma. His father met his mother while he was attending Snowhill Academy, just outside Selma. His father became a civil engineer in 1918, which is no ordinary accomplishment given the fact that blacks had achieved their freedom from slavery only within fifty or so years prior to that. Nevertheless, his father worked hard, persevered, and received his engineering degree from Howard University in Washington, D.C. He was also quite a good football player. When Madison was born in 1923, his father could not get a job as an engineer because of his race. So, he taught physics, math, and chemistry at historically black colleges and universities such as Selma University in Selma, Alabama, and Benedict College in Columbia, South Carolina. He also coached the athletic teams in football and baseball. When I asked Madison about the impact of his family on his eventual success as an entrepreneur, he stated the following:

I came from pretty good stock. My mother graduated from Morris Brown College and my father from Howard University. My maternal grandmother had migrated to Cleveland from the South, and therefore when it was time for me to be born, my mother came to the home of her mother, which was in Cleveland. That's how I got born in Cleveland. But my brother Julian was born in Selma. My dad was a teacher there. Stan was born in Columbia, South

Carolina, because my dad was teaching there. Bernard was born in Washington, D.C., because at that time [my father] had a job in the War Department of the federal government.

Religion and the church were significant in Madison's family background as his paternal and maternal grandfathers were both preachers. Although they had never attended seminary, they could read. But, it was really their reading ability and their passion for learning that influenced Madison to acquire an education. The challenges his father faced in society also had an impact on him. To quote Madison, "[The] one other thing that influenced me more than anything else, if you really want to get down to it, is the failure of my father that drives me today. By that I mean this: I saw my father with all the credentials, with all the education, with all that anyone could ask for try to get a job, and they said no, we don't hire colored people. I think that my drive is a result of the disappointment he felt. I'm going to make up for what they did to my daddy, and that's why I take them on."

One day when Madison came home in the second grade with a drawing of a boat, his mother was particularly impressed with his drawing skill and complimented him on the drawing. She said to him, "Son, you will be an architect."

He responded, "If you say so, that's okay with me." This was really the beginning of what has become a remarkable career. At the age of seven, he had no idea of what architects really did. "But, that's what she said, and that's what you believed in, whatever mother said."

He had three brothers, Julian, Stanley, and Bernard. When Julian came along, his mother told him that he would be an engineer, and he said, "Yes, mother." After Stanley was born, she told him that he would be a preacher, and he said, "No, mother." When Bernard was born, she stated that she had two engineers (meaning his father and her son Julian). She had one architect (meaning Robert). She needed another architect in the family and that would be Bernard. His father had such difficulties getting employment in the field as an engineer that his mother said, "One day, we will have our own firm. We will never have to ask anybody for a job again."

"Now back in the 1920s, that seemed like a very wild prediction. But, in effect, we have always been pointing toward that goal. The only thing I've ever known is architecture. I went through high school and into college and the war came along, and when I came back I finished reserves, I went to architectural school. I finished Harvard and Paris and then we said, we're going to start the firm, because I too could not find a job when I graduated college with a degree because [he was told] we don't hire colored people."

Madison excelled in his courses in elementary and high school. In fact, he performed so well that there was a concern between him and his cousin about whether they should go into medicine or not. But Madison could not stand the sight of blood. Although his mother was an educated woman and had attended college, she stayed at home to raise her children. Yet, she was very entrepreneurial. She was a salesperson going about in the community to sell cosmetics to her friends in order to supplement her husband's income. She was also a devout church person, a member of St. John's A.M.E. Church. I asked Madison whether he thought he would have become an architect without the strong intervention of his mother. He replied in the following way: "I think that it's difficult to say what path I would have taken, but there's no question, I'm an architect because of that. There's no doubt you would have to conclude that my family are educated or intelligent people in their background. We could have done anything if we set our minds to it."

He graduated in 1940 with a high school diploma from East Technical High School in Cleveland, Ohio. Thereafter, he attended Howard University, where he studied architecture. His studies were interrupted however, by the onset of World War II. Madison left Howard University to serve as a second lieutenant in the Army during the war. After he was wounded in Galicano, Italy, in 1944, he received the Purple Heart and various other battle recognitions. He came back to Cleveland and decided to return to his studies in architecture. This time, he turned his attention to Case Western Reserve University (CWRU) in Cleveland in 1946.[4]

However, he received a chilly reception at the university. In fact, when Madison talked to the dean of the architecture school about pursuing study there, he was informed that no colored individual had graduated from the university's architectural school before and they were unclear as to whether his college credits from Howard University could be transferred. Madison's response to the situation was to come back several days later wearing his military uniform. He informed the dean that because he had been injured for his country, he did not understand why he could not be admitted to study at CWRU. One of the architectural professors analyzed Madison's work from Howard University and became an advocate for his admission into the program.[5]

Before he was finally admitted into the program, he was required to take examinations every Saturday during the summer months in order to see if the credits from Howard would transfer. He finished his requirements and was granted formal admission to Case Western Reserve University one day before fall classes began.[6] He received his bachelor of architecture degree from the school in 1948.

I asked why he decided to become an entrepreneur, most particularly in terms of his ability to take risks. He stated quite frankly that one of the most compelling reasons that pushed him into entrepreneurship in addition to his mother's prodding was that in spite of the fact that he received his master of architecture degree from Harvard University in 1952, he, like his father, was unable to find a job in his area of expertise because of his race. In his own words:

First of all, there was no option. They wouldn't hire me. I had the option of going to work in the lumber yards or work someplace else or start my practice. It just wasn't like today. Nobody would hire, so if I'm going to be an architect, I'm going to teach or take the big risk and do it. And that risk was taken in concert with my wife, who also believed in me, and also worked for the first six years in order to survive because those first years, I didn't have any work. I think I made six hundred dollars a year. You can't live on that. But, she was a teacher. I have to give all the credit to her and my mother at that time, too. They were both teaching. They said, "Yes we support you. We believe in you." I wasn't out there all by myself.

Madison and his wife persevered. Eventually, they had two children, and when the children were born, his wife stayed home and took care of them. Madison's father, whom he adored, died in 1951 at the age of fifty-two. He and his brothers were still in school at that time, and he started out in 1954 as Robert P. Madison, architect. In 1956 his brother Julian, an engineer, became a partner in the firm, which then became known as Madison and Madison Architects and Engineers.

I would say this, that the inspiration of my mother, as a Christian person and she believed that if we trusted and prayed, all things were possible. So, between my mother and my father who was a brilliant intellectual, almost genius, and my mother, who was the believer, the combination of these two is who I am. Those were my beginnings. People thought I was crazy for studying architecture in college. [They said] you're crazy. There are no black architects, and when I graduated they said, what are you going to do now? And I said I'm going to practice architecture, so when I came back to Cleveland [after graduating from Harvard] to open my practice, people said this fellow's going to starve before too long. The other thing was that the professors at Harvard University did not want to see me leave because I was going to be "the dean" one day and [they] said, "What are you going to do when you get out there trying to practice architecture? Are you going to starve?"

Madison told them he did not know for sure whether he was going to starve or not. However, because there's a bottom, he could always rise. It was a challenge to him. He would either have to starve to death or make some progress in his life. And, that's really what he's been doing all of these years since. That is how he started thinking about architecture and how he came to love it. He stated, "I did not have the opportunities that my classmates had at Harvard, and Harvard is Harvard. I studied with Walter Gropius. All the major firms descended upon Harvard University, wanting to interview their graduates, especially from the masters class, but nobody interviewed me. We don't hire blacks. No interview, no nothing." It was a period of much political upheaval and racial polarization, as well as violence and unveiled hostility.

> In 1954, when Rosa Parks didn't get off the bus, the civil rights movement came about, but more importantly the political climate changed. Carl Stokes was elected mayor of Cleveland; Maynard Jackson, mayor of Atlanta; [Kenneth A.]Gibson, mayor of Newark; [Richard G.] Hatcher, mayor of Gary, Indiana. Political power became a part of the black people's environment. At that time, they said, "We need an architect." I was prepared. We were prepared to be able to do what they wanted. So, it was a combination of time and our society that provided opportunities when these men took the helm of government because they could give me a job. They could say, we're going to build a post office here. We'll let Madison do one and let somebody else do one. Before that, there was no such thing, but they had the power. When they gained the power to influence contracts, we were ready, and that was something that was important to my success.

Madison benefited greatly from his political contacts. He believes Carl Stokes demonstrated quite clearly that blacks have the capability to govern effectively. In his autobiography, Stokes mentioned the work of Robert and his brother Julian in their architectural firm as a success story. Stokes noted that their success was also enhanced by their participation in minority set-aside programs. Madison's relationship with George Forbes was more professional in nature. "I respected him and he respected me. I didn't ask for anything from him. He didn't ask for anything from me. It was just a matter of our professional courtesies and relationships." Mr. Madison also benefited from his participation in Ohio's minority set-aside programs. He elaborated thus:

> First of all, you have to understand that it is very true, up until those years, black entrepreneurs had no access to the marketplace, no matter what their occupation was. There was no access because it was the good old boy system. We will take care of our own. When the minority set-aside program and the MBE programs came into being, it was simply to say this: Everybody pays taxes and these dollars that you pay in taxes are returned to the marketplace in terms of abilities to perform as contractors and architects. So, if you couldn't get the work through the normal sectors, and if you're paying the taxes, let's set aside some projects that only minorities can work on. They can bid against themselves, and we're sure one of them can get that project. And that was an

equalizer in order to permit the taxation. It provided an opportunity for us to develop a portfolio of work. When I designed the Cleveland State Office tower, it was not a set aside, but it was a team of minorities and whites who were equal partners, and have done that building. We then put that in my portfolio, which could lead to some other opportunities.

Although the set-aside program was developed to provide access to minorities so that they could prove their competence, he has been interviewed by private schools to work on architectural projects for building schools. Representatives from those schools told him,

Mr. Madison, you've done wonderful work, but how many private schools have you done? Well, no private schools, but at least we have a portfolio to say we've done great work, and they can figure out any way they want to squeeze you. But, the point is that the program is intended to a) provide opportunities for those tax payers, which is what we are and b) an opportunity to develop a portfolio because in my field you can't have designed one building until you've proved that you've done one before that. I think it was a great program, and yes, there are benefits because we proved that we were as good as anybody else.

One characteristic that is noticeable in Madison's work is his creativity. He stated the following:

Please understand, architecture is commissioned work. I just can't say, let me build something. I have to have somebody say I want you to design something for me. Now having received the commission, then our creativity is to develop a building or project that our client likes, that wins design awards, so we have to work within the framework of the client. So, architects are somewhat confined by the constraints of their client. But, what's in those constraints is where the creative juices and energies flow and to develop a product, an object that is exciting and challenging. . . . Architecture has a purpose, even though someone may not pay me; it is directed at doing something which is housing mankind from the elements, but I think I like doing what I'm doing, and I'm doing things right now that are unique, [that] I've never done before.

Madison has designed a number of facilities through the years, including the Nuclear Facility at Tuskegee Institute in Tuskegee, Alabama; the Science Research Center at Cleveland State University; the Frank J. Lausche State Office Building; Cuyahoga County Jail II; the Continental Airlines Expansion at Cleveland Hopkins

International Airport; the Cleveland Browns Stadium; the RTA Waterfront; the United States Embassy in Dakar, Senegal; the Cleveland Public Library; and the State of Ohio Computer Center in Columbus.

The American Embassy in Senegal, West Africa, was his most satisfying masterpiece because "it was not just a building. It was a symbol for Africa and it was a coming together of Africa and America in one facility. For me, personally, it [gave me] the opportunity to develop a project that represents the American government on the soil of Africa, and I created it; that was number one." Madison has also helped develop various buildings in downtown Cleveland during the administration of Mayor Mike White. For example, he was the associate architect in designing the Rock 'n' Roll Hall of Fame, and he also worked on the Gund Arena.

Last, I questioned Madison about the role of skin color and race in his success equation.

During my early years, in Washington, D.C., when I went to school, the elementary was inhabited by all the colors of the rainbow in that school, because if you had 1/64th, you were colored. We had kids in my class that were white, near white, brown, near brown, etc. We all played and mixed together and in that milieu, there was not a difference, but when we got out into the free world, how other people looked at you, I began to realize later in life, that even among ourselves, there is yet a prejudice, and I started thinking about it, and that goes back to how did these kids get to be light skinned? Because the slave master had a relationship with a slave woman, and sometimes those young offspring were reared in the house, and they were called house niggers, and those children of slaves and those children with both parents being black were dark skinned and they were reared in the field, and they were called field niggers, and so as time progressed, I was shocked to realize that some of these light-skinned blacks began to look down upon those dark-skinned blacks because they were different. I will tell you that as far as I'm concerned, I couldn't care less if I were some other color.

Yet, Madison has paid a penalty for being black. In 1979, he interviewed for a job at the courthouse in Painesville, Ohio, and was told, "You know, Mr. Madison, you're the best qualified person for this job, but I can't hire you. This town's not ready for a black architect."

Based on the success model discussed earlier in this study, several key factors contributed to Madison's success. First, he attained a high level of educational training, and statistical tests performed in this study indicated that entrepreneurs who were more educated were more successful. Second, he received educational training in the area that the business focused on, which was architecture. Third, he is an older entrepreneur, and entrepreneurs who were older were also more successful.

Fourth, he participated in minority set-aside programs and entrepreneurs who participated in these programs were also more successful. Additionally, he was able to complete his architectural assignments successfully, and he developed a good track record that subsequently enabled him to acquire more work.

Entrepreneurs who had a high percentage of steady customers were also more successful, and steady customers make up 31–50 percent of Madison's total customer base. Marital stability was also positively correlated with success, and Madison has been married for many years. Last, employing relatives to work in one's business operation was positively correlated with success, and Madison has several of his relatives working with him in his company. Among these are his daughter, Jeanne, nephew Kenny, niece Sandra, in addition to his brother Julian.

In spite of all of the obstacles Madison has had to overcome, his work is locally, nationally, and internationally known. He employs more than fifty staff members and operates a very profitable business in the six-figure range. He is a member of the Cleveland chapter of the American Institute of Architects, the Architects Society of Ohio, and the College of Fellows of the American Institute of Architects. He has received numerous honors and awards through the years, including the Distinguished Architect Award from Howard University; the Distinguished Service Award from Case Western Reserve University; the Northeast Ohio Entrepreneur of the Year Award; the Ohio Assembly of Council Corporate Hall of Fame Award; the Architect of the Year Award, as well as the President's Social Responsibility Award from Kent State University "for excellence and creativity in professional endeavors and a commitment to furthering cultural diversity." He has also been listed in *Who's Who in America, Who's Who in the World,* and *Ebony* magazine's list of 1,000 Successful African Americans.

DEBORAH THIGPEN WALLER
President, Thigpen and ADsociates, Inc., advertising and public relations company

I'm on a mission. I have goals. I know what my goals are and when you know what your goals are and your outcome, then you work toward meeting those goals. I've always known, since I was in the ninth grade, what my goals are. And, I have a professional credo I live by. I have a mission statement for the office, the company, but then I have a personal mission statement, and my personal and professional credo is that I am a visionary. I will serve my clients' needs. I will lead, not follow. I will create, not destroy. I am a force for good. I am a force for God. I will defy the odds, step up, step up, and I do. So, that's my personal credo and if you have your credo and your goals that you live by, then that helps see you through.[7]

From left: Michael Waller, President Bill Clinton, and Deborah Thigpen Waller, who is here receiving the 1997 SBA Small Business Person of the Year Award. *Photo by Nannette Bedway*

Deborah Thigpen Waller is the president of Thigpen and ADsociates, Inc., an advertising and public relations firm. The company is located in Twinsburg, Ohio, which is a part of the greater Cleveland metropolitan community. Thigpen Waller is included in this chapter because she is the most successful African American female entrepreneur that I have interviewed in either of my studies on local African American business owners. There was a big gap between the economic success levels of black male and female entrepreneurs. One goal of this study is to develop intervention programs that are specifically designed to deal with factors that constrain black female entrepreneurs in the economic marketplace. There is also the need to perform more research on this subject in the future. Hence, Thigpen Waller's inclusion in this chapter can help us understand more clearly one of the key issues that this study seeks to examine: the role that gender plays in the economic equation.

Thigpen Waller is very warm, friendly, and modest. She was very easy to talk to and humble in spite of her enormous successes. Adorning the walls of her office are the numerous awards and plaques that she has received through the years. She also has several photographs of her, her husband, and various prominent political leaders such as former presidents Bill Clinton and George Bush Sr., former secretary of commerce Ron Brown, and others. The interview began by discussing her early childhood and family life in order to assess some of the earlier influences on her development. She was born in 1956, during the early days of the modern civil rights movement in this country.

> I am the fourth child of six children and I was born in Cleveland, Ohio, in the inner city, and when I was a youth we lived in the Longwood Projects, and I attended Longwood Elementary School. I gather, when I was in the third grade or so, we moved to 106th and Union which is still [the] inner city of Cleveland, but it was more of an integrated area. It was mostly people of eastern European descent, and we were the first African American family on our street. And, I remember all the for-sale signs going up at that time and people just started moving out and more Afro-American families started moving in. So, that was in the early 60s and I just remember that vividly.

Thigpen Waller was very much affected by this white flight as a young child as she observed people moving away and leaving the community as soon as she and other members of her family moved in. It was during this time period that she began to notice there was a difference between black people and white people. After all, she had just moved from an all-black school to one that was predominantly white. Three years later, by the time she entered the sixth grade, her new school had become about half white and half black. She observed that there was a big difference between the racial groups, and she and other blacks were treated differently at the new school. Certain psychological and possibly physical scars remain because she also got into fights with white students. The fights were very physical: "pulling hair, punching, scratching, kicking, you know actual fights." Those episodes were especially traumatic because she had always been a peaceful person. However, basic survival in her new school environment demanded that she stand up and defend herself against the attacks. Thigpen Waller was influenced by the activities of her parents as well during her early years.

> My mother, well, in many ways, I would consider her an entrepreneur. She had a home-based business doing hair in the basement of our home for a number of years. And, then she also worked in a beauty salon and she owned a beauty salon, but then she came back home and was working in the home for the cosmetologist and she ran a beauty shop. My mom was the entrepreneur and my dad was a steady worker, a laborer. And, what I remember best about my dad, and by the way, my mother and father are both still alive and are celebrating their 52nd anniversary this year [2002]. But my dad never missed a day

of work in his life. So, he has had perfect attendance for work, and I don't see that these days. He retired from Republic Steel, which is now LTV Steel.

Thigpen Waller grew up in a working-class neighborhood even though she was exposed to middle- and upper-class ideas later on in her life. She was an excellent student in school, and she had a good attendance record. She usually sat in the front of the class and was involved in several extracurricular activities. All her teachers knew her. One of the most interesting programs that she participated in, one that subsequently provided her with good solid mentoring opportunities, was Junior Achievement. Here, she and other students, with help, developed their own businesses, and they also sold stock in their companies. It was basically a mini-entrepreneurial course. Her older siblings had also participated in Junior Achievement. That experience helped her decide at an early age, during her high school years, that she wanted to become an entrepreneur. When asked about that and other factors that influenced her decision to become an entrepreneur, she responded in this way:

> I decided to become an entrepreneur because in my business life and employ-
> ment working for other firms, the other jobs that I've had, I was basically
> always putting in twelve-hour days, fourteen-hour days, and there just didn't
> seem to be enough gratification from it, at least not from the people that I was
> working that hard for. I felt that if I could work that hard for someone else,
> indeed, I should be able to do something for myself. And, even when I was
> employed, I always kept, I always worked more than one job. [I would] either
> volunteer doing something, or have a job and intern something else. I worked
> two jobs, so I had a lot of energy, and I knew that if I could use that energy for
> my own business, I should be able to be successful because I wasn't a 9:00–
> 5:00, eight-hour day person. . . . I was giving so much more.

She graduated early, at the age of sixteen, at the end of eleventh grade, from John Adams High School and was admitted to Bowling Green State University with a financial aid package. There, she pursued a degree in journalism through the business school. Eventually, she took classes in both journalism and business. While at Bowling Green, she discovered she had a love for and interest in public relations and broadcast journalism. During her junior year, another wonderful opportunity presented itself: an internship with "Up with People," an organization that focused on international theater. As an intern, she traveled to about forty of the United States and also to parts of South America. She had a chance to do public relations work for the organization and received college credits for the internship as well as a per diem. She also had more responsibilities associated with her new work. After returning to Bowling Green to finish up her last year of undergraduate work, she worked at a television station, where she was on the air reporting consumer news and information.

Then, in September 1978, she came back to Cleveland because she didn't get a job when she graduated. Later on, she got a position with Sears and Roebuck as part of their executive management training program. Although executive management was not really an area she was interested in, she was attracted by the possibility that at some future time, she might be able to go to work at the Sears Tower headquarters in their public relations department in Chicago. She did learn a lot about business management, as well as how to supervise people. All that information would be valuable to her later on when she started her own business.

After leaving Sears, in August 1979, she decided to attend graduate school and enrolled at Boston University for two years. There, she worked on her master's degree in mass communications. Although she completed the coursework, financial difficulties kept her from receiving the degree. She also had yet another opportunity to become involved in an internship program, this one at an NBC affiliate station. She also participated in an internship with a friend and colleague who attended Harvard University. Her friend had established a concert promotion business. After attending Boston University, Thigpen Waller was hired as an associate professor/instructor to teach an introductory class in communications and public relations at Texas Southern University in Houston, Texas. She worked in this capacity from 1982 to 1985.

And, all the time that I was working, I was an associate professor, and I freelanced with public relations firms and advertising agencies. Again, I could not do just one job. I just had to be busy all the time with work. I gather you would call me a workaholic. And, I was freelancing and getting another feel for what it was like in the advertising industry, the public-relations industry, and also teaching. Texas Southern wanted me to go to school and get a Ph.D. so I could become a full-fledged professor, and I was not ready to go back to college. I didn't want to go back to school, at least not to study again, so from Texas Southern, I landed another job at Prairieview A&M working in their athletic department, as sports information director.

While working in that job, Thigpen Waller was meeting people who were trying to get her to do work for them in selling magazines and developing ads for their businesses. She decided that now was the appropriate time for her to do this type of work for herself. So, she established her advertising and public relations firm in Houston, Texas, in 1988. Prior to starting the business, she took about a year to plan the business and decide on the name she wanted to use. She also held focus group

sessions with students who had received their master's degrees in business administration. Those students advised her on what steps she needed to take to go into
business. She also started saving capital for the business. She developed a business
plan and handed in her notice to the Prairieview athletic director, who didn't want
her to leave. As fate would have it, the Prairieview athletic department ended up
being her first client because she gave them two weeks notice, and they didn't have
anyone else close by who could promote their big game, which was coming up
soon. She worked with them and negotiated the specifications of her contract.
According to Waller, "I made more on working for them in three months than I did
on my contract as a sports director." The gross amount of money she made on that
contract was about $30,000, although her profit was less after her expenses were
paid. She then started reaching into the network of people and contacts she had
met through the years. When she started her business in 1988, she used money
from her IRA account that she had accumulated while she was working in the area
of higher education. She had saved about $20,000 over a period of eight years.
Thigpen Waller moved her business to the Cleveland area later on largely because
romance entered her life.

> My reason for moving into Cleveland was that I met a businessman, Michael
> Waller, there [in Houston] who was attending a conference that my company
> was doing public relations for. And, I met him and he was from my home-
> town and we got to know each other, fell in love, and within six months, we
> were married. So, I moved back to Cleveland. I would characterize it as love at
> first meeting rather than first sight because I was ignoring him for two days at
> this event because I was working. I wasn't interested in talking to the people
> attending there. But, then he found out that I was from Cleveland so it was
> love at first meeting when we got to sit down and talk to each other.

Thigpen and ADsociates is a full-service advertising and public relations company. Thigpen Waller reviews advertising campaigns and meets with her creative
director and various artists whom she employs to look at their ideas and concepts. She is also very much involved in trying to market their work and acquire
new contracts for the company. They have both national and local clients.

> We've done ads for Huron Hospital and Metro Health Systems and Southpoint
> Hospitals that have run on the RTA bus lines. So, we've done things also for the
> Ohio Lottery where we've had the whole bus ads, painted like a billboard ad. And,
> we worked on creating that design. Throughout the state of Ohio, we've been
> working with NASA Planned Research Center for four years and we actually
> managed the visitor's center there. . . . NASA grants contracts out to us to run the

visitor's center which is their eye on the community, their PR piece to the world, and we're in charge of their exhibit and getting the visitors to come in, promoting the place, tours of NASA facilities, the speaker's bureau, publications that are distributed in a five-area region about what's going on to NASA educators.

Thigpen and ADsociates has worked with numerous clients through the years and has developed an impressive track record. They have worked for corporate clients, health and medical organizations, technological entities, political campaigns, publications, and sports programs. Some of these include Cooper and Lybrands (now known as Price Waterhouse); Goodyear Rubber and Tire Company; Key Corporation; LTV Steel; Magic Johnson Theaters; the Ohio Lottery Commission; the Cleveland Clinic System with Huron Hospital, Metro and Mount Sinai Medical Center; Solar Technologies and the Environmental Protection Agency. The company has also worked on political campaigns for former congressman Craig Washington of Houston; the late congressman Mickey Leland of Houston; former congressman Louis Stokes, as well as Joel Hyatt, who ran unsuccessfully for the United States Senate.

Thigpen and ADsociates has developed a diverse list of clients through the years. She has actually met about 95 percent of her clients personally, although, in some cases, other members of her staff go out to meet and interact with them. Their ability to access federal clients through the federal government's 8(a) program came about because her company is a certified minority business enterprise (MBE). According to Thigpen Waller, "in the 8(a) program you work, you read the *Commerce Business* and other federal publications and we find out about what other types of jobs are coming up for bid in our area of concentration. And, so I bid on jobs and because I am a certified MBE for the state, for the county, for the city, we're sent information about open bids, and that's how we get 50 percent of our business, through the bid process. The other is through marketing and networking and solicitation, giving presentations to sell them our company." Thigpen Waller's company has benefited greatly from minority set-aside programs.

The participation has helped me tremendously as I think that the programs have been excellent because they offer you a lot of support. I think that until I got that first contract with NASA, the banks wouldn't give me a credit line. I mean, you have to have a certain amount of business or dollars or a big client, before they will believe in you and give you financing. So, it really helped. They were like a lifesaver, a lifeline for my business. They helped me to understand business and to be able to really compete on price. If it wasn't for the set-aside business, I wouldn't have been able to compete successfully for the other 50 percent of the corporate work that I was doing that was non-set-aside, that I competed against [in] the open market. So, it really helped me because I had to have all my ducks in order, all my financial statements, my marketing plan, my business, just everything that they wanted to know. You know, when you do these contracts and when you bid on them, your life is an open book to the point that you have to be fingerprinted for some of the certifications for some of the processes.

Thigpen and ADsociates has an excellent portfolio, and if the ideas they present to their potential clients are what they are looking for, then they have a good chance of securing that particular contract or client. However, the economic marketplace is very competitive and hence, their firm, like many others, has to offer creative products to their customers in a cost-effective manner. They also want to get the product to their client in a timely way and to make a profit at the end of the process. Creativity, obviously, has to play a big role in developing advertising and marketing campaigns for such a diverse group of clients. We discussed the role of creativity in this business.

For Thigpen Waller and her staff, the creative process is very much interwoven with psychology itself because it is important for them to understand various conceptions of how to get people to want to buy their clients' products. The whole process of getting people to associate their demand to a certain brand is a big job. Her creativity comes from various sources such as having an exposure to many things and ideas and to having an open mind. She also realized that she could make a paradigm shift, if necessary. "There is so much involved in it and it's not like mathematics that's such an exact science. So, you have a chance to go over the edge, go over the top, or be subtle about it. So, it just depends on who you're dealing with. And, I enjoy that because I like hiring people who are experts in their area. So, I don't know how to draw these concepts or do that, but I can sit down and look at them and say that will work or that won't work."

Because Thigpen Waller is the only female entrepreneur that I included in this life history chapter, I wanted to discuss more fully the impact of gender on her business success. In particular, I wanted to know more about constraints or impediments that she had experienced in the economic sphere because she was a woman. She indicated that she had encountered a number of obstacles along the way because of her gender, especially when she first started out. In some of her previous experiences, the male executives would oftentimes be invited to go to saunas with top executives and would often come back with new job assignments. "Women were not a part of the country club, old-boys network." She, did, however, learn to play golf later on, but she wasn't invited to some events because she was a woman. She also had to fight off unwanted male advances on various occasions. But, she learned to handle those situations in a diplomatic way, and she became stronger because of it. Also, her feminine identity has been interwoven over time with her name, which is Deborah. Her male counterparts have always liked to call her "Debbie," which she believes placed her in a box as someone who was not to be taken seriously. She changed the pronunciation of her name in order to denote someone who was very serious. In effect, it was part of the recreation of Deborah Thigpen Waller. She clarified during our interview, "I grew up with DEB-or-ah and Debby, and to gain respect of my colleagues and the business world, I decided to go by De-BOR-ah because I didn't like people calling me Debby or, there were so many Deborahs so it was a way of setting myself out from the rest of the pack . . . De-BOR-ah is an extension of who I am because De-BOR-ah is a public relations creation."

I asked Thigpen Waller to elaborate on factors that contributed to her success along the way as an entrepreneur. She credited her family for her wonderful up-bringing. They encouraged her in her various endeavors. She also had a lot of "hard knocks" as well and sometimes was told that she could not do certain things because of her skin color, which made her fight even harder to succeed. "So you know, having hard knocks and when you land on your back, you're look-ing up and you know where your help is coming from. I just kept going. And then, my strong commitment in my faith." While we were on the subject of im-pediments that she had experienced because of her race, I wanted to know more about how the issue of skin color and hair texture had impacted on her success as an entrepreneur. The issue of skin color, hair texture and hair length has been particularly problematic for black women, especially when their beauty and at-tractiveness have been judged in comparison with Caucasian women, who have been put on a pedestal in this society. Numerous articles and reports have fo-cused on the fact that darker African American women have more problems getting jobs on television stations, in movies, and other frontline visible posi-tions in comparison to their lighter-skinned counterparts. She answered the ques-tion in this way: "My skin color, no matter what it is, has always just been looked at as black. So, not that I'm light-skinned, African American, or dark-skinned. I've always just been looked at as African American. . . . The skin color thing, most of the differences with that has come from among my own people. So, just socially. But, businesswise, the skin color factor hasn't bothered me at all."

I asked her if she felt that if she were of a lighter skin color with more Euro-pean-type features, whether more doors would have been open for her in the world of business and entrepreneurship. She said,

> That's hard for me to make an assessment on because the doors that I went
> through that I knocked [on] they were open, and when they were closed and
> they weren't open wide enough, I think those had other things that I did not

go in there prepared for. I don't think that it had anything to do with the tone of my skin. People are still prejudiced against you or think you are one thing because of your skin. I notice it all the time but even about the skin, the hair has a lot to do with it. You could write a whole other set on hair. You know, the hair ticks, the hair-skin color, yeah right. So, I wear my hair in its natural state. I have for years, but there are things to make it look European or whatever, but there has been the highlight of how people perceive me is through the texture of my hair. You see, I wear it as natural as it can get.

Thigpen Waller has had the opportunity to interact with a number of well-known and significant political figures through the years. She had the opportunity to work with former Secretary of Commerce Ron Brown, who took a delegation of small business owners to Mexico when the North American Free Trade Agreement was being signed. Thigpen Waller was part of that group. She and her husband Michael Waller, who is also a very successful entrepreneur, had an opportunity to meet former president Bill Clinton when they attended the White House Conference on Small Businesses and later when she received the 1997 Small Business Administration Person of the Year Award. She was honored by former president Clinton and former vice president Al Gore.

Thigpen and ADsociates is a profitable business enterprise with fifteen full-time and ten part-time employees, with profits in the seven-figure range. Her clients are diverse and include individual consumers, other businesses, the government, nonprofit organizations, and politicians. Fewer than 10 percent of her clients are minorities. Mrs. Waller is very philanthropic and has made contributions to various organizations, including the Black Professional Association of Greater Cleveland, the Make-A-Wish Foundation, and Junior Achievement. She and her husband have also established the Michael and Deborah Waller World Development and Humanitarian Evolutionary Fund with the Cleveland Foundation.

A number of variables in Thigpen Waller's life are consistent with my success model, outlined earlier. First, she attained a high level of education, and entrepreneurs who where highly educated were more successful. Second, her education and training were in the area that her business concentrates in, advertising and communications. Third, entrepreneurs who had a high percentage of steady customers in this study were more successful, and 31–50 percent of Thigpen Waller's clients are steady customers. Fourth, Thigpen Waller has participated in and benefited from minority set-aside programs, and the statistical analysis performed in this study indicates that entrepreneurs who participated in set-asides were more successful. Fifth, Thigpen Waller had a business mentor and having a mentor was positively correlated with success. Sixth, Thigpen Waller is married and marital stability was positively correlated with success; in addition, Thigpen Waller is in her mid-years, and entrepreneurs who were older were also more successful. Last, being involved and participating in internship programs was very helpful to Thigpen Waller. She learned a great deal in those programs that later helped her to develop her company.

Thigpen Waller has been the recipient of numerous honors and awards through the years, including the SBA Small Business Person of the Year Award; the Women in Communications' 1997 Cleveland Communicator's Award; and the Emerging Business of the Year Award, 1996, by the Greater Cleveland Growth Association's Cleveland Regional Minority Purchasing Council. She was selected as one of the Women Entrepreneurs of the Year in 1991 in Houston by the Association of Urban Women Entrepreneurs. She was also selected as one of Houston's Young Achievers by the Human Enrichment of Life Program in 1991 and received the Outstanding Agency Coordinator Award from the United Way in 1990.

LEROY OZANNE
Founder and CEO, Ozanne Construction Company

It is very, very confusing to me that since we started, let's talk about slaves and whatever you want to call it. Let's go way back. But, let's go back after some of the good things happened to us and we got beyond slavery and we were able to participate in the economy. Why didn't we qualify as an initial investor on roads, transportation of any kind, stagecoaches, I don't care? Somebody needed another $500 dollars, but they didn't ask us for it. Because they knew that if they asked us for it, we would become participants in the ground level of business that would probably grow into a large empire. We can skip all the way back to before airlines and utility companies and steel mills and see why none of the original investors were solicited in the black community. Certainly, we could have gotten fifteen of us together and gotten together a hundred-dollar bill to invest, because that's about all it took.[8]

Leroy Ozanne has experienced many things in life. He is very reflective on various issues and possesses a lively wit and a delightful sense of humor. Ozanne Construction Company was included in this chapter for several reasons. First, it is one of the very few family-based business enterprises in this study that has survived across time. Second, the business is in an area in which African Americans traditionally have been underrepresented.

Ozanne Construction Company was established in 1956. Most black-owned businesses have not survived past the lifespan of the initial owners and founders. Consequently, most African American entrepreneurs in the contemporary period

Leroy Ozanne with granddaughter Lisa Ozanne.

had to start their businesses from scratch. As chapter 6 indicated, black entrepreneurs who inherit their businesses from their parents are more successful than those who do not, which is intuitive and is what one would expect to find. Often no business succession plan is formulated so that family members have no clear-cut plan or strategy to ensure that the business continues from one generation to the next. The Ozanne family has already dealt with this contingency and has developed a plan that ensures the smooth transition of the business from Leroy Ozanne to his son Dominic. At present, Leroy Ozanne is the CEO of the company, while Dominic serves as the president. Finally, Ozanne Construction Company is included here because it is the most successful business in this entire study in terms of its total sales and profitability. Its inclusion, therefore, helps us more clearly understand the realms of possibility for black entrepreneurs in the Cleveland metropolitan area.

Leroy Ozanne was born in Beaumont, Texas, in 1925. Both his parents were born in southwest Louisiana, Cajun country, and during his childhood, he had the opportunity to meet the relatives of both of his parents who lived in Louisiana. His mother's parents grew up in New Iberia, while his father's parents were from Oppaloosa. In the 1920s and earlier, farming was an important occupation. Everybody wanted to become a farmer when they grew up. Ozanne's father left the farm and moved to Beaumont, Texas, where gold had been discovered. Oil was found in the city, and this created a rush for gold. Ozanne's father jumped on his pony and moved to Texas to set up an operation there. His mother's father was a carpenter and also moved to Texas, which is where his parents met.

Although Ozanne grew up in Texas, he had the opportunity to get to know his grandfather who owned a store in Louisiana.

> When I first met him I was amazed at him because he could run a store and make a living at it and support a family on it and he could know what to stock and what to purchase and what to sell to people in this rural area, and nickels and dimes and quarters were big things for people to spend on, and I was amazed by that. He must have been in business there for thirty years. That's why I get upset. Why didn't they check with him? He had a hundred dollars. I know he had a hundred dollars he could have invested somewhere if someone had asked him, but he was ignored and we don't want you to be investors because we don't want you to be a part of this state. And they're talking about affirmative action and this is where I get upset because I say this reverse affirmative action that you claim was always in reverse for us because we never were asked.

Ozanne stayed in Beaumont and completed high school. He went to Alabama State University for his first year of undergraduate work. As a freshman at Alabama State University, he received a music scholarship in the form of a stipend. One condition of the stipend was that he had to play in the band and teach music to elementary school children. He indicated that during his first year at Alabama State, he had a little too much fun. In other words, he did not apply himself to his work. "I think that's not speaking well of a minority college, because I should have been directed better. But, I think I would have been directed better had I stayed there my sophomore year." He was drafted into the military after his first year of college in 1944 at the age of eighteen. He was supposed to be drafted earlier but was able to get a six-month deferment because he had tried to volunteer for the Tuskegee Air Force. He was finally drafted and served in the United States Navy in 1944. After he returned from serving in the military, he came to Cleveland and enrolled at John Carroll University. "I went into pre-engineering studies at John Carroll. Before [that] I was in music. I was going to be a musician, because you've got to realize by 1944, if you wanted to think about what you wanted to do with your future, you wouldn't think about, 'I think I'll be an architect, I'll be, maybe, a doctor.' That was way down the line. But, a musician was about the closest thing you could get, to get started on something really fast because as musicians, they were young and were able to earn a dollar and even as badly as I played [the trumpet], I was able to earn a few bucks."

He finished his pre-engineering program at John Carroll and began to look for a school of architecture to attend. He applied for entrance at Case Western Reserve University, and because they curtailed their architectural program, he didn't make the cut. They were taking only twenty-two students at that time. Ozanne was number twenty-three on their list. "I didn't know any politicians or preachers, anybody to stand by and give me a blessing. I went on to the same college in a few other areas where you could get some architectural courses." He did not finish his bachelor's degree. He received his associate degree in pre-engineering. He did pursue further study, but it wasn't in any organized program to finish the bachelor's degree in architecture. I asked him why he decided to become an entrepreneur, and he answered me in the following way:

> I worked for the city of Cleveland as a result of putting together a dossier—"a resume." I learned how to draw, to do some architectural drafting. I studied all these courses. I thought that I could. Then, they were looking for building inspectors when they were desperately trying to condemn a part of the city to build the Tri-C campus downtown. So, in order to acquire this land, the city hired a new group of inspectors to go out and help them acquire through condemnation these homes and businesses and horse stables and bars and restaurants in that area. So, I was hired to do that, and as a result of working for the city in the building department, it became very clear to me by observing the cadre of people in business in Cleveland who were contractors that they were far and removed from what I thought the level should be. I'm not calling anybody dumb or nothing but they came in with very poor credentials, so I looked beyond that and said who else is doing this, and one or two of them had to have you fill out his building permit application because he could not read. This was a man making a living building buildings in the city of Cleveland who was a minority. Then, I looked at the white population coming in there to see what kind of intellect they had, and it was something that was not, you know, they had a lot of friends. They didn't have to stand in line like the black contractors did because the guys would say, "just leave your application and I'll take care of it for you." So, I noticed that, and I said, maybe this is something that I can do. So, I decided that "I think I can do it." So, I said, yep. I said to myself, "Self: I think that I can do this."

At the same time this idea came to him, he was still in school and was doing some architectural drafting on the side for various people who needed to acquire building permits. Sometimes, they would want to put an addition on their home, to put an addition on their garage, or build a new garage. He provided them with good working drawings. And, things worked out well for him. He had quite a bit of business on the side. So, when he decided to go into business, it was just automatic. It didn't take him long to get other jobs. He had some friends who needed to have things done. They gave him some work, and he has been self-employed ever since.

His earlier courses in pre-engineering in addition to his studies at John Carroll University complemented his work with the building department at the city of Cleveland. In that job, he gained experience in the industry area that he was going to start his business in. According to Ozanne,

> It was total exposure because you had to help people get building permits. You had to go in to observe the reasons why they needed a permit and what had to be done as a result, and they had to get architectural drawings to provide the city with evidence that they were going to obey the code, the building code and the plumbing and electrical and heating permits that had to be associated with a new addition or a complete new structure. All this was even better than most people getting an education. I stayed there for four years, almost five, and that kind of exposure, believe me, when you needed to move on, can't be a better vehicle. There was no way.

Although he had planned to start his own business, his own departure from city hall after working for almost five years was to some extent precipitated by the fact that some of his colleagues had reported to his boss that he was doing work on the side, and they didn't like that very much. In fact, when the new mayor of Cleveland came into office, he said to Ozanne, "I understand that you've been drawing these things on the side. You shouldn't be doing that. I'm going to get rid of you. Goodbye." And, the next morning, Ozanne went into business. "I left city hall, put on some dungarees, and went to work in my shop."

Ozanne's dismissal was ironic, given the fact that doing consulting jobs on the side in one's area of expertise was really nothing new in the building department in Cleveland city hall. On the contrary, many of the employees in the department were architects and engineers, some of whom were retired, who were making extra money on the side. According to Ozanne, "I was only doing what everybody else was doing. They could do their work so well that they weren't doing a thing after 1:00 P.M., and that's what makes these kinds of city hall jobs so lucrative because people want them because they know they could get full pay for half-time work. It hasn't changed." When asked if his race had anything to do with his reprimand by the mayor, he responded by saying that he believed that some of the big complaints about him were coming from people who were doing drawings just like him. Thus, he was taking work from them. They perceived him as a competitor. There were a couple of black architects, in particular, who had just started out and didn't like the competition that Ozanne was offering.

When Ozanne first started his business in 1956, his office was located on Crawford Road in the Hough area, largely a white community at the time. One source of capital for his new business was his savings account. He had began to save money that he earned from his freelance work. He walked into the Cleveland Trust Bank, across the street from his office, and asked if he could set up a line of credit. When the bank refused, he went to its Miles Avenue branch and opened a commercial account. He was able to get a line of credit there that enabled him to hire staff and pay them each week until he got paid on some of his construction contracts. He asked for less than five hundred dollars from the bank.

Another critical factor that aided Ozanne in successfully securing capital was that one of the white bankers took him under his wing, so to speak, and mentored him about how to develop a good financial relationship with the bank. He showed him how to establish a good credit history that would enable him to access even more capital in the future. But, the banker wanted to make sure that Ozanne took his advice. It was a very good mentoring relationship because Ozanne began to understand how bankers operated and how to successfully access more credit over time. One of the most important lessons that he learned was "to always borrow money when you don't need it. You can never get a dime when you're broke." He would borrow a small amount of money, put it in his account, and pay it back in three months time. In this way, he was creating a credit history. The next time he wanted a loan, he could borrow more than he had during the previous time. Today, some bankers invite Ozanne to play golf with them at various clubs, which is ironic given the difficulty he had accessing money from the bankers in the early days.

Ozanne was a friend of Carl Stokes before he became mayor and also contributed to Stokes's political campaigns. He never actually went to Carl Stokes's office while he was mayor, but did continue to help him financially. Ozanne also was a supporter of George Forbes, most particularly when he ran for mayor against Mike White in 1989. Ozanne Construction Company benefited enormously from participating in federal and state set-aside programs. One strategy that Ozanne used to great benefit was to develop a joint venture with Turner Construction Company, a very successful white-owned business. When the set-aside programs were first established, many large or majority-owned companies tried to develop ties with minority-owned firms in order to show that they had some compassion and get contracts when they made bids. Ozanne's own personal experience in the set-aside program was very much influenced by his work with Turner Construction Company, which at that time was probably ranked fourth in the country in terms of its construction contracts. Turner Construction Company had opened an office in Cleveland and was looking for someone to mentor with. Ozanne was invited to Washington, D.C., in the 1970s, along with a larger group of minority entrepreneurs by President Jimmy Carter to focus on the issue of set-asides. This meeting provided them with relevant information on various aspects of the construction industry. It was at this meeting that he met representatives of the Turner Construction Company. After a brief discussion, they expressed an interest in possibly working with him in the future. At this time, as a result of the Hough riots in Cleveland, members of the minority community were talking about building a shopping center. The timing was right, and members of the staff of Turner Construction Company met with Ozanne and members of his staff. Ozanne interacted most with Turner employees Ralph Johnson, Alphonso Sanchez, and Joseph A. McCullough. As Ozanne explained:

> I exposed them to my expertise and my personnel, people, and my good abilities, and they said well maybe, you look to be all right so we agreed to be partners. So, as a result of that we had a joint venture relationship on this shopping center, and then we went into building a police building, airport, and maybe $100 million worth of other stuff around here. As a result of being involved with Turner [Construction Company] in Cleveland, I got called to Atlanta [and met] with Mayor Maynard Jackson. I went to Atlanta, and they were getting ready to build their airport, and [I] formed a joint venture with two major contractors there—not Turner—and we got together as one company and built the airport for the city of Atlanta, and these are the kinds of things that set-asides do. While I was in Atlanta, we also built their new main library and a couple of jailhouses that they've got sitting up there right now. And, as a result of that, we were able to go into things that we would continue to do ourselves, and we managed to go from building little buildings into getting major contracts.

There is no doubt that the business relationship Ozanne established with Turner Construction Company ensured the eventual success of Ozanne Construction Company. So, in essence, it was similar to the earlier apprenticeship role Ozanne had experienced when he worked in the building department in the city of Cleveland. In both these situations, he learned things that would help him overcome many obstacles in the real world of entrepreneurship. There were simply so many things that he learned while mentoring with Turner Construction Company that he could never learn from reading books. And, a very interesting truth emerged after he worked with them for a while: Ozanne was already using some of these techniques in his own business operation on a trial-and-error kind of basis, and no one had ever given him credit for them or legitimized them. The moment he realized this fact was truly a turning point in his life because, for the first time, he began to realize he could operate among the best of them, in the "big league." So, his mentoring relationship with Turner Construction Company was a win-win situation. In describing what he learned and its impact on his own company's success, he stated the following:

> There would have been no way to know how things are done in construction, how it's really done in construction, unless you are associated with a major contractor like Turner. Now, I got exposed to the way they do business, how they operate, their main nuts and bolts operation from zero to the top, where they started writing checks to give out dividends for profits. So, I got a chance to witness every one of those steps which I would bring back here [and] say, no fellows, this is not the way to do this. Here's how you do it. This is what I brought back as a result of elbow-rubbing with some of the meanest guys in the world.

During his years of participating in joint ventures with Turner Construction Company, Ozanne stressed that he was never a subcontractor. He was always a partner, a co-contractor on the various jobs. He would not tolerate being a sub-contractor on any of their assignments. They would make an agreement and draw up papers specifying who would be responsible for what on each assignment as well as how the profits were to be distributed—whether they would be divided up 60–40, 35–65, or 50–50.

In analyzing the Ozanne-Turner relationship more fully, I had the opportunity to interview Ralph W. Johnson, who served as the project executive for Turner Construction Company in Cleveland at the time the Turner-Ozanne relationship first developed. According to Johnson, their first project together involved developing a commercial base in the Hough area, which desperately needed shopping centers, grocery stores, automobile stores, and other types of businesses. The Hough area had been destroyed by the riots. Turner Construction Company had been approached by a minority developer to build a shopping center. They investigated various firms in the area and selected Ozanne Construction Company as the best choice because of its reputation and the quality of its work.[9]

Johnson further stated that he and Leroy Ozanne developed procedures on how to make things work. Some of Turner's people were brought in to work with Leroy's people. Turner Construction was a publicly held corporation. Although the distribution of profit varied somewhat through the years, in the early period Turner Construction received 70 percent of the profit while Ozanne Construction got 30 percent. Johnson believes this distribution was commensurate with each company's contribution to a project. He also stated that during the joint-venture relationships, Ozanne Construction carried its own weight.[10]

Although some local Cleveland entrepreneurs have suggested that Ozanne was merely involved in the joint-venture relationship as a silent partner, Johnson did not agree with this. He stated that Ozanne was always involved in the decision-making processes during their joint ventures. In fact, in recent years, Ozanne has competed with Turner Construction Company on several jobs and has won the contracts over Turner Construction Company.

The partnership was a great success. Ozanne Construction Company has an average annual volume of work in the $40–$50 million range, and their construction management volume exceeds $100 million.[11] In terms of their profitability, they like to maintain 6–7 percent of their volume in profits. The construction industry is very volatile, however, and profits vary from year to year. Weather conditions and sometimes legal entanglements get in the way. Currently, they have two offices, a main office in Cleveland and a satellite office in Atlanta, Georgia. They employ eleven to twenty workers in their businesses. I asked Ozanne what other factors have contributed to his business success along the way.

Without hesitation, he pointed to his son's efforts in the company as a major contributor to their overall success. He also felt that having continuity in their personnel and staff members had also enhanced the company's success. Efforts were made to get commentary from Dominic Ozanne for this study, but he declined to participate. Leroy Ozanne stated:

> I was lucky enough to have a son who could step in, and since he's been in charge, the volume of this company has grown tenfold. Just because he's better educated and he's got more business ideas than I do, they like him out there a lot better than they like me, and he's just a good manager and person and I would attribute that [he's] a big part of our success. We would have done something if he had not been around, but I don't think it would have been as volume-related as it turned out. The other thing [is] we have managed to keep some real good people around for a long period of time. We've got some workers who have been with us for fourteen years. That says something. We've got workers here that have left and come back, and we've got management people who are really dedicated to their work. I would say that our people have been the other contributing factor to keep this thing going.

Another issue that was discussed centered on the role of race and skin color in the struggle for success. Leroy Ozanne is also a striking-looking man who is very light in complexion. He said that he doesn't give skin color much thought. There have been many occasions when he was the only black person in the room. Yet, he felt like he belonged there because he believed that he was just as good and as smart as others were. His family has always lived in a neighborhood where it was understood that he was black. He doesn't feel that his skin color has helped him to succeed as an entrepreneur or allowed him to get any special benefits. "I had a friend who's a contractor, and he's dark and he and I had about the same level of struggling. He's a carpenter, a subcontractor, and I never considered myself as a subcontractor. I always wanted to be 'the man.' I'm in charge here and I'm going to hire you as a carpenter, but I'm not going to be one."

Several key factors from my model can be used to analyze the economic success of Leroy Ozanne. These include the fact that although he did not complete his college degree, he did attend college for several years, and his training was in an area that directly related to the area of focus for his business, engineering. Second, he had several years of experience in an industry area, construction, when he worked for the city of Cleveland. This was very useful to him because he later established a construction company. Third, Ozanne employed his son Dominic to work in the family business, and employing one's relative to work in one's business is also correlated with success. Fourth, older entrepreneurs in the study were also more successful and Leroy Ozanne is fairly advanced in age. Fifth, Ozanne has participated in numerous set-aside programs, and entrepreneurs who participated in set-asides were more successful. Sixth, Ozanne is married, and marital stability was correlated with economic success. Seventh, steady customers make up 31 to 50 percent of Ozanne's total customer base, and entrepreneurs who had a high percentage of steady customers were also more successful. Eighth, Ozanne had business mentors, and this variable was correlated with success. Last, there is little doubt that Ozanne's participation in a joint-venture relationship with Turner Construction ultimately enhanced the firm's overall success.

Dr. Oscar Saffold
Physician, CEO of Metropolitan Dermatology, Inc.

I think that there's an innate quality in people that causes them to want to become entrepreneurs. You can have people with the same level of education, finishing Harvard's MBA program. One has a burning desire to go back and begin his own business, and the other has a burning desire to achieve as an African American in "corporate America." Both of their ambitions are worthwhile, but one leads you down the path to entrepreneurship and one leads to corporate America.[12]

Dr. Oscar Saffold.

My first encounter with Saffold was as a patient. A colleague of mine had told me about his services as a dermatologist, and he came highly recommended. Since I was looking for a good dermatologist, I made an appointment and went in to his office on Lee Road. He was very courteous and professional. His office was overflowing with patients. It was almost standing room only. I was curious to know what kind of doctor was able to secure such a loyal following among his patients. I was soon going to be able to answer that question for myself.

I was impressed with the dermatological results I achieved, but effective treatment did require several office visits. After observing Saffold for several weeks and noticing that he had many of the attributes for success that I had observed over time while performing this study, I asked if I could interview him, and he politely assented. The name of his company is Metropolitan Dermatology. One of his offices is located in downtown Cleveland, at 2475 East 22nd Street, while another office is on Lee Road. I interviewed him in spring 2000. I wanted to know first and foremost why he decided to become an entrepreneur. "I became an entrepreneur because of my grandfather as a role model. He was an entrepreneur in Cleveland during the Depression, and my role model was always to be in business. I chose medicine because I particularly was fascinated with the art of healing and the knowledge that [there] was something that one could do to make other people better."

His grandfather owned drugstores, buildings, and a bowling alley. Although his father worked for his grandfather, he did not inherit the family business. "They were pretty much gone by then." Dr. Saffold was born in 1941. He attended the public schools in Cleveland and later attended Kent State University (KSU) because, at that time, he believed he wanted to become a pharmacist to work in his grandfather's drugstores. While studying at Kent State University, he worked during the summer as an orderly, and that's when he discovered he really enjoyed working with people and was fascinated with the art of healing. Because of that discovery, he changed his major to medicine and transferred from KSU to Fisk University in Nashville, Tennessee, where he received his bachelor's degree in science in 1963. He entered Meharry Medical School, an African American school, also in Nashville, in 1963 and received his medical degree in 1967. Then he went to Boston to serve as an assistant resident in dermatology from 1968 to 1969 at the Tufts University School of Medicine and Boston City Hospital. A few years later, he returned to Cleveland to practice medicine. I asked Saffold why he thought he had been so successful in practicing medicine.

> I think understanding that medicine is a service industry has probably been the most significant. I think that becoming well-trained is a backdrop for the success, but I like to say people are human beings before and after they're educated. It's the kind of human being that you are [that] determines the level of success. The education puts you in a position to be successful, but the ability to relate to people is what I refer to as the art of medicine. The background of education is the science of medicine, but the art of medicine is even more important, in my opinion, than the science of medicine. I think it's the two together, the preparation and the skill I've acquired through education together with the feelings I have for people as a service industry.

Saffold believes an innate quality exists that causes some individuals to want to become entrepreneurs. Some people may want to start their own business while others desire to work for someone else. Saffold's medical practice is very profitable and employs six to ten staff members. Even though his practice is successful, he did experience a business failure. That business enterprise was a health maintenance organization (HMO) called Personal Physician Care, Inc. The business was a for-profit HMO. He had part ownership in the company, serving as the medical director of Personal Physician Care of Ohio from 1987 to 1993 and the president of Personal Physician Care, Inc. from 1993 to 1998. The HMO started around the same time period as Hough/Norwood and Total Healthcare, which still operates as a nonprofit entity. Dr. Saffold's HMO was for profit, as was Daymed, which was located in Dayton, Ohio. Both the for-profit HMOs went out of business. In describing the challenges of the African American–owned HMO, he stated: "We were basically a single payer business. And that payer was the State of Ohio. About 93 to 94 percent of our business was paid for by the state of Ohio through welfare recipients. At one point, we were making a 3 to 4 percent profit through 1995–1996. In mid-1996, the state decided they were paying too much to life insurance companies and over a two-year period, cut 14 percent of the revenue off the top. It took us two to three years of struggle to try to decrease our expenses, but we couldn't decrease our expenses fast enough, so the business became unprofitable, and financially, we went bankrupt in late 1997."

In other words, the business went from having a 3 percent profit margin to an 11 percent loss. I asked Saffold if he saw the end coming, or whether he ever believed that could happen as a result of actions by the state. "We were informed that it was about to happen, but we thought we'd be able to convince them we were not being overpaid. So, a lot of our efforts and activities went into lobbying that they were about to underpay us, and we thought we'd be able to get the increase, the revenue back at the same time. On the other hand, we fought to decrease our expenses. But, we were unsuccessful in getting the revenue returned and were unsuccessful in getting our expenses back."

The state took over the company because the business was regulated by the Department of Insurance. Because the entity was a corporation, Saffold did get some protection from his liability with the business. I asked him if he felt any other factors other than the role of state intervention affected the ability of the business to succeed. He stated: "This is an instance where we thought that there was some institutional racism by the part of the hospitals. We had ideas that were sound ideas to partner with hospitals that would cause us to be able to decrease our expenses and still have a rate of income that would be profitable for the hospitals. They turned us down categorically. Yet, other insurances came along with the same ideas and schemes and they were embraced with these ideas. So, we were either ahead of our time or there was some institutional racism."

According to a March 27, 1999, article published in the *Cleveland Plain Dealer,* a lawsuit was filed in Franklin County Common Pleas Court by the Ohio Insurance Department (OID) against Dr. Oscar Saffold, president and CEO of Personal Physician Care (PPC) and Wilton Savage, the chief financial officer for the company. The lawsuit included allegations that improper business practices were used by Saffold and Savage in operating the HMO. These practices included being slow to renegotiate agreements with providers after PPC's Medicare payments were reduced, mismanagement of claims put through the existent processing systems, and financial irregularities.[13] I made efforts to contact Wilton Savage, who now lives in another state, but was unable to reach him for comment.

Dr. Saffold has developed a very successful medical practice through the years, in which he has earned a profit in the six-figure range. Based on an analysis of my success model, numerous factors have enhanced Saffold's medical practice. First, he possesses a high level of education, having received an M.D. degree. Second, his degree was in the same area that the business focused on, which was medicine. Third, he had a business mentor, and having a business mentor was positively correlated with success. Fourth, Saffold is married, and marital stability was also correlated with success. Fifth, entrepreneurs who were more advanced in age were also more successful, and he is an older entrepreneur. Sixth, he came from a background in which other members of his family were involved in business, and that was also correlated with success.

With regard to the failure of his HMO, several issues are important. Although Saffold had acquired extensive education to become a physician, he didn't necessarily have any experience which would help in launching an HMO. There is a big difference between being a physician in private practice and charting the development of a healthcare maintenance organization. It may have been appropriate for Saffold to have taken additional course work in the area of healthcare management. In more recent years, several colleges and universities in the United States have developed joint medical doctor/juris doctor programs and curriculums. The goal is to train medical doctors for the changing demands of the healthcare arena. Such programs would have greatly benefited Saffold.

Second, it is unclear whether he had the appropriate management skills to run the operation. Running an HMO effectively necessitates having many skills, among them administrative skills, management skills, budgeting skills, knowledge of how to delegate responsibilities to staff, and possession of an efficient claims-processing system. Third, the company was overly reliant on a single customer, the state of Ohio, for its survival. Having a more diversified client base would have been meaningful in that situation, as they would have been able to fall back on other clients after the state of Ohio reduced its Medicare payments. Last, although Saffold had a business plan to assist with the development of his company, it is unclear to what extent the plan incorporated alternative scenarios to fall back on when the business began to experience difficulties. Personal Physicians Care, Inc., earned profits in the seven-figure range.

BRIAN HALL
CEO of Industrial Transport, Inc.

Now, it's a documented fact that we have less access to capital than our white counterparts with the same amount of education and the same role [or position] in the same neighborhood. One of the things that's overlooked and that is our homes because our homes are in areas that are valued less than those of

Brian Hall.

our counterparts. We start off in the equation with less net worth if we both own a home. If I own one in the East and they're in the West, and it's the exact same square footage and the same type of neighborhood, my home will be worth less than their home. Then I walk into the bank and the bank proves that they've discriminated. So my chance of getting money with a home that's worth less than their home, I'm continually falling behind in the race. I obviously think that race has to play a factor. You just can't ignore that. You can't get capital at the same rate as your white counterpart.[14]

My first impression of Brian Hall, in January 2000, was that he was courteous and efficient as I interviewed him in his office. I started the interview by asking him what kind of services his company provided. He indicated that it is essentially a transportation company. They move trailers in and out of assembly plants and out of various distribution centers. They are the last part of the process in transporting the freight. His business is located in the inner city at 2330 East 79th Street in Cleveland. Hall grew up in Cleveland, Ohio. His father came from Green County, Alabama, and moved to Cleveland during the 1950s. His mother was born in Wellsville, a small town in southern Ohio. She also moved to Cleveland during the 1950s. His parents met, married, and started a family. Hall was born in Cleveland, Ohio, in 1958.

Hall is a product of the Cleveland public school system. He graduated from John F. Kennedy High School in 1976 and went to college at the University of Cincinnati, where he studied architecture before he realized that he wished to go home and go into his father's business. He changed his course of study and received a bachelor's degree in business. He worked in Cleveland for four or five years and then attended the MBA program at Baldwin Wallace College. He received his MBA degree from Baldwin Wallace College in 1987. I was interested in knowing whether there was a tradition of entrepreneurship in his family background. He stated:

> Yes, my father has been in business as long as I can remember. He did work for some period of time in the insurance business. That was still like being an independent contractor. Then, he was the manager for an insurance office, and he left that some time in the mid 1960s and went back into the trucking business, which brought him to Cleveland. When he originally came here, he and his brothers had a truck and were always using that truck to supplement their income. They began to grow their business from one truck to two, three, and [he] became a freight broker eventually, having his own transportation business.

Other members of his family were also involved in business, such as his brother and his brother-in-law. He said he was positively influenced toward the virtue of being an entrepreneur because they understood and valued being their own bosses, and even when he was studying architecture, he knew his real goal was to one day own a business.

> Either he [my father] would give us an opportunity to make money through his company, or we could make money by cutting grass for neighbors, or paper routes. I had a wagon. I got bottles from people and would take bottles back to the store. I'd go around and that was the way to get money to buy candy. So, I exchanged bottles for candy. That's part of it, and the other part of it was the desire for the creation of wealth and to decide how it was going to be created. I never felt like I was going to work for anybody for a long period of time. It was always, I was going to figure out how to have my own business and sell my talents. In particular, when I decided to leave the field of architecture, it was because I realized my father's business was becoming successful, and growing up, it was always a struggle for him to meet household expenses, and it was a battle about whether he should be in business or whether he

should go get a job somewhere. He was not going to get a job, and it was something he and my mother would have discussions about. So, when I was in my second year of college and saw that his business was doing almost a million dollars, I decided that there was something there that I could add to it, and also a way for me to start making an income without having to worry about who was going to hire me. So, I asked him if he would hire me, and that's when he told me that this was what he'd been doing all this work for, so that I could come back and contribute. So, I decided to become an entrepreneur, but I decided to come back and join the family business.

Hall's business is currently located on East 79th, which is part of the inner city in Cleveland. Even though it is located in a predominantly black community, Hall has few minority clients. Fewer than 10 percent of his clients are minority. I was curious to know why he had decided to located his business in this area. He noted:

I talked about growing up and working in the family business or with the family truck or whatever it might be, and we had been located in and around this area since as far as I can remember. Just around the corner, we owned a gas station. A few blocks away, we owned a truck stop and 76 station. When I say owned, it's a point of being advantaged, disadvantaged, struggling to keep these businesses running. But my father was either involved with a partner [or was striving forward] at the same time with these other businesses. But, we've been in and around these neighborhoods. But, the way we ended up here [is] when I got back from college, the business was on Harvard and 110th street. We were still in the city of Cleveland, closer to the inner suburbs, a more middle class neighborhood, but we were renting space there. This [current] building was vacant. A business had left and moved south and we could get the business reasonably, so the big decision was to get the real estate and the economics of being here were less expensive than being somewhere else, and it was something that we could acquire.

In addition to that, some of the employees Hall had hired through the years were from the inner city and the community. For him, there was also a sense of wanting to be there so they could channel employment opportunities to the community. Yet, having a business in the inner city is a double-edged sword. The real estate is cheaper and one can help provide employment opportunities for members of the community, but often crime rates are higher. Hall's business has been burglarized, and drug-related violence has a strong impact on the community. He also experienced criminal activities at his previous location on 110th and Harvard.

We have drug sales that are going on across the street from us on the corner. So it does impact our employees that come to work, that they are in the environment to see this and some people may not want to be, they may in fact become wary. We have not had burglaries in this location. As a matter of fact, we have had fewer burglaries since we've moved here than we've probably had in one year at that last location where we were burglarized frequently. Not the building, but our trucks were vandalized where we were, or professional thieves were coming in and taking the tires off the trucks or taking the batteries. We haven't had the same kind of problems here. We have had a couple of cars stolen from our lot. We've been here twelve to fourteen years and we've had two cars stolen in fourteen years, so fortunately we've not had a break-in the office or violence in the office where we've felt it's not safe here. There's both a perception and reality that makes it difficult to attract people to work in the inner city.

Hall said that he had also experienced criminal activity in an earlier business location which was on 110th and Harvard, a more affluent, middle-class area. It was also more of an industrial area. When I questioned him about whether he had used any special precautions to deal with increasing criminal activity, he stated, "I have personally purchased a gun because there are times I have to come very late at night or very early in the morning. Like I said, there's activity going on the street or if the burglar alarm goes off, they call me to come to the building and sometimes I get there before the police. We do keep the door locked so that people don't just walk in the building, especially the women because they're here alone. They don't want someone to just walk into the building, like a stranger. We have a screening system. We have a burglar system and other things as a precaution."

Hall uses the corporation model. His father and uncle incorporated the business in 1977. Hall has also owned several other business enterprises as well over the years. One of these companies is a maintenance company that used to be their in-house maintenance center. He decided to make it a profit center and developed it as an independent company. He owns 100 percent of the stock in that company and also at present 100 percent of Industrial Transport, Inc. He also owned or co-owned two restaurant/food service businesses. At the present time, he has sold his interest in one of these restaurants and he closed down the other one. I asked Hall why he felt he had been able to achieve success as an entrepreneur. He emphasized his commitment to providing quality service to his customers and delivering on their expectations. "We've delivered on the expectations of our customers, first and foremost. We've had a major customer—Ford Motor Company—that not only has appreciated our meeting their expectations, but they've also had an initiative to say they would like to do business with companies that are minorities and increase their span of experience with minority companies, and that hasn't hurt us. I'm not sure if it's helped us, but it hasn't hurt us at all. But I think first and foremost that we've delivered on the expectations of our customers."

I asked Hall if he had benefited from minority set-aside programs. He indicated that he has benefited from being included in the process rather than for having work set aside for his company. He emphasized his commitment to the quality of the product he produces and the service he provides.

> We have always competed on price [and] competed on service and that competition or the fact that we were a minority has put [us] into the competition, because while Ford has said they want to buy from the lowest cost for the best service, and they're also saying, let's make sure the pool we choose from includes some minority contractors. Unless it's done behind closed doors, I haven't gotten or retained my business because I was a minority contractor. I think that the way I said it hasn't hurt us. There are times where we have been unfairly judged or unfairly treated where we could have lost bids, but the fact that we were a minority business gave us the opportunity to get a closer examination of the facts. Because in order to resource a minority supplier, there are some safeguards that say we want somebody else to come in and take a look and make sure that whatever's being said is really what's going on and that has helped us.

We spoke about the recent court challenges to affirmative action programs and minority set-aside programs. I asked Hall if he believed these programs would soon become part of our historical past. He was very optimistic about the fate of the programs and emphasized that America has much to gain by recognizing the tremendous talent available in its diverse labor force.

> I think the demise of the set-asides, and again you're thinking of the broad picture of development and procurement and everything else, that they will not truly be a demise. The demographics say that minorities are going to be the majority in the next twenty years and because of that, the marketplace will demand that there's a diverse supply base. And it's already doing so. The companies that do the best job are those developing and increasing minority suppliers and those that have already realized the diversity of their companies: Coke, the airlines, K-Mart, J. C. Penney, Sears, Ford, General Motors, Chrysler. They recognize both in the work force and in the people they sell to that they're selling to a diversified [group].

I asked Hall about the role of race on his success as an entrepreneur. Here, I wanted to know what role race has played in the economic marketplace. Hall believes that he and other African Americans have considerably more difficulty having access to financial capital than their white counterparts. He believes this system of unequal exchange is also very evident at the neighborhood level where property values are skewed to a negative degree in assessing the worth and value of black property in comparison to white property of equal size and standard. For him, access to capital will remain one of the major barriers affecting black entrepreneurs as we move forward in this new millennium. Hall's business has been very successful, as he has earned six-figure profits. Several factors from my model are important in explaining Hall's success. First, he is highly educated, having received a postgraduate degree. Second, his areas of concentration were architecture and business administration, which have been useful to him in the development of his business. Third, he had a business mentor, and having a business mentor is correlated with success. Several relatives work in the business, and employing relatives was positively correlated with success. He has participated in and benefited from corporate diversity programs, and this also affected his success. Hall is married and marital stability is correlated with success. Older entrepreneurs in the study were more successful, and Hall is in his mid-level years. Last, steady customers make up a large percent of his total customer base, and entrepreneurs who had a high percentage of steady customers were more successful.

SHELTON L. MOORE
Business partner, The Nelson Group

> There are no contracts that are drawn up by an architect, engineered by engineers, and put out for bids that actually work the way it's shown on paper. There are always field conditions that prevail, so you get out to a job site, and in our case, we make all the steel at once for the foundation for the building. They may have done their soil test samples and started the excavation. After getting into it, they started encountering conditions that they didn't anticipate, take out more dirt, or they may have hit sections where the building is going to be soft. They may have hit a gas line or pocket in the ground. These conditions create change orders. Contractors at times make more money on change orders than they do on the basic contract and they account for that.[15]

Shelton Moore is included here because he truly embodies the spirit of entrepreneurship, as exemplified by the fact that he is now involved as a partner in the Nelson Group, his fourth business enterprise. Moore has also been involved with

Shelton L. Moore.

three unsuccessful construction companies. I am especially grateful to Moore and others for coming forward, as it is not always pleasant to talk about unsuccessful economic outcomes. It is hoped that this story may be of use to other aspiring entrepreneurs.

Moore was born in Cleveland, Ohio, on November 23, 1950, into a family that valued self-employment. His father operated a business on the side all the time he was holding down a regular full-time job. There was a certain amount of enthusiasm associated with generating additional income that inspired Moore. His father owned a photography business and a furniture upholstery business. He re-upholstered furniture and seat covers for automobiles. Moore became interested in construction work as a child. He used to like to build things. No one in his family had that kind of interest, but his grew through the years.

Moore attended at least seven elementary schools; his family moved about thirteen times, mainly within the city of Cleveland, before he reached the age of fourteen. When he was about five years old, his parents got a divorce, after which he was raised largely by a single mother and various members of his extended family. In 1969 he graduated from Glenville High School and was in the Glenville area when the riots broke out. He attended Wittenburg University in Springfield,

Ohio, and graduated in 1973 with a bachelor's degree in economics with a minor in accounting. While Moore was at Wittenburg, one of his professors agreed to help minority students get jobs in public accounting firms. Largely because of his professor's assistance, Moore was able to secure a position as a public accountant and worked for Ernst & Ernst, which is now the Ernst & Young public accounting firm. This was no small feat, given that this company was one of the largest CPA firms in the United States.

As an employee of the company, Moore had the opportunity to work on projects with many clients at the national office in Cleveland. Thus, he worked on projects with colleges, manufacturing businesses, retail businesses, construction companies, and was the staff auditor for various clients in the Cleveland area. He also took other professional courses that were offered each year and was certified as a public accountant. He performed the tax work for his clients and became a member of the Association of Black Accountants. His interest in business was further heightened from his interactions and association with other African American entrepreneurs.

> My interest in becoming an entrepreneur primarily started in discussions with other black accountants who were in business for themselves, who had African American businesses as a client base and some of the issues and problems that they were having during the 1973–1978 period. A lot of the discussions involved capital formation, business professionalism, and marketing, and how these businesses could grow. This was also a period during which minority business legislation was being drafted. Near the end of 1979, a lot of interest was developed by myself and other minority businesses to go down and lobby in Columbus for the state minority business legislation because of the fact that the state of Ohio had been found guilty of practicing discrimination in the award of contracts for construction and goods and services, so there was legislation pending to enact a program to remedy that past discrimination. There was a study and public hearings, and as a result of all that, the state of Ohio developed House Bill 584 which was at the time ground-breaking, and it was grass root minority business legislation in the country. Ohio wound up being a very strong advocate for minority business legislation that many other states have tried to emulate.

Moore's interest in entrepreneurship was further deepened by his work with other black accountants. They would assist in the preparation of tax returns and would help other businesses deal with their tax problems as well. He gradually began to increase his own client base and became very knowledgeable about the various types of cash flow problems that exist and how to solve these problems. "My experience with public accounting gave me a lot of exposure to the construction industry here in Cleveland, and I began to gravitate toward companies that had contracting opportunities, seeing that there was room for a company to grow in quantum leaps in a short period of time if it had the knowhow and the management supervisory skills to manage multiple jobs. So the ability to get larger or grow became a factor of their ability to estimate progress and complete jobs on time and satisfactorily."

He was eventually approached by an African American friend, who was an accountant, to take over the bookkeeping of a large construction company in a nontraditional African American area—structural steel and steel erection. He became directly involved in steel erection, working with the project owners and construction managers, as well as the higher level hierarchy of the construction business itself. This business was Minority Steel Erectors, Inc., a corporation established by twelve tradesmen who had worked previously for other contractors. Some of the shareholders were minorities, and some were not. Although the business had been established in 1977, Moore did not become involved until 1979. He was initially hired as the treasurer for the board of directors and eventually purchased enough shares in the company to secure 5 percent ownership. The business operated in the skilled and semiskilled trade areas where unionized crane workers worked alongside other tradesmen to develop the main superstructure of buildings, sewage treatment plant facilities, bridges, and other areas that utilized steel. He also helped the company secure a line of credit for the supplies and materials they needed. He met a lot of other minority contractors in all the other trades.

> There are roughly thirty-three disciplines of trades—plumbing, electrical, drywall, floors, roofers, HVAC. All the trades would basically come on job sites after the steel frame was erected, so while we were there finishing up, other trades were coming in, and I met the minority contractors. After a certain time in the business, about two to three years in the business, many of them invited me to come to different meetings where they were trying to formulate organizations to address some of the problems they were having and penetrating other public sector markets, getting county work, getting work from the city of Cleveland, getting work from the different agencies (CMHA, RTA, Cuyahoga County), who were spending billions of dollars but had no program implementing or incorporating participation of minority businesses. Many trips to Columbus and different other government agency offices were set up to make them aware of and sensitive to the need to have minority participation on projects when there previously was none.

Many minority companies had problems because some of them were not large enough to take on bidding. Some of them also had trouble acquiring adequate bonding and financial capital for their projects. Another problem was bringing in first-year apprentice programs. The company informed the union members that the programs would be opened up so they could tell their friends that the programs would be initiated on a certain date and they could go out into the open and the public and get additional members who were interested or individuals who were interested in the trade union. A certain number of positions were to be filled. There was also a requirement that a person had to have a high school education and a valid driver's license as well as a certain amount of knowledge in order to become an apprentice.

Minority Steel Erectors used union workers. Moore indicated that in the construction area, you have to hire union people. When I asked him how many African American workers were part of the unions or unionized in Cleveland, he was unsure. "That's the biggest question to find out. There have been many legislative requests from contractors of what their registers are. They won't come to you or they will not provide that information." I also had difficulty acquiring local data and statistics on extent of union participation by African Americans. We contacted the Construction Builders Trade Association.

Different projects are solicited for bidding by owners of construction companies. Their construction documents would clarify in some detail the specifications for their job assignments. For example, these documents would indicate if the project was going to be a union project and whether it would use particular trade unions, as well as the prevailing wage provisions that should be paid for particular trade areas. The location of the project would also be listed on the document. Moore mentioned that they would have to rely on hiring workers from the local union. They would also have to make sure they had a certain number of minority workers on the work force. Unions would have to supply different men to different contractors so they could use the minority workforce utilization strategy.

Minority Steel Erectors, Inc., failed and was closed down in 1982. According to Moore, one of the major factors precipitating the eventual demise of the company was the refusal of one of the other owners to allow himself to be indemnified for insurance and building purposes. In other words, the president of the company, who owned the largest share of the company's stock (i.e., about 20 percent), would not personally sign for loans for the company or for insurance purposes in order to bid on work or to secure financing.

Another problem Moore ran into was that after his company obtained a contract or after they were successful in bidding, he would go to the union and tell officials they needed thirty men and that at least five of them had to be minorities. Sometimes, the union officials would tell Moore that the minorities were already out on projects and they would be unable to supply the number of minority males he requested. Moore would then be in a position where his minority workforce on the project would be less than the contract documents specified to meet the company's goals. When this happened, Moore would have to contact other unions. I also questioned him about other external factors that affected the construction industry, such as the weather.

> Construction is primarily seasonal. I would say 75 percent seasonal. Not much construction goes on during rain. Not much goes on below 25 degrees or in the snow in the trade I'm in. We've worked in many instances through the winter, but you have to have lost days due to weather. That factor has to be brought into the bids if you know the project is going on through winter. If the men show up, some unions say you must pay them two hours [work] to show up even if they show up and it's raining. If they work more than two hours, then you'd have to pay them at least for four hours. There are significant amounts of exposure working with the trade unions at times when the weather is inclement.

Other factors as well affect one's ability to be profitable in this industry, including the availability of manpower with the appropriate levels of skills needed for each project, the weather, and the capability of the contractor you may be working for. All these variables can affect the overall success and profitability of the project. Some contractors have multiple contracts going at the same time. "One project may be shut down for a few days when they will take the manpower from that and send them around dispersing to the other projects to catch up on who's ahead of schedule." Things seldom go according the written plan. Many unforeseen problems can develop on site which may have far-reaching consequences. For example, they may encounter conditions that they did not anticipate. They may hit a gas line or a pocket in the ground. This may lead to an increase in their cost to actually do the project even though they have already made a bid to do the work for a certain specified amount of money. This raised the question of what happens to the business owners if they underbudget or overbudget. If you underbudget,

> It winds up being profit for you. The construction manager has responsibilities for the whole thing. Their job is to get a general contractor to handle all the general trades work. You would have a concrete contractor who would pour it and finish it. A steel contractor who just put all the steel rods down that the concrete would be poured on. You would have an erection contractor

who would install the steel beams, metal stairs, framing for elevators, and everything. Those are basically semiskilled contractors, doing the rough structural work. Then, you would have contractors who would come in to do the waterproofing, fireproofing. They would take every place that would have exposure to fire and spray fire proofing material all over it. That's all they would do. Then you would have the plumbers come in and all the major piping for the sanitary, the plumbing, fire protection.

The other side of the coin is that if you are over budget, this becomes a financial liability to you. Underbidding is prevalent because black owners are never in the advantageous position with the company to which they're bidding. Consequently, the company they're bidding to is accepting prices so when they make a decision to choose which subcontractor they want to accept, they don't necessarily tell the rest of the subcontractors that they have already selected the one they are going to use. However, they will take the other subcontractors' bids for doing a particular job. They'll go back and tell the other bidders,

I've got XYZ company down the street that tells me they will do the job for $100,000, and he'll come up to me and say what's your price on this project and I'll say I come down to $105,000 and he'll say you're still higher than my budget. I don't have that much in this job. I already have a job. I bid it already. My package for this skill is $94,000 and I'll look at my figures and I'll determine if it's worth it for me to cut my price to get the job, because maybe I don't have anything else going. I'm going to have to lay my men off. I'd really rather work for a smaller margin of my cost. I'll say okay. I'll do it for $94,000.00. The same contractor may go to two or three of my competitors and say I got Moore to come down to $94,000.00. I really want you to have the job. Do you think you can match that? It depends on the level of ethics and integrity of the contractor whether he's going to play one against the other and how long he does it. Sometimes they'll do it until the owner says get me a steel erection company on that job site, and then he has to make a decision. But, I've seen prime contractors play subcontractors one against the other for weeks, and some subcontractors, if they're desperate, will cut their own throat to get on the job site thinking that they'll make up the profit they lose on one job by getting another later.

This process is called bid shopping. I asked Moore if it were illegal for bids to be discussed in this way. He indicated that bid shopping is very common in the construction industry. While prime contractor bids are sealed and opened by the agency to which that business submits the bid, once the prime bidder is selected,

Moore indicated, he or she plays a bid shopping game, which enables him or her to make a layer of profit. He said that bid shopping was not illegal and was a commonly accepted practice in construction.

Pre-bid meetings are held, and a person has the opportunity to look at the contract documents, the plans, actual narrative requirements, etc. Hence, he can develop a list of questions and things to ask that are not answered by the contract documents at the time the meeting convenes. Contractors and subcontractors attend the pre-bid meetings. However, entrepreneurs generally do not let their competitors know what they're bidding at that meeting. I asked Moore what type of training he would recommend for would-be construction company owners. He said, "A lot of individuals in construction are there because they have a predecessor through family relationships. They've developed the experience of being in the construction field at a young age and they've carried it forward. There's a certain amount of logical training that they've been able to acquire over a period of time by being in the field."

Another major criterion for construction owners is to have bonding for their firms. One type is bid bonding which basically protects the entrepreneur's bid. If a person is in a situation where he cannot satisfy or maintain his bid, the bid bond comes in and he can keep his price. Second, a performance bond is necessary. This bond indicates that a person will perform and the bond will support him. This is the hardest bond to acquire. Moore stated that it was based on the entrepreneurs' experience and who they're dealing with. In most cases, all government projects must have a performance bond. The rule of thumb for bonding is whatever your net liquid assets are, that is cash, near cash, and receivables over excess, take current liabilities times a factor of ten to find out what the size of the performance bond should be. For example, if you had ten thousand dollars net liquid assets, you should be able to get a one hundred thousand dollar bond. If you had one hundred thousand dollars, you would get a million dollars.

After Minority Steel Erectors, Inc., was dissolved, it was reorganized, still in 1982, to become a new company, which Moore established, called North Shore Iron Way, Inc. This was also a construction company, and it performed the same basic operations as Minority Steel Erectors, Inc., had. Seven individuals followed from the old company, helping Moore establish his second business enterprise. Moore owned about 15 percent of the company's stock. This business closed in 1992.

In 1993 Moore started Complete Metal Contracting and Supply, Inc. He owned 100 percent of the company's stock. The business performed the same operations as North Shore Iron Way, Inc., had. And this business, too, did not succeed. With its closure, Moore had been involved with at least three different business operations that did not succeed. I asked him why he felt that these businesses failed, given that he has acquired considerable experience in the world of construction and that he is highly educated. He responded this way: "The devastating financial problems were due to lack of financing. To the overall manifestation of minority business and especially in the construction field as it related to having the community and the political structure to work with us. We were functioning, and they had been functioning as an island unto themselves and did not understand the political connections." Failures also result from the inability to collect the full amount of receivables billed for work completed.

In his new business enterprise, the Nelson Group, he is a computer consultant, a completely new environment for him. He works on the basis of contracts. He believes that this area is more defined and is based on one's ability to produce the desired result primarily involving information services. His company is also a computer system reseller, so it takes products from manufacturers and assembles them, thus providing a value-added service to those products. He then sells them to his customers. Moore's company upgrades, repairs, and installs computers.

Moore state that one reason for the failure of his first three businesses was "financial considerations. It took a lot of money to start a construction company, to amass all the tools, human resources tools, as well as the materials to run a construction [company]." Also, while the debts of his second and third businesses were very high, his profits were fairly low. He reported that the profits of each of these businesses were less than $40,000 per year.

Last, I wanted to know his opinion about why some business owners succeed in their business operations. "Tenacity, having the right combination of opportunities presented to them if they take advantage of it, they happen to have maximized the potential and were able to take that and use it as a marketing springboard to put themselves in a favorable lighter position for the next level that they're going to. It has a lot to do with being in the right place at the right time and having a lot of energy to push your agenda. Service, it's about providing your customer with as much needed assistance and service beyond the physical, tangible product."

Several factors from my model are useful in analyzing the situation of Shelton Moore. First, although he possesses a college degree in economics, he did not have the highest level of education, and entrepreneurs in this study who had higher levels of education were more successful when controlling for other variables in the model. Second, even though he earned an undergraduate degree, it was in accounting. While accounting skills would be useful to any business, Moore did not have educational training in the areas of engineering or construction, which would have been very beneficial for him in the development of his construction companies. The construction industry is a high-risk one, and it is advantageous for one to have as much knowledge as possible about the industry. Third, a small portion of his company's clients were steady, and entrepreneurs in my model who had a high percentage of steady customers were more successful. Fourth, external problems such as uncertain weather conditions were also problematic for construction companies. Fifth, he and his co-owners would have to deal with unanticipated problems. It is unclear whether he had included detailed backup plans in his business plans. Sixth, the construction industry typically requires more start-up capital than do many service-related busiesses. Yet, in several cases, Moore started his companies with between $10,000 and $50,000. In accumulating his start-up capital, he relied on his personal savings for both businesses. He also experienced problems with lack of funding for some of his projects.

Moore is one of the founding trustees for the African American Chamber of Commerce of Northeast Ohio. The mission of the organization is to develop economic strategies in order to support wealth creation and the attainment of economic self-sufficiency for African American businesses.

CHAPTER EIGHT

Conclusions and Public Policy Recommendations

This study has focused on African American entrepreneurs in Cleveland, Ohio, 1795–2002. One of its major strengths has been to analyze the contributions of African American entrepreneurs at the grassroots level of society. It has also provided a comparative analysis of local business activity with national data. Four major questions were examined: How successful are African American entrepreneurs? What are the predictors of success? What unique problems are faced by this group? And what role does gender play in the economic equation? In other words, are firms owned and operated by men more successful than those owned and operated by women?

This study has unearthed a strong tradition of black entrepreneurship at the local level that is in some respects similar to that discussed by scholars such as Juliet E. K. Walker and John Sibley Butler. The data examined here indicates that a strong tradition of black business activity has survived against almost insurmountable odds. The title of this book seeks to convey a sense of the struggle, toil, and determination exemplified in the life experiences and histories of the entrepreneurs included in the study. To some extent, the survival of this business tradition reflects the indomitable spirit of African American people. As I collected data on African American business owners for this study and for an earlier pilot study, it was apparent that even those who would be considered most marginal or at great risk for failure were not about to give up. On the contrary, through ceaseless attempts at trial and error and by learning by doing, most were determined to stay the course as we move forward in this new millennium.

Although black business owners in Cleveland share much in common with other black entrepreneurs in the United States, clearly some particular nuances are interwoven with locally specific conditions in which they find themselves. In the Cleveland area, these include the following:

(1) Until recently, Cleveland ranked second in the country, behind Chicago, in terms of the degree to which citizens experienced the effects of racial segregation in their residential areas.[1] More recent information compiled by researchers at the

Lewis Mumford Center at The University at Albany (State University of New York) indicates that residential segregation between racial groups, particularly blacks and whites, is still relatively high in many cities and suburban communities in the United States. Although the degree of racial residential segregation has declined somewhat in Cleveland in recent years, among other large cities with substantial African American populations, the city is still considered one of the ten cities in the United States with the highest levels of racial segregation.[2] Segregated residential patterns also severely circumscribed the economic space that minority entrepreneurs were allowed to occupy. Segregation also constrained their ability to be competitive with white entrepreneurs in the economic marketplace. Although more research on this issue is needed, the findings from this study tentatively suggest that, to some extent, both black and white entrepreneurs may operate within the confines of a fairly segregated marketplace. Minority communities, where many black businesses are located, are also coincidentally the areas that typically have lower per capita incomes, increasingly higher levels of criminal activity, and growing levels of unemployment, particularly for black male workers.

(2) Cleveland's economic restructuring process over the past few decades has had an impact on the increasing levels of poverty in minority communities. African Americans have been disproportionately affected by the loss of blue-collar and other manufacturing jobs.

(3) The increasing inability of the Cleveland public schools to deliver quality education to students in the modern period has had a deleterious impact not only in terms of providing skills and knowledge to would-be entrepreneurs, but also to individuals who wish to enter the wage-sector economy. The dropout rates for African Americans in Cleveland's public schools has been high. While other national studies indicate that contemporary black entrepreneurs have high levels of educational attainment, this phenomenon is not borne out by the Cleveland data. Although most of the highly successful entrepreneurs in chapter 8 had high levels of education, this is not true for most of the entrepreneurs in this study. Some had not finished high school, and only 47 percent earned an undergraduate college degree or higher. This was in stark contrast to the white entrepreneurs in the study, of whom 80 percent earned a bachelor's degree or higher. The results of the OLS regressions performed in this study indicated that entrepreneurs who had higher levels of education were more successful than those who did not. Hence, lower levels of education can be a significant barrier in attaining economic success in the entrepreneurial world.

The issue of race was important in this study. This variable manifested itself in numerous ways and greatly affects the condition of the African American entrepreneurs. The data presented here has demonstrated that, both in the historical past and in the present, African American entrepreneurs and citizens, more broadly speaking, have not been valued in the American economy. In spite of their contributions, accomplishments, and creativity, they have not always been treated with respect. The examples are legion and are too numerous to mention individually, but a few particularly deserve some discussion. They include Garrett Morgan. Although he was one of the most outstanding entrepreneurs and inventors of his time, available data and historical records indicate he was not regarded as such during his lifetime. Moreover, in spite of the fact that he invented the gas mask (and several other products) and used it to save the lives of several men who were trapped inside crib number 5 under Lake Erie during the tunnel disaster of July 24, 1916, when nineteen people lost their lives, he was virtually ignored when bravery awards were presented by the Carnegie Hero Fund Commission.

Rather than give an award to Morgan, who not only created the gas mask that saved the men's lives but who risked his own life to personally go inside the tunnel with other volunteers to help to save the victims, Mayor Harry L. Davis remained silent and allowed the Carnegie Hero Fund Commission to give awards only to men who followed Morgan into the tunnel. Morgan and many others who were alive at that time, considered this an affront to Morgan. Morgan was embarrassed by this lack of acknowledgment, and he and various organizations and concerned citizens protested to Mayor Davis about the way he had been treated. In a letter dated October 26, 1917, Morgan wrote to the mayor, articulating his own concerns and grievance about the situation. He stated, "The treatment accorded me in the particulars set out in the questions asked above is such as to make me and the members of my race feel that you will not give a colored man a square deal." One can only wonder how he would have been treated had he been a white inventor like Thomas Edison. Equally as perplexing was the situation of Robert Madison, who, even armed with a masters degree from Harvard University and a prestigious Fulbright Award, could not find employment as an architect on the open market when he graduated, simply because he was black. This sad reality ultimately propelled him into the world of self-employment where he now enjoys local, national, and international acclaim. In the contemporary period, many entrepreneurs in this study reported that they have been discriminated against by financial lending institutions because of their race. Ironically, even the most highly successful black owners who make profits in the six- or seven-figure range indicated that they still experience difficulties acquiring economic support from formal lending institutions.

The findings reported in this book demonstrate that African American businesses continue to make notable contributions toward both national and local development efforts. The development of successful African American business enterprises, thus, spins off numerous benefits to the communities in which they are located because business owners pay taxes; develop new sources of capital;

help develop a solid infrastructure in their communities; create new jobs and employment for the citizenry; and provide important goods and services. Their assistance in improving the standard of living in these communities also helps alleviate poverty and underdevelopment. Thus, African American firms at the local level, like their national counterparts, are creating job opportunities. The evidence demonstrates that at both the local and national levels, black-owned firms tend to have a workforce that is made up of predominantly minority workers. The findings of my study in this area are consistent with the earlier conclusions advanced by economist Timothy Bates regarding the racial/ethnic composition of employees in black-owned enterprises.

The 1994 State of Small Business Report to the President of the United States pointed out that small businesses were responsible for the creation of more than one million jobs in the American economy in 1993, while employment actually decreased by two hundred thousand jobs in large firms. Additionally, companies that had four or fewer employees created about 2.6 million jobs in 1994. The small business sector is worthy of more intensive research for a number of reasons such as the fact that it employs roughly 60 percent of the workforce, contributes to 54 percent of sales, makes up about 40 percent of the Gross Domestic Product, and is responsible for approximately 50 percent of the output in the private sector.[3]

Although more African Americans are starting businesses at a higher rate than before, their participation level in business compared to their numerical percentage of the national population is still less than that of whites, and also much less than that of some of the other minority groups in the United States.[4] For example, national statistical data on business development shows that a serious disparity still exists when comparing black and white business ownership rates. In 1987, blacks owned and controlled less than fifteen businesses for every one thousand African American people in vivid contrast to more than seventy-two businesses for every one thousand whites. Moreover, blacks brought in $795 in revenue per employee, while whites brought in $56,120 per employee.[5]

Walker and Butler have provided important historical information that affirms the important role blacks have played for centuries in developing indigenous enterprises. They have also uncovered a lively tradition of self-help that was operationalized through the development of indigenous black institutions such as the church and credit rotating societies. One explanation they offer for the decreased involvement of blacks, relative to other groups in self-employment activities, is the increasing racial hostility they encountered from whites, exemplified in the passage of Jim Crow laws, state legislation, and many other activities that prevented blacks from being more effective in the economic arena. John Sibley Butler even discusses the theory of the "economic detour" that developed historically as blacks took avenues to protect themselves by trying to go around the legalistic and other types of barriers erected against them. Because the impact of racism was to some extent insurmountable for them, Butler argues that many blacks ventured into other areas of the economy, including working for others rather than becoming self-employed.

One ongoing enigma that needs further analysis regards African Americans' continued diminutive presence in the world of entrepreneurship in spite of the significant gains they have achieved in the civil rights and post–civil rights periods. We have also witnessed the creation of governmental programs designed to enhance the condition of disadvantaged groups, including the enactment of civil rights and affirmative action legislation; minority set-aside programs; the establishment of programs by the SBA to guarantee loans made to qualified minority entrepreneurs by financial lending institutions in order to enhance their access to, and accumulation of, capital; the development of block grant programs for disadvantaged communities; and the establishment of enterprise and empowerment zones in many American cities. We have also witnessed a noticeable increase in the size of the black middle class.

Nevertheless, in spite of all of the above developments, African Americans are still falling behind in the economic sphere, relative to other groups in the population. In spite of the fact that blacks earn a collective income that exceeds $400 billion each year, they are more consumer-oriented today than they were in the past. During the first few business days of each month, millions of dollars flow out of the black community into the white community, in some cases, never to return. In short, we need examine more fully why blacks still face so many challenges with regard to achieving economic parity with whites, given the fact that opportunities for black success are better today than ever before in this country's history, and some of the "racial barriers" have been eliminated.

The major issue that this study has concentrated on has been why some businesses succeed while others fail. This question has been examined by analyzing data from the nineteenth, twentieth, and twenty-first centuries, with primary emphasis on the contemporary period, 1960–2002. The data indicate that many complex factors, which are both internal to the entrepreneurs and external to their firms, affect their ability to succeed. One of the most important variables is the level of education of the entrepreneur. The results of the OLS regressions performed in this study indicate that entrepreneurs who have higher levels of education are more successful, when one controls for other variables in the model. In some cases, the entrepreneurs were highly educated in the area that their businesses focus on. In other instances, the entrepreneurs may have had degrees in areas that are unrelated to the business focus. Having a degree in any field may still be better than having no degree at all because education provides a conceptual framework that assists in solving day-to-day problems. In the absence of such a framework, it becomes much more difficult to operate in an economic marketplace that is becoming increasingly more complex.

Entrepreneurs who had more years of experience in industry were also more successful when controlling for the other variables in the model discussed in chapter 6. Some entrepreneurs had worked in industry for several years and gained expertise in areas that were similar to the one that their business concentrates on. For entrepreneurs who had lower levels of education, having many years of experience in an industry area that is similar or closely aligned with the eventual area of the business concentration was the next best trade-off. This shows up clearly in an analysis of the data. Entrepreneurs who were older were also more successful. This finding may suggest that as entrepreneurs mature and become more experienced, they may be likely to implement strategies in their business operations that will enhance their business survival. This finding is intuitive.

Entrepreneurs who inherited their firms from family members were more successful than those who did not. This means that individuals who started out with property and resources were more advantaged in entrepreneurship than those who did not. The intergenerational transfer of assets is a very important factor for African American entrepreneurs, as well as for entrepreneurs of other racial/ethnic groups. This finding is also intuitive and is what one would expect to see. Entrepreneurs who had a high percentage of steady customers were also more successful, when controlling for the other variables in the model for success.

The results of the Pearson r Correlations indicated that nine independent variables were positively correlated to success when it was measured as years in operation. These variables were the education of the entrepreneurs; years of experience in industry; percentage of steady customers; inheriting one's business from a family member; employing relatives to work in one's business enterprise; participating and benefiting from minority set-aside programs; the age of the entrepreneur; marital stability; and the level of business debt.

Five independent variables were positively correlated with success when success was measured in terms of the profits of the firms. These were years of experience in industry; level of business debt; percentage of steady customers; having a business mentor; and marital stability.

Highly successful African American entrepreneurs work long and arduous hours in order to succeed. They are also determined to stay the course and have a passion for their work. The data indicate that having ties to politicians and other highly placed elites has enabled some entrepreneurs in both the past and the present to develop patron-client networks and to move in highly exalted circles which enhanced the overall longevity of their firms and their profitability. Moreover, one strand that runs from the earlier historical period to the present is the importance of creativity. Highly successful owners are very creative, and this creativity is manifested in different ways that range all the way from creating new products and acquiring patents for them to developing a sense of the big picture. Everything was linked to everything else. The success from one business enterprise had significant spin-off effects for entrepreneurs to develop other businesses. This is why in some many cases, highly successful owners had more than one business enterprise. Some had several successful business operations. Having a successful experience also led to higher levels of self-esteem.

In addition to Pearson r Correlations and OLS regressions, bivariate analyses were also performed in the study. The results of the bivariate analyses demonstrated that entrepreneurs who participated in minority set-aside programs were more successful than those who did not. This finding is particularly important given the uncertain future of minority set-asides in the state of Ohio as new disadvantaged business programs are being put into place. As George Forbes noted when discussing the impact of the new "disadvantaged business programs," one central question to be examined is whether the black slice of the proverbial economic pie will be now much smaller as people from Appalachia and others, who now claim that they are "economically disadvantaged," are included in the equation when the amount of dollars to be allocated is not necessarily increased. This study supports the continuation of set-aside programs because even with the programs in place, a sizeable number of black enterprises are still very marginal in terms of their profitability. How many more of these businesses will be at risk for failure in the future if these programs are completely eliminated?

There is no doubt that skin color has played and will continue to play an important role. In the United States, lighter-skinned blacks were given rights and privileges denied to their darker-skinned counterparts. Nevertheless, some entrepreneurs who were darker in color were also highly successful, which suggests that hard work, determination, intelligence, and high self-esteem are also important variables for success.

Just as many factors affect the entrepreneur's ability to attain success, other variables also have impact on his or her potential for failure. Lack of access to capital and inadequate capitalization are still problem areas for black owners. African Americans in this study have problems acquiring capital at both the front end of their operations (when the business is first established) and at the back end (as the business begins to expand and grow). Not only do blacks have problems acquiring loans from financial lending institutions, they also frequently don't get the amount they request or actually need. This factor reduces the likelihood that they will be able to develop and expand their business at the rate that they should. Consequently, many blacks have to rely on their personal savings accounts, income tax refunds, or credit cards to come up with the start-up capital for their businesses. They may not have to go into debt immediately to jump-start the business enterprise. However, if the business does not fare well and fails, all their life savings disappear. Moreover, because of the high levels of poverty in the African American community and the residual impacts of historical inequalities that prevented them from accumulating wealth and income to the same degree as their white counterparts, many blacks who might otherwise have the necessary skills and education will not be able to become self-employed because of their lack of economic resources. Lack of capital continues to be a major barrier to black entrepreneurship. Several of the entrepreneurs studied declared bankruptcy. In some cases, it was because of significant cash flow problems in the business. In other cases, the bankruptcy was the result of a combination of factors associated with the overall management of the business.

Analysis of the data collected in this study indicates that many African American entrepreneurs are using the trial-and-error method in business rather than the education and training route. This is linked to the fact that less than half of the entrepreneurs in the study had a college degree or higher, although some entrepreneurs did report having some college training that did not meet the requirements to actually earn a degree. Concomitantly, many had not taken courses in business management, accounting, or taxation issues. Many were operating businesses without having a written business plan that would serve as a blueprint for the development of their businesses. This factor also affected their ability to get bank loans because banks now require solid business plans as part of the deliberation process before providing business loans. Business plans should include information such as the mission of the company, the business philosophy of the entrepreneur; income and profit statements; and a host of other important information, such as an assessment of their competitors, their marketing strategies, advertising methods, etc. More significantly, a solid plan of action must be included that articulates in great detail how the owner plans to expand the business. A related issue that emerged during the course of this study is that many blacks decide to go into business because they feel that they have talent or skill in a particular area. However, having a skill or talent in an area related to the area a person wishes to start a business in is a necessary, but not a sufficient, condition for becoming an entrepreneur. For example, being a good cook is not a sufficient condition for opening a restaurant. In addition to having skills in cooking, it would be useful to study restaurant management or to acquire educational training in business and accounting.

In many cases, black entrepreneurs also try to grow/develop their businesses too fast and this can have devastating consequences. There is a tendency to do this particularly because entrepreneurs in the early days are eager to expand and grow and some have innovative products and services that are instantly popular with the public. But, the first few years in operation are also the most precarious, and most businesses fail during the first few years of operation. Also, growing a business too fast can be challenging because as an entrepreneur enhances the production of his or her product in order to respond to public demand, he or she is also going to need to get qualified staff to do the work. That means entrepreneurs must be able to pay them, and this may be a problem in the early stages of the business when they are building up their product sales and the profits are still low. Moreover, entrepreneurs need to have good management skills to communicate to the employees what the job expectations are so that employees can be productive. Lack of good management skills is another reason some businesses fail. Some owners don't see the big picture and hence do not understand the interrelationship between various parts of the business. All parts of the business have to be moving toward the same goal. So, many things are done on an ad hoc basis rather than in an integrated manner. Not having a written plan of action also affects the overall management of the operation because the owners have not really thought how the whole enterprise should work and how all parts of the organization fit together.

Some businesses fail because of a lack of patronage from the group that most of their goods and services are targeted to. For example, some entrepreneurs who rely on a largely black clientele, may not receive sufficient patronage from them to achieve the profit necessary to keep their business afloat. The issue of black patronage of their own indigenous business enterprises is an important one and will be addressed more fully in my future studies. However, the data presented in this study indicates that the issue of black patronage is complex. While some highly successful entrepreneurs in this study have a predominantly black clientele, other successful owners have an almost exclusively white clientele. While some blacks do not patronize black businesses with great frequency, some black businesses get a very high patronage level from African Americans. These businesses tend to be medical doctors and dentists in private practice, beauty salons, barber shops, and funeral homes. Some of the reasons for black consumer loyalty in these areas has to do with history and culture. Many blacks, for cultural and historical reasons, simply prefer someone from their community to handle their hair care and family burials. It also has to do with trust and having a good comfort level. Nevertheless, the data suggest that newly emerging entrepreneurs should explore developing and marketing their services for a more diversified clientele because so much of black wealth is not spent in black-owned enterprises and flows outside of the African American community. A related problem that affects the likelihood for failure is that some blacks start businesses in market areas that are already oversaturated with individuals producing the same type of product. Hence, when these same producers are relying on a clientele that is drawn from the same geographical area and a similar mile radius, it can cause problems for future growth, development, and profitability.

African American businesses, like any other businesses, have also been affected by cycles of economic prosperity and economic decline. Many black businesses failed during the Great Depression, for example. The First Bank and Trust was established during the 1970s. This was a period of high inflation and unemployment. The First Bank and many other banks and savings and loan institutions were negatively impacted by the overall economic climate because it affected interest rates determined by the Federal Reserve as well as the ability of individuals and entrepreneurs to borrow and repay their loans.

Although all business activity involves some element of risk, some areas of business have a higher level of risk than others. For example, the construction industry, particularly industrial construction, is a high-risk area. The capital needs are also greater for construction activities than for many personal kinds of service areas. Not only do construction workers have to deal with many internal variables that affect the day-to day-operation of their businesses, they also must contend with external factors such as prevailing weather conditions.

In spite of the increase in the number of agencies and business centers that have developed through the years to assist black entrepreneurs, many blacks at the local level simply do not know where to go for help. There appears to be a big gap between the established programs and the provision of assistance to black entrepreneurs. Since I established the Minority Business Program at Kent State University in November 1998 to assist black businesses, I have had numerous phone calls and e-mail messages from entrepreneurs who are seeking business assistance in one form or another. They have called me from Ravenna, Akron, Cleveland, Elyria, Youngstown, and Athens, Ohio. I even received a letter from an African American male who was incarcerated in a prison facility in Ohio. The one common message they have articulated to me is that they simply don't know where to go for help. In some way, they came to hear about the Minority Business Program either through word of mouth or in various newspaper and magazine articles that have publicized my work. They need counseling and various types of business assistance. They need help acquiring capital and developing a solid plan of action for their business activity. For some of these entrepreneurs who have been around for a while, one frequent reality that I see is that they often don't know how to take their businesses to the next level. All these facts suggest that more effort should be made by existing business centers to proactively seek black entrepreneurs. We must find where they are and what their needs are. It is my goal to provide good quality assistance to minority entrepreneurs under the umbrella of the Minority Business Program created at Kent State University in 1998. The goal of the Minority Business Program is to "help minority businesses become economically efficient and self-reliant in the twenty-first century and beyond."

Although minority set-aside programs have greatly enhanced the success levels of black business owners, the data indicates that many blacks simply do not know how to access the set-aside programs, and sometimes, the owners who do get the contracts do not follow through on their assignments specified in the contracts. This fact can have negative, long-term implications as some entrepreneurs lose their credibility, and that prevents them from securing contracts at a later date. Several black owners in this study have confided to me the details of their personal experiences as participants in set-aside programs, and the data indicate that in some cases, their business failure was precipitated to some degree by the fact that they sometimes underbid on contracts in order to get the set-aside dollars. Consequently, they had to eat their losses, which were quite substantial. In some cases, this led to eventually filing bankruptcy for their businesses as the owners were unable to pay their creditors. Last, increasing levels of criminal activity have also affected the survival of many black business enterprises. Although this is an issue that I will assess to a greater degree in several forthcoming publications, the evidence indicates that almost one out of every two black entrepreneurs in this study were victimized by crime. This criminal activity had economic, psychological, and physical consequences as some entrepreneurs moved from one community to another in search of peace and stability.

The issue of the use of technology among African American entrepreneurs is deserving of future enquiries. Although this study did not focus particular attention on technology use among African Americans, during the course of my research and analysis of black business owners, it became apparent that many of them are not accessing certain types of technology, such as computer technology, to any large degree. Some are not yet conversant with e-commerce networks and the World Wide Web. This may have serious and far-reaching consequences for their future development and should be examined more fully in future works. Additionally, the extent to which blacks are using technologies appropriate to their level of development in their business operations should be assessed. During a face-to-face interview with one of the entrepreneurs in my earlier pilot study, I discovered he owned a telephone answering service and was using the old switchboard model, popular some decades ago. As I interviewed him in his facility and watched him operate this switchboard, I asked him how he was faring in relationship to competitors like Ameritech, AT&T, and other companies that were using more sophisticated voice mail systems, etc. There are also other cases deserving of further analysis on a larger scale.

African Americans have been characterized in the literature as a group of individuals who do not possess a vibrant economic culture. They have also not been given credit for the contributions made by the black family unit to entrepreneurial success. The data in this study refutes some of the major arguments or stereotypes that have been advanced by other scholars in the literature. African Americans in this study possessed a vibrant economic culture. For example, many of the highly successful entrepreneurs received strong support from their families when they decided to become entrepreneurs; most had business mentors; and some have relatives working for them in their business enterprises. The overwhelming majority of black entrepreneurs in this study strongly agree that entrepreneurship is a rewarding profession.

Society perceives that blacks do not give back to their community once they become successful. This was not reflected in my data base. On the contrary, most of the black owners strongly agreed that while making a profit was important, giving back to their community was equally important. Black owners also indicated the various ways in which they give back to their communities, which include being mentors and role models; accepting interns in their companies; volunteering their time in worthy causes; donating money to various activities; and providing employment opportunities.

In determining exactly how successful black businesses are, it is important to note that there are varying levels of success within the universe of black business owners. A sizeable number of the businesses are marginal enterprises, earning less than forty thousand dollars per year in profits. There were also a number of entrepreneurs who were making good profits of more than one hundred thousand dollars per year. All the entrepreneurs included in the biographical chapter made profits of six or seven figures. Yet, few blacks are making more than a million per year in profits. The conclusions in this study also challenge the tendency of some scholars to treat black entrepreneurs as a monolithic category or unit. In so doing, they have tended to overgeneralize the problems of black entrepreneurs to the entire universe of participants. The data suggests that although there are clearly important characteristics that all African American entrepreneurs share in common, there are also important differences. There was a good degree of variation among the black owners in this study. These differences were manifested in a number of areas, including the number of hours worked per week; the years of experience they have in industry; their ability to access financial and social capital; the degree to which they have a strong economic culture; their level of educational attainment; domestic stability; the degree to which they experience racism in their daily lives, etc.

There were also important similarities, however, with respect to the degree to which they remain undercapitalized in relation to other racial/ethnic communities; the degree to which they experience residential segregation in their lives; the degree to which they have difficulty developing a clientele that is not almost exclusively black; and the degree to which they tend to locate their businesses in predominantly black communities, etc.

RESEARCH RECOMMENDATIONS

Based on the above discussion, it is recommended that more research be performed in the following areas. I believe that the addition of future studies in these areas will greatly assist us in our efforts to produce knowledge that can be used to ameliorate the condition of African American entrepreneurs and, by extension, the African American community. First, more research should be performed to determine intragroup similarities and differences with respect to economic culture. The data suggest that there is greater differentiation amongst black business owners than previous studies have acknowledged. Second, future studies should analyze similarities and differences between the strategies used by African American, Hispanic, Asian American, and Native American entrepreneurs in the Midwest. This information would be very useful in hands-on seminars with minority entrepreneurs. More research and analysis should also be performed regarding broadening capital ownership in the African American community. This includes the need for more in-depth analyses of the nontraditional methods that blacks can use to access capital. Scholars could examine more clearly the role of the black churches as institutions that promulgate the principles of self-help. In particular, it would be useful to know more about the development of credit unions by some black churches and whether some of these resources are used to provide capital to black owners at low rates of interest. Of interest as well, would be an investigation into the possibility of developing more black venture capital funds that could be used to help talented black entrepreneurs. Last, it would be important to analyze to what extent employee ownership programs and business succession plans can be used to assist black firms. The establishment of employee ownership programs would be a wonderful way to allow black employees to own a stake in the company and to be more vested in the economic outcomes of the minority businesses. Moreover, the data from this study indicates that few black-owned businesses have been self-sustaining through time. One reason was that there was an absence of business succession plans in place; thus, when the owner died, so did the business.

The extended family has had a very important role to play in the African American community. The importance of the extended family is also significant in this study for two basic reasons: First, a significant degree of difference was exhibited between the black and white owners with respect to the number of family members they hired in their businesses. Second, a significant number of the most successful owners had family members working in their business operations. More research in this area could help illuminate differences when comparing black and white owners and could also help us understand differences among black business owners.

More work needs to be done to analyze the impact of remaining minority set-aside legislation on black business success. In particular, one area that is deserving of more work is a comparison of black businesses in the set-aside period versus their progress in the transitional period or, in some cases, post–set-aside period. Are the new disadvantaged business programs working? Are they addressing the needs of minority and female entrepreneurs? It would be useful to establish longitudinal data bases that can chart successes and failures of businesses over time. Additional research should be performed on the social capital resources of the African American community. Scholars such as Gavin Chen and Frank Fratoe have argued that some groups such as Asians and Hispanics rely more heavily on capital that comes from their friends and family members than do black business owners. More analysis should be performed on this phenomenon at the local level. Also, more research should be performed to determine more effective ways to help minority entrepreneurs acquire financial capital.

There is still much we should know about gender differences between black male and female business owners. Future studies should analyze how gender structures economic opportunities in the marketplace and how women can become more effective entrepreneurs. What role do culture, history, and gender play in mediating economic outcomes for African American female entrepreneurs? Last, more studies should be performed that focus on constraints minority entrepreneurs face in specific industries. While my own study has provided important insights on business success in various types of industries, future comprehensive studies should be performed on the construction industry, retail/trade, services, and manufacturing. The construction and manufacturing industries, in particular, have proven to be particularly problematic in terms of entry of minority owners. These studies could provide information on industry-level barriers that prohibit large-scale entry and successful outcomes.

More work should be forthcoming as well on the use of appropriate types of technologies by African American firms. It is important to understand how blacks use and access technologies as we move into this new millennium. Additionally, efforts should be made to provide training and skills to black entrepreneurs so they can develop Internet-based enterprises that can make their products and services available to a wider clientele.

PUBLIC POLICY RECOMMENDATIONS

It is recommended that an economic development task force be established to implement the findings put forth in this study. This task force would consist of politicians, city planners, public policy analysts, financial lending organizations, representatives from development agencies, and academicians who are performing research on this subject. One critical goal of the task force could also be to perform a broader needs assessment for the minority business sector in northeast Ohio in order to develop a strategic plan to drive the development of strategies for the entire region. As an outgrowth of the economic development task force, it is recommended that a center for the study and development of minority businesses be established at Kent State University, which is where I currently teach. The purpose of the center would be to assist in the creation and development of minority business enterprises in northeast Ohio. The center would provide research and technical training for minority business owners. There is an important symbiotic relationship between research and public policy. In fact, one of the primary purposes of performing research is to produce data that will be useful in the debate over the selection of public policy options for implementation. Toward that end, this study has made an important first step in providing a series of recommendations that are grounded in a solid research effort at the local level of analysis. The establishment of this center would greatly facilitate the dissemination and implementation of data related to minority business development.

Another role of the center would be to provide functional types of education courses for the business owners as justified from the findings of this study. The data presented here supports the need to offer black owners specialized types of training and skills in many practical areas of business survival. Now that I have identified some of their needs, the next step is to provide intervention in these areas by providing knowledge and skills to the entrepreneurs over the next three to five years and develop an evaluation tool to measure the degree to which this intervention affects the ability of these entrepreneurs to succeed. Toward this end, I am delighted that the Cleveland Foundation awarded me a three-year grant of $153,358 for 1999–2002 to implement a pilot program to provide technical training and assistance to black entrepreneurs in the greater Cleveland area, based on my research findings. More resources, however, will need to be forthcoming from various entities in the Cleveland area to make this program more comprehensive and available to more entrepreneurs in the future. In this regard, developing partnerships with entities that have a complementary mission to our own, will be essential.

Mentoring programs should be established at every level of the educational system, i.e., elementary, junior high, high school, and college. The purpose of these programs would be to provide positive role models and information on entrepreneurship as a positive career path for African American students. Role models should be provided early in the life of students so that they can gradually be recruited into the area of entrepreneurial activities for the future. In other words, if we do not have large numbers of black students who are currently choosing entrepreneurship as a vocation, we should "grow our own." This program would focus on providing entrepreneurial training and role models for students in grades K–12 and for college students. A specific business curriculum, appropriate for the developmental levels of the students, would be developed. The establishment of a "Grow Your Own Entrepreneurship Program" will have positive long-term benefits for the black-owned business sector. At the college level, interns would be allowed to acquire hands-on knowledge of what being an entrepreneur is really all about, from both a scholarly and a practical point of view.

A shadow program should be established under the umbrella of the proposed center for the study and development of minority businesses. This program would allow the more successful business owners to mentor the least successful group and share with them various techniques of business that have been effective. Much more work needs to be done at the grassroots level to establish more microloan funds and venture capital fund opportunities. Steve Washington, economic development director of the Urban League of Greater Cleveland, has been instrumental in developing a venture capital fund in the Cleveland area. More analysis should also be made of strategies that could be used to access informal credit under the aegis of credit unions that have been established at some of the local African American churches. More important, a community capital investment fund should be created in the African American community. This investment fund would be funded by individuals, corporations, and other entities who wish to make philanthropic donations to the project. The fund could be overseen by the proposed center for the study and development of minority businesses at Kent State University. The purpose of the fund would be to provide capital resources to African American entrepreneurs at the beginning of their business operations or to more established entrepreneurs who need capital to expand their businesses at critical periods of time. The total investment fund would consist of $10 million, which would be used to provide loans to entrepreneurs at a low rate of interest. The center would develop the criteria for the loans as well as establish a loan committee that would be responsible for the allocation of the loans as well as overseeing the repayment process.

Much more work needs to be done in monitoring financial institutions to make sure black applicants for loans are being treated fairly and are not being discriminated against in the formal lending process and that black-owned businesses in poor inner-city communities are not being "redlined." A number of black owners in this study reported that they had been discriminated against by formal lending institutions or agencies in their quest to attain financial capital. It might be possible to establish more creative forms of financing with banking institutions if humanistic criteria could be used more often in conjunction with an analysis of the entrepreneurs' credit history, collateral portfolio, projected strength and weaknesses as discerned from an analysis of the entrepreneurs' business plan, profit and loss statements, etc.

Increasing criminal activity and victimization have had negative consequences for African American business owners in many minority communities. The impacts experienced by the entrepreneurs have been economic, physical, and psychological in nature. There is still much that we need to know about the impact of crime at the neighborhood level of analysis. I have recently received another grant award from the Urban University Program to perform additional research on the impact of crime on African American entrepreneurs. This research proposal was cowritten with Dr. David Kaplan, a fellow professor in the department of geography at Kent State University. This research follows up on my previous work and enables us to look more closely at the interrelationship between race, geographic space, criminal activity, and the economic success of the African American entrepreneur. In this proposal, we look more clearly at the role of geography and space in influencing behavior at the local level of analysis. This project is truly interdisciplinary in nature and is cutting-edge work. Important public policy recommendations are outgrowths of this project, for example the need to establish more effective community policing networks to develop strategies to deal with increasing criminal activity. Such community development projects can be established in close collaboration with local police departments in Cuyahoga County and other areas. The data also indicate the need for more stringent legislation to enable the judicial system to adequately penalize offenders who perpetrate violent acts and illegal behavior. Special tax breaks and incentives should be made available to entrepreneurs who choose to locate their businesses in crime-ridden communities to offset the increasingly higher costs of insurance premiums, security personnel, and surveillance equipment that must be paid for by the entrepreneurs.

Last, a comprehensive data base on minority entrepreneurs in the state of Ohio should be established. This data base would include the names, addresses, and business information for all business entities owned by African Americans, Hispanics, Asian Americans, and Native Americans. At present, no definitive list exists in this area; moreover, special efforts should be made to continually update these lists, with particular emphasis on the number of new business start-ups in a particular area as well as the business area the new entrepreneurs are focusing on. Records should also be kept on the number of business failures. In addition, the reasons why businesses were unsuccessful should be analyzed so that intervention strategies can be implemented on a larger scale throughout Ohio to assist owners who have a high risk for business failure. Annual reports could be written that provide an empirical analysis of the state of the minority-owned business sector in Ohio. The development of such a database will also assist researchers in the future who wish to examine minority businesses.

In addition to developing my own questionnaire and research design, I also had to locate the entrepreneurs to participate in my analysis. More efforts should be made to promote more collaborative efforts and activity between universities, economic development agencies, nonprofit entities, and organizations in the private and public sectors to ensure that there is less duplication of our efforts.

APPENDIX A

Methodology for Chapter 5

One hundred eighty-six business owners were interviewed between spring 1998 and summer 2000. Of these, 136 were black and 50 were white. The following methodological procedures were used in this chapter. First, the black sample and the white sample were equalized. In other words, the size of the black sample was decreased in order to be equivalent to the size of the white sample (i.e., n = 50, utilizing a random number list on SPSS). Hence, the data presented in chapter 5 presents an analysis of fifty black forms, for a total of N=100 firms. Most of the analysis explains how the respondents answered a broad range of questions. This chapter also includes both quantitative and qualitative dimensions of analysis. The qualitative data is largely derived from an analysis of secondary materials, as well as answers that the business owners gave in their questionnaires regarding their feelings and perceptions on a wide range of issues. The quantitative data comes directly from the information the business owners provided on the questionnaires.

APPENDIX B

Research Design, Methodology, and Operationalization of Variables for Chapter 6

RESEARCH DESIGN AND METHODOLOGY

One of the primary purposes of this study was to determine what set of factors promotes successful entrepreneurial outcomes for black business owners. In other words, I wanted to know why some firms succeed, while others fail. In large measure, this is a factor of how economic success is measured (i.e., is success measured in terms of profitability, longevity, or by some other measure). The conclusions that emerge from this analysis reflect, in large measure, the results of a quantitative analysis to determine the factors associated with black business success. They also reflect the incorporation of qualitative analysis in order to understand the larger contextual forces that continue to mediate the economic outcomes for black entrepreneurs.

Efforts were made in this study to analyze the population of black business owners in Cleveland, Ohio. The data reported in this study were collected from spring 1998–spring 2001. A stratified sample was utilized that included four major categories of businesses. These categories were retail/trade, service, manufacturing, and construction. Businesses which could not be easily subsumed under these major categories were placed in an unclassified category. Most businesses in the latter category were in the areas of real estate, distribution, promotion (i.e., marketing), and finance. All the businesses in this study can be characterized as small businesses, which means that they employed fewer than five hundred, utilized fairly small amounts of capital to start up their businesses, and earned moderate rates of profit. By modest rates of profit, I mean that the profit of many of the businesses in the study was less than one hundred thousand dollars per year. Examples of the kinds of businesses generally included under the four major categories used in this study are the following standard industrial classification (SIC) codes.[1]

Construction: contractors, plumbing, heating, painting, masonry, roofing, concrete work, demolition, and installing building equipment

Manufacturing: food products, bakeries, beverages, textile mill products (clothing), lumber, furniture, paper and allied products, printing and publishing, cleaners, chemicals, rubber products, leather, metal industries, stone, clay, and glass products

Retail Trade: selling goods such as those in manufacturing, grocery, apparel and drug stores, restaurants, automotive dealers, gas stations, and newsstands

Service: hotels, laundries, beauty shops, advertising, credit reporting and collecting, pest control, building maintenance, computer and data processing, auto repair, parking, motion picture production and services, dance studios, sports clubs, medical establishments, religious organizations, legal establishments, management and public relations, research, and testing

Geographically, the sample area included firms that were located in downtown Cleveland bounded by East 55th Street to Lake Front Boulevard, to the border of Cuyahoga County on the east side. It also included the city of East Cleveland as well as the following eastern suburbs of Cleveland: Euclid, South Euclid, Richmond Heights, Highland Heights, Mayfield, Mayfield Heights, Gates Mills, Lyndhurst, Cleveland Heights, University Heights, Shaker Heights, Beachwood, Pepper Pike, Warrensville Township, Warrensville Heights, Maple Heights, Bedford Heights, Bedford, Garfield Heights, and Cuyahoga Heights. (See map 2.) Cleveland was selected as the site for the study because it is a large urban area with diverse types of business enterprises.

Business owners included in the study represented two major racial groups: black owners and white owners. White business owners were included primarily to provide a basis for analyzing the similarities and differences between black entrepreneurs and white entrepreneurs in a large urban environment. Developing a sampling list of black business owners who resided within the geographical boundaries of our research project proved to be particularly problematic. One major reason for this was that no definitive list currently exists that includes the names, addresses, and racial identity of our major targeted group, black business owners.

Instead, we decided to incorporate several different strategies to fulfill the requirements of the research project. First, we compiled a list of all businesses included in the *Cleveland Black Pages* that fell within the specified geographic boundaries of our study. The major limitation to relying on this publication as the only source is that participation in the volume is voluntary, and hence, many black businesses who decided not to participate in it are not included.

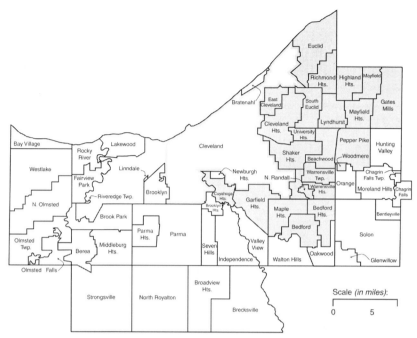

Cuyahoga County, Ohio, 1990 community boundaries. Source: *Cleveland: A Metropolitan Reader,* edited by W. Dennis Keating, Norman Krumholtz, and David C. Perry (Kent, Ohio: Kent State Univ. Press).

To overcome that problem, we acquired the 1997 list of certified minority business owners from the Ohio Department of Development as well as a list of certified business owners from the city of Cleveland. The disadvantage to using those certified minority business lists was that although they include women and minority businesses in which 51 percent or more of the business is owned by Hispanic, Native American, black, and Asian entrepreneurs, the owners' racial identity is not made public on the lists. Hence, a number of business owners included on the lists are obviously not black, but there is no scientific way to determine their ethnicities. Third, it should be pointed out that many black businesses are either not certified with the state of Ohio, decide not to be listed in the *Cleveland Black Pages,* or are too small to be captured in the U.S. Census Reports. Additionally, most of the minority businesses included on the 1997 certified list were located outside our targeted area, in other parts of Ohio, and hence were not relevant for our study.

After merging the various aforementioned lists and discarding businesses that were duplicated or located outside our target area, an estimated population or universe of 544 minority firms remained. Because the compiled list of minority owners was smaller than we had anticipated, the author of this study sent letters explaining the purpose of the study to all of the entrepreneurs in order to enhance the likelihood of securing the participation of owners who identified themselves as black. In addition to that, other informed strategies were also used to expand the size of the sample. This included traveling to African American communities to discover clusters of black-owned businesses in order to encourage them to participate in the study. Also, some entrepreneurs who decided to participate gave me the names and phone numbers of other business owners they believed might want to be included.

Introductory letters (explaining the purpose of the study) were also mailed to 570 white businesses that were selected randomly using statistical software. The random number list was applied to the businesses listed in the *Ameritech Business Directory for Cleveland and Northeast, Ohio*. This procedure was used for the white business owners because they are considerably more numerous than black business owners, and we simply had more white businesses to choose from. Numerous follow-up phone calls were made to encourage the owners to participate in the study. In order to determine our probable black universe of business owners within the larger category of minority entrepreneurs, I used statistical census data regarding the percentage of blacks who resided in our target area. Blacks comprise approximately 40 percent of the residents in my geographically targeted areas. Hence, I took 40 percent of the total minority entrepreneur list, which is 217 firms. My estimated black universe of owners, then, was 217. In the end, 136 African American businesses participated in my study, which is a response rate of 63 percent. Five businesses were a part of the pretest, one entrepreneur's responses were used for narrative purposes only. Statistical tests were performed on the remaining 130 businesses.

To compare African American male owners to African American female owners, the two groups were equalized. Because there were more men than women in the overall sample the male group's size was decreased to be equal to that of the female group. Thus, the data comparing the two groups of entrepreneurs includes an examination of fifty black men and fifty black women. Descriptive data is included in various comparative tables and charts. Ordinary least squares (OLS) regressions were performed to examine the relationship between gender and several independent variables that are discussed more fully in chapter 6. As stated in the Introduction, one of the major strengths of this study is that it includes data on both successful and failed business enterprises.

It was particularly difficult to locate failed business enterprises, but I incorporated the use of several informal strategies to achieve that goal. Letters were sent out to the entrepreneurs who participated in my studies asking them if they knew of businesses that had closed down. Surprisingly, several of the owners gave me the names and sometimes the phone numbers of entrepreneurs whose businesses were no longer in operation. In some cases, owners of failed enterprises agreed to be interviewed. In some cases, they did not. Their reactions were quite understandable, given the fact that most people do not like to talk about failure. Another strategy that I used was to interview some of the owners of existing businesses about previous businesses they no longer operate. Hence, in a very few cases, some owners were interviewed twice to collect data on both their successful and failed enterprises. Hence, the unit of analysis in this study is the business enterprise. In the end, data was collected on eight failed businesses. The inclusion of both groups of businesses (successful and failed) in the analysis helped me to more clearly analyze the central question that this book seeks to address, namely, why some businesses succeed while others fail.

Fifty white owners agreed to participate in this study. It should be pointed out that this book provides an analysis of the data I collected for my second study on black entrepreneurship, which was funded by a grant from the Ohio Board of Regents. My earlier pilot study was performed in 1995, and I interviewed thirty-four black business owners and fourteen white business owners. That study was funded by a grant from the Ohio Urban University Program. Altogether, then, I have performed an in-depth analysis on about 233 business owners in the greater Cleveland area.

Several questionnaires were used to collect data for the study. A standardized questionnaire was used to collect the data for all of the entrepreneurs; that questionnaire included seventy-nine questions designed to elicit answers in order to test the hypotheses that are examined in this study. While some of the questions allowed the business owners to give their personal opinions on various issues, the majority solicited factual information about the personal attributes of the business owners and their organizations. The owners were also asked to give their perceptions and opinions on various issues using a Likert scale.

Most interviews were performed over the phone. Graduate students assisted me in interviewing the owners. These interviewers underwent an intensive training program and all were instructed on the importance of uniformity in reading the questions and maintaining objectivity in soliciting the data. Standardized telephone interview techniques were used by all interviewers. Interviewers were instructed not to lead the respondents to give a particular answer, but were told to ask interviewees the questions in a neutral manner. One of the major difficulties encountered by all of the interviewers was being able to get the owners to commit forty-five minutes of their business day to do a telephone interview. This was largely due to the nature of their business activities and the demands the owners faced to successfully run the daily operations of their firms. Some simply chose not to participate for unknown reasons. In some cases, the interviewers had to call several times to arrange a suitable schedule for the interview.

In short, every possible effort was taken to increase the likelihood of maximum participation by the business owners.

Before the actual interview schedule began, a pretest was performed on five black-owned businesses. Various changes were made to the questionnaires, including rewording some of the questions to make them clearer to the business owners and organizing the questions in a more effective grouping. The five pretest question-naires were not included in the final data set.

In addition to the above interviews, I selected several highly successful entre-preneurs and unsuccessful owners from which to elicit life histories and interviewed them face-to-face in their business facilities. In some cases, those interviews lasted for several hours. A separate questionnaire was used for the life histories and is included on my website (www.minority-business.org).The purpose of these ques-tions was to elicit a life narrative from the entrepreneurs that focused on their historical development and background in order to understand more fully why they decided to become entrepreneurs as well as significant factors that influenced them through the years.

Figures 17 and 18 provide a geographical overview of where the businesses in the sample were located, according to the owners' racial categorization. The vast majority of the black businesses (62 percent) were located in the city of Cleve-land, with smaller numbers located in Shaker Heights, Cleveland Heights, et cetera. The vast majority of the white businesses (54 percent) were also located in the city of Cleveland. This is what one would expect to find, particularly since the city of Cleveland has taken steps in recent years to revitalize the downtown area.

In addition to using primary data, secondary materials were also incorpo-rated into the study. Research was carried out in various university libraries in order to access a number of scholarly articles, reports, and books. Additionally, census data was incorporated in order to include the latest available data sets. Last, I also performed research at the Western Reserve Historical Society in Cleve-land, Ohio, and used the Internet and World Wide Web.

Operationalizing the Variables for this Study

The following areas are the major focus of this study: They are individual-owner characteristics, human capital, financial capital, social capital, economic culture, and race. In developing the hypothesis to be tested, I was guided by the previous research findings of other scholars as well as my own ideas. I expect to see differ-ent outcomes for the hypotheses when different measures of success are used. Therefore, different attributes of business owners will be significant depending on whether economic success is measured by using longevity or profitability.

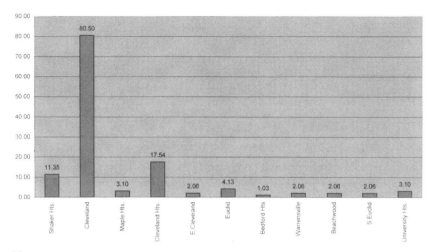

Fig. 17

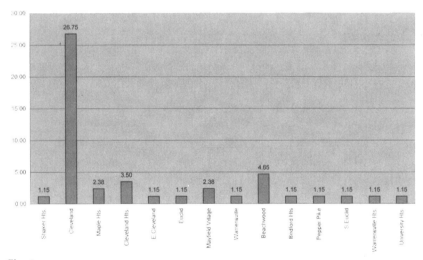

Fig. 18

H1: Entrepreneurs with more years of formal educational training should be more successful.

H2: Entrepreneurs with more years of experience in industry should be more successful.

Rationale for Hypotheses: The above variables measure the importance of human capital. Several previous studies performed by Timothy Bates have found that economic success was positively correlated with the education of the entrepreneur. A study performed by Faith Ando as well concluded that economic success was linked to the education of the entrepreneur and to the years of experience of the owner in industry.[2] Frank Fratoe has also written about the importance of business experience to overall success. Business experience is often acquired by owning a business enterprise, as well as having some previous background in the area of business.[3]

Human capital can be understood as the knowledge that the entrepreneur brings to the work environment by virtue of formal training or informal methods to achieve business experience. It also involves the human energy that the individual uses in the development of his/her enterprise.[4] This term is operationalized by using data on the educational background of the entrepreneur and the years of experience in industry of the business owner.

H3: Entrepreneurs who are older in age should be more successful.

H4: Entrepreneurs who have marital stability should be more successful.

Rationale for Hypotheses: These hypotheses measure the effects of individual-owner characteristics. A previous study performed by Faith Ando found that economic success was positively related to the age of the firm. Here, I look at the age of the entrepreneurs to determine what effect it has on overall success. Another study performed by Frank Fratoe demonstrated that most of the black owners in his study were married.[5] Since I wanted to know whether marital status affected entrepreneurial success, I also examined the impact of marital stability.

Individual-owner characteristics are defined as demographic descriptive data which provided me with background information about the owners. To operationalize, I collected data on the age and marital stability of the business owner. Marital stability was measured by determining whether the owner was married, single, widowed, or divorced.

H5: Entrepreneurs who have not experienced problems securing financial capital should be more successful.

H6: Entrepreneurs who have a low level of business debt should be more successful.

Rationale for Hypotheses: Numerous studies have emphasized the importance of financial capital to the overall survival of the business firm. These include studies written by Timothy Bates, Bessie House-Soremekun, Frank Fratoe, Faith Ando, et cetera.[6] Here I want to examine this issue as it relates to black business owners.

Timothy Bates posited that black business success is affected by the amount of financial capital invested in the business.[7] This variable was more important than other business-owner characcteristics with regard to making a distinction between active businesses and those that were discontinued. In other words, businesses in which entrepreneurs invest more capital should be more successful. In some cases, black entrepreneurs access their savings accounts and receive support from friends/relatives, while in other instances, they secure loans from financial lending institutions which affects their level of business debt. As entrepreneurs borrow more money at the time of start-up, their business debt rises. Here, I wish to look at the relationship between level of business debt and economic success.

Financial capital includes equity capital which is invested at the time the business is formed and debt capital consists of funds which are invested at various intervals throughout the life cycle of the business. To operationalize the variables of financial capital, I collected information on whether the entrepreneurs had experienced problems seeking financial backing for their firms and their level of business debt.

H7: Entrepreneurs who inherit their businesses from family members should be more successful.

H8: Entrepreneurs who received strong family support when they started their businesses should be more successful.

H9: Entrepreneurs who had business mentors should be more successful.

H10: Entrepreneurs who employ their relatives to work in their businesses should be more successful.

Rationale for Hypotheses: Here, I examine economic culture variables. A number of studies performed by Gavin Chen, John Cole, Frank Fratoe, Shelly Green, and Paul Pryde all emphasize the importance of economic culture and social capital for minority and nonminority entrepreneurial success.[8] In particular, these studies have discussed the importance of having business mentors, role models, having other members in one's family unit being involved in business activities, receiving strong family support. Some of these studies have also indicated that in some minority firms, especially in the Hispanic and Asian communities, many of the entrepreneurs tend to hire their own relatives to work in their companies. In some cases, this may help them to keep costs down by employing members of their own family to work (at reduced wages). On the other hand, it keeps the business tradition of entrepreneurship in the family and helps to keep the operation going as a family-based enterprise. I also wanted to analyze the attitude of the business owners toward participating in entrepreneurial endeavors.

Economic culture and social capital are very much interrelated. One way to look at the interaction of these two variables is to note that economic culture refers to the broader set of cultural values, attitudes and behaviors in the black community which underpin and influence their economic behavior. Economic theory has tended to downplay or de-emphasize the impact of culture for a model of "economic man or woman" which stresses principles of rationality and efficiency which are presumably "universal." Social capital, on the other hand, focuses on the social resources which the entrepreneur has in order to move his/her business forward. As stated in chapter 2, social capital can be understood as the social resources which one acquires through kinship networks, members of one's own family or community, business entities, or other groups that provide various types of assistance to the business owner. These may include the provision of entrepreneurial role models, informal training in various community activities, financial support which one may receive outside of the umbrella of formal lending institutions, the development of labor resources (i.e., employees), customers, and business clients.[9] The variable of economic culture is a broad one which encompasses both the economic behaviors of the black consumer community, as well as that of the entrepreneurs. For the purpose of this study, this concept is examined from the perspective or point of view of the black entrepreneurs. A future study should certainly address this issue from the perspective of the black consumer.

In operationalizing the variable of economic culture, data were collected to answer the following questions: Did the owners inherit their business(es) from their parents/ Did they have mentors or role models who encouraged them to become entrepreneurs? Are other members of their family involved in business activities? Did they receive support from their family members when they decided to become entrepreneurs? Do they employ their relatives to work in their businesses?

H11: Entrepreneurs who have steady customers should be more successful.

H12: Entrepreneurs who received capital from friends/ relatives should be more successful.

Rationale for Hypotheses: These hypotheses focuses on social capital. Some scholars have argued that black entrepreneurs do not access "friendly capital" in the same way as Asian or Hispanic entrepreneurs.[10] Friendly capital often comes from friends and relatives, and in some cases, may not have to be repaid. I examined this issue by looking at to what extent black entrepreneurs receive support from friends/ relatives. I also examine the impact of steady customers on economic success. The results of my previous pilot study on black businesses showed that having a steady clientele was an important factor in achieving business success. I want to examine this variable here in this larger study. Social capital is operationalized by analyzing the amount of capital the owner received from friends/relatives and the percentage of steady customers that he/she had.

H13: Entrepreneurs who have participated in, or benefited from minority set-aside programs are more successful.

Rationale for Hypothesis: Several authors such as Timothy Bates and Thomas Boston have published work which argues that minority set-aside programs have helped black businesses to succeed. Boston's study provides a detailed analysis of set-aside programs in Atlanta, Georgia.[11] I wish to analyze the impact of set-aside programs on the economic outcomes of black entrepreneurs in Cleveland, Ohio. The independent variable for hypothesis thirteen was operationalized by collecting information on whether the entrepreneurs had participated in, or benefited from minority set-aside programs.

Testing of Hypotheses: Pearson r Correlations were performed as well as OLS Regressions. I performed the OLS Regressions in the following way. First, I examined and tested the predictive ability of the independent variables in my model on the dependent variables. Then I performed a test to see if multicollinearity existed between the independent variables. The multicollinearity test revealed that two of the independent variables were related to each other. These variables were age and years of experience in industry. Hence, in chapter 6, for table 4, years in operation is deleted and age is included, while in table 3 years in operation is included and age is deleted.

Notes

INTRODUCTION

1. See, for example, Juliet E. K. Walker, *The History of Black Business in America: Capitalism, Race, Entrepreneurship* (New York: Macmillan, 1998), 1–50; John Sibley Butler, *Entrepreneurship and Self-Help Among Black Americans: A Reconsideration of Race and Economics* (Albany: State University of New York Press, 1991), 1–50; Timothy Bates, *Race, Self-Employment, and Upward Mobility* (Washington, D.C.: Woodrow Wilson Center Press, 1997), 1–100; Timothy Bates, *Banking on Black Enterprise: The Potential of Emerging Firms in Revitalizing Urban Economies* (Washington, D.C.: Joint Center for Political and Economic Studies, 1993), 1–50; Shelly Green and Paul Pryde, *Black Entrepreneurship in America* (London: Transaction Publishers, 1990), 1–50; Bessie House and Ilon Alon, "An Exploratory Analysis of Factors which Promote Black Business Success: A Pilot Study of Cleveland, Ohio," *The Ohio Journal of Economics and Politics* 11, no. 1 (1997): 21–27; Frank A. Fratoe, "Social Capital of Black Business Owners," *The Review of Black Political Economy* 16, nos. 1–2 (Fall 1993): 33–50.

2. See, for example, Claud Anderson, *Black Labor, White Wealth: The Search for Power and Economic Justice* (Edgewood, Md.: Duncan and Duncan, 1994), 31–32, 184–88; Green and Pryde, *Black Entrepreneurship in America*, vii–viii, 10–12; Sol Ahiarah, "Black Americans' Business Ownership Factors: A Theoretical Perspective," *The Review of Black Political Economy* 22, no. 2 (Fall 1993): 15–16.

3. See, for example, several important studies that have examined entrepreneurs at the local level of society. Thomas D. Boston, for example, examined black entrepreneurs in Atlanta, Georgia, in *Affirmative Action and Black Entrepreneurship* (London: Routledge, 1999); David Caplovitz, *The Merchants of Harlem: A Study of Small Business in a Black Community* (Beverly Hills: Sage Publications, 1973); Bessie House, "African-American Businesses, Economic Development, and the Puzzle of Success: A Pilot Study of Cleveland, Ohio," Executive Summary and Final Report for the Ohio Urban University Program, Kent State University, Kent, Ohio, Oct. 1997; House and Alon, "An Exploratory Analysis"; Patricia J. Cirillo, "Business Environment of Minority Business Owners in Cleveland," Minority Economic Opportunity Center, Oct. 1993; George Erickcek, "The Role of Small Business: A Tale of Two Cities," Employment Research, W. E. Upjohn Institute for Employment Research, Fall 1997.

4. 1990 census data on Cleveland's population indicates that there were about 500,526 inhabitants in Cleveland, and about 50.5 percent, or 252,766, were nonwhite. Of this nonwhite group, more than 92 percent, or 233,245, were African American. See David C. Perry, "Cleveland: Journey to Maturity" in *Cleveland: A Metropolitan Reader,* edited by W. Dennis Keating, Norman Krumholz, and David C. Perry (Kent, Ohio: Kent State University Press, 1995), 23. See also Alon Achkar, "Cleveland Population Drops Below 500,000: Blacks Largest Racial Group in City, Census Shows," *Cleveland Plain Dealer,* Mar. 17, 2001, 1. Ac-

cording to this article, the 2000 census puts Cleveland's population at 478,403 inhabitants. The African American population increased to 244,000, making it the city's largest racial group, with 51% of the population.

5. Small Business Administration, government documents, http://www.sbaonline. sba.gov/starting/indexwhatis.html.

6. Bates, *Banking on Black Enterprise*, 6–7.

7. Ron Kirksey, "Professor Receives Cleveland Foundation Grant for African-American Entrepreneurs Program," *Call and Post*, Dec. 16–22, 1999, 7C.

8. Office of Advocacy, U.S. Small Business Administration, *Minorities in Business* (Washington, D.C.: 1999), 12.

9. See, for example, Green and Pryde, *Black Entrepreneurship in America,* 32–33; Paula Mergenhagen, "Black-Oriented Businesses," *American Demographics* 18, no. 6 (June 1996): 24–25; Office of Advocacy, U.S. Small Business Administration, *Minorities in Business,* 1.

10. Mergenhagen, "Black-Oriented Businesses," 33. See also Green and Pryde, *Black Entrepreneurship in America,* 33.

11. Green and Pryde, *Black Entrepreneurship in America,* 33.

12. Mergenhagen, "Black-Owned Businesses," 30; U.S. Department of Commerce, Economics and Statistics Administration, U.S. Census Bureau, *1997 Economic Census, Survey of Minority Owned Business Enterprises,* 71.

13. When black entrepreneurs in the eastern suburbs of Cleveland are added, the total number of business owners increases. These areas include Beachwood, Bedford Heights, Cleveland Heights, East Cleveland, Euclid, Maple Heights, Shaker Heights, University Heights, and Warrensville Heights.

14. U.S. Census Bureau, *1997 Economic Census,* 14.

15. See Timothy Bates, "Do Black-Owned Businesses Employ Minority Workers? New Evidence," *The Review of Black Political Economy* (Spring 1998): 51–58; House, "African-American Businesses," 6.

16. Lucius J. Barker, Mack H. Jones, and Catherine Tate, *African-Americans and the American Political System,* 4th ed., (Upper Saddle River, New Jersey: Prentice Hall, 1999), 18–24.

17. Ibid., 19–20.

18. Ibid., 19; see also Thomas D. Boston, *Affirmative Action and Black Entrepreneurship,* 10.

1. African American Entrepreneurship at the National Level

1. According to the Office of the Advocacy of the Small Business Administration, black-owned businesses increased by 108 percent between 1987–97. Their estimates indicated that by 1997 there were approximately 881,646 black-owned businesses in the United States. Results from the 2000 census will provide additional information on black business ownership and participation rates.

2. House and Alon, "An Exploratory Analysis," 21–22.

3. For example, Jesse Jackson's Rainbow/Push Coalition Wall Street Project, his 9th Street Project in Cleveland, Ohio, as well as other conferences such as the International Conference on Black Businesses in Africa and the United States, held in Arlington, Texas, in 1999 have focused on economic development issues.

4. Proceedings of the 1998 Wall Street Project Conference, Windows on the World,

New York, New York, Jan. 14–16, 1998. See also Jesse Jackson's speech entitled "Expanding the Marketplace: Inclusion, the Key to Economic Growth," http://www.rainbowpush.org, accessed Jan. 11, 2002.

5. Proceedings of the 1998 Wall Street Project Conference, 13.

6. See, for example, Ahiarah, "Black Americans' Business Ownership Factors," 15–16; Barker, Jones, and Tate, *African-Americans and the American Political System,* 18–24.

7. Melvin L. Oliver and Thomas M. Shapiro, *Black Wealth/White Wealth: A New Perspective on Racial Inequality* (New York: Routledge, 1997), 24.

8. U.S. Census Bureau, Current Population Report, "Money Income in the United States: 1999," http://www.census.gov.

9. Oliver and Shapiro, *Black Wealth/White Wealth,* 7–8.

10. See, for example, a large body of literature on African American businesses.

11. Butler, *Entrepreneurship and Self-Help Among Black Americans,* 1–78; Walker, *The History of Black Business in America,* 1–82.

12. Butler, *Entrepreneurship and Self-Help Among Black Americans,* 143–154.

13. Bates, *Banking on Black Enterprise,* 41.

14. Ibid., xix–xx.

15. Gavin Chen and John A. Cole, "The Myths, Facts, and Theories of Ethnic, Small-Scale Enterprise Financing," *The Review of Black Political Economy* (Spring 1988): 115; R. S. Burt, "The Contingent Value of Social Capital," *Administrative Science Quarterly* 42 (1997): 339–65; J. S. Coleman, "Social Capital in the Creation of Human Capital," *American Journal of Sociology* 94 (1988 Supplement): S95–S120; R. D. Putnam, "Bowling Alone: America's Declining Social Capital," *Journal of Democracy* 6, no. 1 (1995): 65–78; Fratoe, "Social Capital of Black Business Owners," 39–49; Frank A. Fratoe, "Rural Minority Business Development," *The Review of Black Political Economy* 22, no. 2 (Fall 1993): 41–72.

16. Chen and Cole, "The Myths, Facts and Theories," 111.

17. Ibid., 117–118.

18. Fratoe, "Social Capital of Black Business Owners," 33–40.

19. Ibid., 37–40.

20. Ibid., 42–44; Ando, "Capital Issues," 78–107.

21. Ando, "Capital Issues," 86.

22. Ibid., 91–92.

23. Bates, *Banking on Black Enterprise,* 90–91; Bates, "Do Black-Owned Businesses Employ Minority Workers?" 51–56.

24. Ibid.

25. Arthur G. Woolf, "Market Structure and Minority Presence: Black-Owned Firms in Manufacture," *The Review of Black Political Economy* (Spring 1986): 79–87.

26. Bates, "Do Black-Owned Businesses Employ Minority Workers?" 55.

27. Michael E. Porter, "The Competitive Advantage of the Inner City," *Harvard Business Review* (May–June 1995): 55–71.

28. A number of scholars contributed to *The Review of Black Political Economy* 24, nos. 2–3 (Fall 1995–Winter 1996), an issue devoted to responding to Michael Porter's arguments. These included among others, Susan S. Fainstein and Mia Gray, "Economic Development Strategies for the Inner City: The Need for Governmental Intervention," 29–38; John Sibley Butler, "Entrepreneurship and the Advantages of the Inner City: How to Aug-

ment the Porter Thesis," 39–49; Timothy Bates, "Political Economy of Urban Poverty in the 21st Century: How Progress and Public Policy Generate Rising Poverty," 111–22; James Peoples, "Potential Welfare Gains from Improving Economic Conditions in the Inner City," 207–12; Margaret C. Simms and Winston J. Allen, "Is the Inner City Competitive," *The Review of Black Political Economy,* 213–22.

29. See Cirillo, *Business Environment of Minority Business Owners in Cleveland, Ohio,* 1–50; Erickcek, *The Role of Small Business: A Tale of Two Cities,* 1–4; House, "African-American Businesses," 1–30; House and Alon,"An Exploratory Analysis," 21–27.

30. House, "African-American Businesses," 1–50.

31. Ibid.

32. House and Alon, "An Exploratory Analysis," 21–27.

33. Erickcek, *The Role of Small Business,* 1–4.

34. Ibid.

35. Bates, *Banking on Black Enterprise,* xviii; Fratoe, "Social Capital of Black Business Owners," 44–46.

36. Fratoe, "Social Capital of Black Business Owners," 47.

37. Ibid., 35–37.

38. Fratoe,"Social Capital of Black Business Owners," 40–41; Chen and Cole, "The Myths, Facts and Theories," 117.

39. Bates, *Banking on Black Enterprise,* 41.

40. Ibid., 17–18.

41. Bates, *Banking on Black Enterprise,* 90–91; Bates, "Do Black-Owned Businesses Employ Minority Workers?" 51–56.

42. Bates, *Race, Self-Employment and Upward Mobility: An Elusive American Dream* (Baltimore: Johns Hopkins University Press, 1997), 21–22; Bates, *Banking on Black Enterprise,* 41; Ando, "Capital Issues," 91.

43. Bates, *Banking on Black Enterprise,* 11.

2. The Historical Development of the African American Community

1. Carol Poh Miller and Robert A. Wheeler, "Cleveland: The Making and Remaking of an American City; 1776–1993," in *Cleveland: A Metropolitan Reader,* edited by W. Dennis Keating, Norman Krumholz, and David C. Perry (Kent, Ohio: The Kent State University Press, 1995), 31.

2. Ibid.

3. David C. Perry, "Cleveland: Journey to Maturity," 14.

4. Ibid.

5. Miller and Wheeler, "Cleveland," 32; see also Kenneth L. Kusmer, "Black Cleveland and the Central-Woodland Community, 1865–1930," in *Cleveland: A Metropolitan Reader,* 266.

6. Russell H. Davis, *Memorable Negroes in Cleveland's Past* (Cleveland: Western Reserve Historical Society, 1969), 5, 7.

7. Ibid., 5.

8. Russell H. Davis, *The Negro in Cleveland's Political Life* (Cleveland: Western Reserve Historical Society, 1966), 1; Eric J. Brewer, "The Struggle: Gaining Political Power," *Renaissance Magazine* (Feb. 1989): 5.

9. Russell H. Davis, *Memorable Negroes in Cleveland's Past,* 5, 7.

10. See also Eric J. Brewer, "Entrepreneurs Build with Vision," *Renaissance Magazine* (Feb. 1989): 20. See also Samuel Black, Associate Curator, African-American History, Western Reserve Historical Society, interview by author, Dec. 12, 1999, Cleveland, Ohio.

11. Miller and Wheeler, "Cleveland," 33; Christopher Wye, "Black Civil Rights," in *Cleveland: A Metropolitan Reader,* edited by W. Dennis Keating, Norman Krumholz, and David C. Perry (Kent, Ohio: Kent State University Press, 1995), 120.

12. Miller and Wheeler, "Cleveland," 32–34; Kusmer, "Black Cleveland," 266.

13. Davis, *Memorable Negroes in Cleveland's Past,* 7; Black, interview.

14. Davis, *Memorable Negroes in Cleveland's Past,* 7.

15. Davis, *The Negro in Cleveland's Political Life,* 1.

16. Ibid.

17. Kenneth L. Kusmer, *A Ghetto Takes Shape: Black Cleveland, 1870–1930* (Urbana: University of Illinois Press, 19760), 18; see also Davis, *Memorable Negroes in Cleveland's Past,* 13.

18. Davis, *Memorable Negroes in Cleveland's Past,* 17.

19. Kusmer, *A Ghetto Takes Shape,* 18; Black, interview.

20. Kusmer, *A Ghetto Takes Shape,* 11; Miller and Wheeler, "Cleveland," 35.

21. Perry, "Cleveland: Journey to Maturity," 11.

22. Kusmer, *A Ghetto Takes Shape,* 19.

23. Ibid.

24. Ibid., 22.

25. See Angela Davis, *Women, Race and Class* (New York: Vintage Books, 1981), 5, 87.

26. Ibid, 90.

27. Kusmer, "Black Cleveland," 269.

28. Kusmer, *A Ghetto Takes Shape,* 22.

29. Ibid., 16, 22–23.

30. Miller and Wheeler, "Cleveland," 37.

31. Wye, "Black Civil Rights," 120–21.

32. Miller and Wheeler, "Cleveland," 35, 39–40.

3. BLACK BUSINESS DEVELOPMENT, 1895–1960

1. Black, interview; Brewer, "Entrepreneurs Build with Vision," 21; Kusmer, *A Ghetto Takes Shape,* 193; Davis, *Memorable Negroes in Cleveland's Past,* 45.

2. John A. Garraty, ed., *The Barber and the Historian: The Correspondence of George A. Meyers and James Ford Rhodes, 1910–1923* (Columbus: Ohio Historical Society, 1956), xvi–xvii; Brewer, "Entrepreneurs Build with Vision," 20.

3. Black, interview, 99.

4. Brewer, "Entrepreneurs Build with Vision," 20.

5. Garraty, *The Barber and the Historian,* xvi.

6. Ibid., xvii–xviii; Russell H. Davis, *Memorable Negroes in Cleveland's Past,* 30–31.

7. Kusmer, *A Ghetto Takes Shape,* 76.

8. Ibid.

9. Black, interview; see also Kusmer, *A Ghetto Takes Shape,* 117.

10. Black, interview.

11. Kusmer, *A Ghetto Takes Shape,* 77; Carol Poh Miller and Robert Wheeler, *Cleveland: A Concise History, 1796–1996* (Cleveland: Case Western Reserve University, 1990), 11.

12. Cliff Thompson, *Charles Chesnutt* (New York: Chelsea House Publishers, 1992), 43–51; 79–85; Black, interview.

13. Ibid.

14. Davis, *Memorable Negroes in Cleveland's Past,* 28.

15. Ibid., 43.

16. Ibid.

17. Ibid.; Black, interview; Kusmer, *A Ghetto Takes Shape,* 82–83.

18. Kusmer, *A Ghetto Takes Shape,* 82–83.

19. George Fraser, taped interview by author, Jan. 7, 2000, Cleveland Heights, Ohio.

20. Fratoe, "Social Capital of Black Business Owners," 36.

21. Kusmer, *A Ghetto Takes Shape,* 81.

22. Ibid., 193–94; Black, interview.

23. Black, interview.

24. Garrett Morgan Collection, African American Archives, Microfilm collection, Western Reserve Historical Society Historical Archives, MS3534. See also Louis Haber, *Black Pioneers of Science and Invention* (New York: Harcourt, Brace and World, 1970), 61–63.

25. Haber, *Black Pioneers,* 63.

26. Ibid., 64; see also Black, interview; Garrett Morgan Collection.

27. Haber, *Black Pioneers,* 63–64; Garrett Morgan Collection.

28. Black, interview; Garrett Morgan Collection.

29. See Haber, *Black Pioneers,* 67; see also "Heroism Has No Color Line, Local Men Prove," *Cleveland Advocate,* Saturday, July 29, 1916; "Tunnel Blast Kills 21, Injures 9, City, County, U.S. Probe Disaster," *Cleveland Plain Dealer,* July 26, 1916.

30. Garrett Morgan Collection; see also David D. Van Tassel and John L. Grabowski, eds., *The Encyclopedia of Cleveland History* (Bloomington: Indiana University Press, 1996).

31. Garrett Morgan Collection.

32. Black, interview.

33. Ibid.; Garrett Morgan Collection; Kusmer, *A Ghetto Takes Shape,* 142.

34. Black, interview.

35. Garrett Morgan Collection; see also Black, interview.

36. Kusmer, *A Ghetto Takes Shape,* 83, 194.

37. Van Tassel and Grabowski, *The Encyclopedia of Cleveland History,* 1105–6.

38. Ibid., 1107.

39. Edward M. Miggins, "Between Spires and Stacks: The People and Neighborhoods of Cleveland," in *Cleveland: A Metropolitan Reader,* 192.

40. Ibid., 192; see also Brewer, "Entrepreneurs Build with Vision," 20–21.

41. Kimberly L. Phillips, *Alabama North: African-American Migrants, Community, and Working Class Activism in Cleveland, 1915–1945* (Urbana: University of Illinois Press, 1999), 17; Black interview.

42. As a native Alabamian myself who now resides in the state of Ohio, I could certainly identify with many of the arguments that were advanced by Phillips in her noteworthy book. Southern culture is indeed distinctive, and yet, some of it did in fact survive the migration period of southern migrants who moved here. As she rightfully mentions, the

southern African American culture has historically existed largely as an oral rather than as a written regime. In other words, the spoken word has always been more dominant than the written word. To some extent, this reflects our history and circumstances in America, which date all the way back to the arrival of Africans in the southern states as a result of the transatlantic slave trade. Africans were severely punished for their efforts to learn to read and write and to master what we today refer to as "the process of becoming functionally literate." Although some Africans did secretly learn to use the written word, many continued to transmit their culture via the oral route, which persists even today and is a carryover from African traditional culture. Hence, southern black migrants who came to Cleveland used various strategies to keep their cultural beliefs alive, including forming their own churches and social clubs and keeping their history alive through the use of oral discussions and verbal interaction.

43. Phillips, *Alabama North,* 3.

44. Kusmer, "Black Cleveland," 274.

45. Black, interview.

46. Ibid.

47. D. L. Beavers, "Somebody Somewhere Wants Your Photograph," *Legacy* (Feb.–Mar., 1995), 42.

48. Ibid.

49. Ibid.; see also "The Cole Calendar," published by The Western Reserve Historical Society.

50. Beaers, "Somebody Somewhere," 42; "The Cole Calendar."

51. Davis, *Memorable Negroes in Cleveland's Past,* 53.

52. Kusmer, *A Ghetto Takes Shape,* 195

53. Davis, *Memorable Negroes in Cleveland's Past,* 53.

54. Louise D. Freeman, "Cleveland's Future Outlook League Carried Light into the Dark Days of the Depression with Nonviolent Tactics that Won Jobs for City's Blacks," *Renaissance Magazine* (1990): 15.

55. Kusmer, *A Ghetto Takes Shape,* 148–50; Davis, *Memorable Negroes in Cleveland's Past,* 50.

56. Davis, *Memorable Negroes in Cleveland's Past,* 50.

57. Phillips, *Alabama North,* 3.

58. Black, interview.

59. Wye, "Black Civil Rights," 121.

60. Anderson, *Black Labor, White Wealth,* 185.

61. Ibid.

62. Black, interview.

63. Ibid.

64. Ibid.

65. H. J. Lowry, *Vocational Opportunities for Negroes in Cleveland,* National Youth Administration in Ohio, Vocational Study for Negroes, no. 1 (Mar. 1938): 1

66. Ibid.

67. Black, interview; Davis, *Women, Race, and Class,* 5, 87; Marian J. Morton, *Defining Women's Sphere* (Cleveland: Case Western Reserve University, 1995), 10, 41–59.

68. Black, interview.

69. Ibid.

70. Ibid.

71. Ibid.

72. Brewer, "Entrepreneurs Build with a Vision" 21.

73. Wye, "Black Civil Rights," 121.

74. Ibid., 123; Brewer, "Entrepreneurs Build with a Vision," 21–22.

75. Brewer, "Entrepreneurs Build with a Vision," 22.

76. Black, interview.

77. Van Tassel and Grabowski, *Encyclopedia of Cleveland History,* 1107–8.

78. Brewer, "Entrepreneurs Build with a Vision," 22.

4. Black Economic and Political Development in the Contemporary Period, 1960–2002

1. Barker, Jones, and Tate, *African Americans and the American Political System,* 103; see also Boston, *Affirmative Action and Black Entrepreneurship,* 10.

2. Boston, *Affirmative Action and Black Entrepreneurship,* 10–11.

3. William E. Nelson Jr., "Cleveland: The Evolution of Black Political Power," in *Cleveland: A Metropolitan Reader,* 6; Wye, "Black Civil Rights," 128–29.

4. Nelson, "Cleveland: The Evolution of Black Political Power," 284–85.

5. Ibid.

6. Ibid, 285.

7. Ibid., 286.

8. Brewer, "The Struggle," 7.

9. Wye, "Black Civil Rights," 127–28.

10. Ibid., 128.

11. Ibid.

12. Ibid., 129.

13. Ibid.; Brewer, "Entrepreneurs Build with Vision," 22.

14. William E. Nelson Jr., "Cleveland: The Evolution of Political Power" (unpublished paper), 4.

15. Carl B. Stokes, *Promises of Power: A Political Autobiography* (New York: Simon and Schuster, 1973), 118.

16. Ibid., 124–25.

17. Ibid., 252.

18. Ibid., 126. See also William E. Nelson Jr., "Cleveland: The Rise and Fall of the New Black Politics," in *The New Black Politics: The Search for Political Power,* ed. Michael B. Preston, Lenneal J. Henderson Jr., and Paul Puryear. 2d ed. (New York: Longman, 1987), 191–92.

19. Stokes, *Promises of Power,* 252.

20. Robert P. Madison, taped interview by author, Aug. 2, 2000, Cleveland, Ohio.

21. Stokes, *Promises of Power,* 125–26.

22. Nelson, "Cleveland: The Evolution of Black Political Power," 286; see also Brewer, "The Struggle," 7.

23. Nelson, "Cleveland: The Evolution of Black Political Power," 287.

24. Ibid.

25. Ibid.

26. Ibid.

27. Ibid.

28. Ibid., 288.

29. Bart Greer, "Passing the Reins of Power: Carl B. Stokes and Michael R. White Represent the City's Black Political Evolution from Old Guard to New," *Renaissance Magazine* (February 1991): 19; see also Nelson, "Cleveland: The Evolution of Black Political Power," 294. George Forbes hosted the radio program "People Power" on WERE AM.

30. George Forbes, taped interview by author, Nov. 3, 1999, Cleveland, Ohio.

31. Nelson, "Cleveland: The Rise and Fall," 199.

32. Boston, *Affirmative Action and Black Entrepreneurship*, 10–11.

33. Ibid., 84–85.

34. Timothy Bates, "The Impact of Preferential Procurement Policies on Minority-Owned Businesses," *The Review of Black Political Economy* (Summer 1985): 53.

35. Ibid.

36. Boston, *Affirmative Action and Black Entrepreneurship*, 84–85.

37. Ibid., 11.

38. Ibid.

39. Condensed version of House Bill 584 retrieved from the Supreme Court Library.

40. Ibid.

41. Nelson, "Cleveland: The Evolution of Black Political Power," 288.

42. Resume of George Forbes.

43. Boston, *Affirmative Action and Black Entrepreneurship*, 4.

44. Ibid., 17, 33–38; see also Mitchell F. Rice, "State and Local Government Set-Aside Programs, Disparity Studies, and Minority Business Development in the Post-Croson Era," *Journal of Urban Affairs* 15, no. 6 (1993): 529–53.

45. Rice, "State and Local Government Set-Aside Programs," 532–33.

46. Ibid.; John Nolan, "Appeals Court Rejects Ohio's Contract Program for Minorities," *Call and Post,* June 8, 2000.

47. Newsletter from Governor George Voinovich's office.

48. Forbes, interview.

49. Joe Hallett, "Ohio's Race-Based Contracts 'Unlawful': Need Should Count for More than Ethnicity, Says Magistrate," *Cleveland Plain Dealer,* Oct. 31, 1996.

50. Albert C. Jones, "Commissioners Shut Out Minority Bidders, Repeal 1993 Equal Opportunity Program" (Jan. 20–26, 2000): 1, 2A.

51. Nolan, "Appeals Court Rejects Ohio's Contract Program for Minorities."

52. Ibid.

53. Boston, *Affirmative Action and Entrepreneurship*, 39–40; see also Rice, "State and Local Government Set-Aside Programs," 536; see also David Bennett, "Disparity Study Widens in Scope," *Crain's Cleveland Business,* Jan. 8, 2001, 6.

54. Julian Chow, "The City of Cleveland in the Eighties: A Decade of Multifaceted Changes," Center for Urban Poverty and Social Change, Mandel School of Applied Social Sciences, Case Western Reserve University, Apr. 1992, 2.

55. Ibid.

56. Keith McKnight, "Ohio's Big Cities Losing Residents," *Akron Beacon Journal,* Oct. 21, 2000, 1, A8.

57. Todd Swanstrom, "Urban Populism, Fiscal Crisis, and the New Political Economy," in *Cleveland: A Metropolitan Reader,* 99.

58. Black, interview.

59. Brewer, "Entrepreneurs Build with Vision," 22.

60. John Bustamante, taped interview by author, Apr. 22, 2001, Beachwood, Ohio; *Call and Post,* July 6, June 29, 1974; Van Tassel and Grabowski, *Encyclopedia of Cleveland History,* 426.

61. Bustamante, interview; *Call and Post,* July 6, June 29, 1974.

62. Bustamante, interview; *Call and Post,* July 6, June 29, 1974; see also *Annual Report 1984,* First Intercity Bank Corporation Cleveland, Ohio, 1985.

63. Bustamante, interview; Van Tassel and Grabowski, *Encyclopedia of Cleveland History,* 426; *Annual Report 1984,* 3.

64. *Annual Report 1984,* 3.

65. Bustamante, interiview; Van Tassel and Grabowski, *Encyclopedia of Cleveland History,* 426.

66. Leroy Ozanne, taped interview by author, Aug. 1, 2000.

67. Ibid.; Bustamante, interview.

68. Ozzane, interview.

69. Judge George W. White, taped interview by Bessie House, Apr. 22, 2001, Lodi, Ohio.

70. Miller and Wheeler, "Cleveland," 45.

71. Wye, "Black Civil Rights," 130.

72. Nelson, "Cleveland: the Evolution of Black Political Power," 289–94.

73. Greer, "Passing the Reins of Power," 19; Nelson, "Cleveland: the Evolution of Black Political Power," 293–94.

74. Cleveland Empowerment Zone Performance Report, 1995–1996, 1–8; Cleveland Supplemental Empowerment Zone Executive Summary, 2.

75. Madison, interview.

5. The Contemporary Condition of Black-Owned Businesses in Cleveland

1. Bates, *Banking on Black Enterprise,* 14, 41; Bates, "Do Black-Owned Businesses Employ Minority Workers? New Evidence," 51–58.

2. Fratoe, "Rural Minority Business Development," 47.

3. Bates, *Banking on Black Enterprise,*12.

4. Butler, *Entrepreneurship and Self-Help among African Americans,* 311.

5. Green and Pryde, *Black Entrepreneurship in America,* 170.

6. Chen and Cole, "The Myths, Facts and Theories," 111–21; Fratoe, "Social Capital," 35–38; Green and Pryde, *Black Entrepreneurship in America,* 70–75; Oliver and Shapiro, *Black Wealth/White Wealth,* 45.

7. Oliver and Shapiro, *Black Wealth/White Wealth,* 45.

8. Gavin M. Chen, "Minority Business Development: Where Do We Go From Here?" *The Review of Black Political Economy* 22, no. 2 (Fall 1993): 6.

9. Fratoe, "Social Capital," 44.

10. Oliver and Shapiro, *Black Wealth/White Wealth,* 193.

11. Ahiarah, "Black Americans' Business Ownership Factors," 33.

6. Continuum of Black Business Success: Why Some Firms Succeed While Others Fail

1. In this book I report unstandardized regression coefficients rather than standardized values. Here, I adopt the methodological approach advocated by Gary King in "How Not to Lie with Statistics: Avoiding Common Mistakes in Quantitative Political Science," *American Journal of Political Science* 30 (1985): 672. Here, King points out that standardized coefficients are harder to interpret and do not necessarily provide information that could help to compare the effects from different explanatory variables. Moreover, standardized coefficients may provide unreliable or misleading information.

7. Biographical Sketches of African American Entrepreneurs

1. Fraser, interview.

2. T. S. Peric, "Overcoming Bad Moves: How a Comeback Is Possible, Even after a Knockdown," *Managing Small Business: Ideas for Small Business Success* 1, no. 2 (1999): 4.

3. Madison, interview.

4. Carlo Wolff, "Madison's Avenue" *(Case Western Reserve University) Alumni Review* 9, no. 2 (Feb. 1997): 39, 42–45.

5. Ibid.

6. Ibid.

7. Deborah Thigpen Waller, interview by author, Sept 15, 2000, Twinsburg, Ohio.

8. Ozanne, interview.

9. Ralph W. Johnson, telephone interview by author, Apr. 30, 1991.

10. Ibid.

11. Dominic Ozanne, e-mail, Jan, 18, 2002.

12. Dr. Oscar Saffold, interview by author, spring 2000.

13. Troy Flint, "Ohio Insurance Department Sues Personal Physician Care," *Cleveland Plain Dealer,* Mar. 27, 1999, 2C.

14. Brian Hall, interview by author, Jan. 4, 2000, Cleveland, Ohio.

15. Shelton Moore, interview by author, Dec. 11, 1999, Cleveland Ohio, and Jan. 20, 2002, Beachwood, Ohio.

8. Conclusions and Public Policy Recommendations

1. Claudia J. Coulton and Julian Chow, "The Impact of Poverty on Cleveland Neighborhoods," in *Cleveland: A Metropolitan Reader,* 212.

2. Lewis Mumford Center, The University at Albany (State University of New York), "Ethnic Diversity Grows, Neighborhood Integration Lags Behind," www.albany.edu/mumford/census, accessed Jan. 22, 2002.

3. "The State of Black Business," *Black Enterprise* 26, no. 4 (Nov. 1, 1995): 77.

4. Robert W. Fairlie, *Ethnic and Racial Entrepreneurship: A Study of Historical and Contemporary Differences* (New York: Garland Publishing, 1996), 11, 55.

5. "The Key to Black Wealth: Ownership," *Black Enterprise* 24, no. 12 (July 1994): 24.

APPENDIX B

1. *Standard Industrial Classification Manual* (Washington, D.C.: Office of Management and Budget, 1987), 61, 67, 313, 353.

2. Bates, *Banking on Black Enterprise,* 14, 41; Timothy Bates, *Race, Self-Employment, and Upward Mobility,* 22; Ando, "Capital Issues."

3. Fratoe, "Rural Minority Business Development."

4. Ibid.

5. Fratoe, "Social Capital, 47; Ando, "Capital Issues."

6. Bates, *Banking on Black Enterprise,* 40–44; House, "African-American Businesses," 3, 7; Fratoe, "Social Capital," 39–42; Ando, "Capital Issues," 77–80.

7. Bates, *Banking on Black Enterprise,* 54.

8. Chen and Cole, "The Myths, Facts, and Theories"; Fratoe, "Social Capital"; Green and Pryde, *Black Entrepreneurship in America,* 70–75.

9. Chen, "Minority Business Development."

10. Chen and Cole, "The Myths, Facts, and Theories," 111–21; Fratoe, "Social Capital"; Fratoe, "Rural Minority Business Development," 47.

11. Fratoe, "Social Capital," 41; Boston, *Affirmative Action and Bleck Entrepreneurship,* 12–32; Bates, *Banking on Black Enterprise,* 93–100.

Selected Bibliography

Achkar, Alon. "Cleveland Population Drops Below 500,000." *Cleveland Plain Dealer,* Mar. 17, 2001, 1, 8A.

"Heroism Has No Color Line, Local Men Prove," *Cleveland Advocate,* July 29, 1916.

Ahiarah, Sol. "Black Americans' Business Ownership Factors: A Theoretical Perspective." *The Review of Black Political Economy* 22, no. 2 (Fall 1993): 15–39.

Ahoud, John. "Characteristics of Successful Entrepreneurs." *Personnel Psychology* 24 (1971): 141–53.

Aldrich, Howard P., J. Jones, and D. McEnvoy. "Ethnic Advantage and Minority Business Development." In *Ethnic Communities for Business: Strategies for Economic Survival,* edited by R. Ward and R. Jenkins, 184, 189–210. Cambridge: Cambridge University Press, 1984.

Aldrich, Howard P., and Roger Waldinger. "Ethnicity and Entrepreneurship." *The Review of Sociology* 16 (1990): 111–35.

Anderson, Claud. *Black Labor, White Wealth: The Search for Power and Economic Justice.* Edgewood, Md.: Duncan and Duncan, 1994.

Ando, Faith H. "Capital Issues and the Minority-Owned Business." *The Review of Black Political Economy* (Spring 1988): 77–109.

Barker, Lucius J., Mack H. Jones, and Catherine Tate. *African Americans and the American Political System.* 3d ed. Upper Saddle River, N.J.: Prentice Hall, 1999.

Bates, Timothy. *An Analysis of Income Differentials Among Self-Employed Minorities.* Los Angeles: Center for Afro-American Studies, June 1988.

———. "An Econometric Analysis of Lending to Black Businesses." *The Review of Economics and Statistics* (1973): 272–83.

———. *Banking on Black Enterprise: The Potential of Emerging Firms for Revitalizing Urban Economies.* Washington, D.C.: Joint Center for Political and Economic Studies, 1993.

———. "The Changing Nature of Minority Businesses: A Comparative Analysis of Asian Non-Minority and Black-Owned Businesses." *The Review of Black Political Economy* 18, no. 1 (Fall 1989).

———. "Characteristics of Minorities Who Are Entering Self-Employment." *The Review of Black Political Economy* (Fall 1986): 31–49.

———. "Do Black-Owned Businesses Employ Minority Workers? New Evidence." *The Review of Black Political Economy* (Spring 1988): 51–64.

———. "Impact of Preferential Procurement Policies on Minority-Owned Businesses." *The Review of Black Political Economy* (Summer 1985): 51–65.

———. *Major Studies of Minority Business: A Bibliographic Review*. Washington, D.C.: Joint Center for Political and Economic Studies Press, 1993.

———. "Political Economy of Urban Poverty in the 21st Century: How Progress and Public Policy Generate Rising Poverty." *The Review of Black Political Economy* 24, no. 2/3 (Fall 1995/ Winter 1996): 111–21.

———. *Race, Self-Employment and Upward Mobility: An Elusive American Dream*. Baltimore: Johns Hopkins University Press, 1997.

———. "Self-Employed Minorities: Traits and Trends." *The Review of Black Political Economy* (Spring 1988): 51–60.

Bates, Timothy, and William Bradford. *Financing Black Economic Development*. New York: Academic Press, 1979.

Bates, Timothy, and Darrell L. Williams. "Racial Politics: Does It Pay." *Social Science Quarterly* 74, no. 3 (Sept. 1993): 507–22.

Beavers, D. L. "The Phillis Wheatley Association." *Renaissance Magazine* (Feb. 1991): 7–9.

———. "Somebody, Somewhere Wants Your Photograph," *Legacy* (Feb.–Mar. 1995): 42–45.

Bennett, David. "Disparity Study Widens in Scope." *Crain's Cleveland Business*, Jan. 8, 2001.

Black, Samuel. Curator, African American Archives, Western Reserve Historical Society. Interview by author, Dec. 12, 1999.

Borjas, George G. "Ethnic Capital and Intergenerational Mobility." *Quarterly Journal of Economics* 107, no. 1 (Feb. 1992): 123–50.

———. "Ethnicity, Neighborhoods, and Human Capital Externalities." *The American Economic Review* 85, no. 3 (1995): 365–390.

———. "The Self-Employment Experiences of Immigrants." *The Journal of Human Resources* 21 (1986): 485–506.

Boston, Thomas D. *Affirmative Action and Black Entrepreneurship*. London: Routledge, 1999.

Boston, Thomas D., and Catherine L. Ross. "Editors' Introduction." *The Review of Black Political Economy* (Fall/Winter 1996).

Boyd, Robert. "Black and Asian Self-Employment in Large Metropolitan Areas: A Comparative Analysis." *Social Problems* 37 (1990): 258–74.

Brewer, Eric J. "Entrepreneurs Build with Vision," *Renaissance Magazine* (Feb. 1989): 20–22.

———. "The Struggle: Gaining Political Power." *Renaissance Magazine* (Feb. 1989): 5–7.

Brimmer, Andrew F. "Income, Wealth, and Investment Behavior in the Black Community." *The American Economic Review* 78, no. 2 (1988): 151–55.

———. "Trends, Prospects, and Strategies for Black Economic Progress." *The Review of Black Political Economy* 14 (Spring 1986).

Burt, R. S. "The Contingent Value of Social Capital," *Administrative Science Quarterly* 42 (1997): 339–65.

Burton, David J. "An Innovative Approach to African-American Business Development." *Business and Economic Review* 41, no. 4 (July 1995): 24–26.

———. "Non-Traditional Business Education for Black Entrepreneurs: Observations from a Successful Program." *Journal of Small Business Management* 28, no. 2 (1990): 30–36.

Bustamante, John, Founder of First Bank, Inc. Interview by author, Apr. 22, 2001.

Butler, John Sibley. *Entrepreneurship and Self-Help Among Americans: A Reconsideration of Race and Economics*. Albany: State University of New York Press, 1991.

————. "Entrepreneurship and the Advantages of the Inner City: How to Augment the Porter Thesis." *The Review of Black Political Economy* 24, no. 2/3 (Fall 1995/Winter 1996): 39–49.

Caplovitz, David. *The Merchants of Harlem: A Study of Small Business in a Black Community.* Beverly Hills: Sage Publications, 1973.

Charles Waddell Chesnutt Collection. African American Archives, Microfilm Collection, Western Reserve Historical Society.

Chen, Gavin M. "Minority Business Development: Where Do We Go From Here?" *The Review of Black Political Economy* 22, no. 2 (Fall 1993): 5–10.

Chen, Gavin M., and John A. Cole. "The Myths, Facts, and Theories of Ethnic, Small-Scale Enterprise Financing." *The Review of Black Political Economy* 16, nos. 1–2 (Spring 1988): 111–23.

Chow, Julian. "The City of Cleveland in the Eighties: A Decade of Multifaceted Changes." Cleveland, Center for Urban Poverty and Social Change, Mandel School of Applied Social Sciences, Case Western Reserve University, Apr. 1992.

Cirillo, Patricia J. "Business Environment of Minority Business Owners in Cleveland." Cleveland Minority Economic Opportunity Center, Oct. 1993.

City of Cleveland Empowerment Zone Performance Report, 1995–1996, Cleveland Supplemental Empowerment Zone Executive Summary. <www.hud.gov/cpd/ezec/clohperf.html>. Accessed Oct. 6, 2000.

Coleman, J. S. "Social Capital in the Creation of Human Capital," *American Journal of Sociology* 94 (1988 Supplement): S95–S120.

Cooper, Ernest C., and Roger Mitton. "The Negro in Cleveland, 1950–1963: An Analysis of the Society and Economic Characteristics of the Negro Population." Cleveland Research Department, Cleveland Urban League, June 1964.

Coulton, Claudia J., Julian Chow, Edward C. Chong, and Marilyn Su. "Geographic Concentration of Affluence and Poverty in 100 Metropolitan Areas, 1990. *Urban Affairs Review* 32, no. 2 (Nov. 1996): 182–210.

Coulton, Claudia J., Julian Chow, and Shanta Pandey. "An Analysis of Poverty and Related Conditions in Cleveland Area Neighborhoods." *Technical Report.* Cleveland, Ohio: Center for Urban Poverty and Social Change, Mandel School of Applied Social Sciences, Case Western Reserve University, Jan. 1990.

Davis, Angela Y. *Women, Race and Class.* New York: Vintage Books, 1981.

Davis, Russell H. "Civil Rights in Cleveland 1912 through 1961." In *An Account of the Cleveland Branch National Association for the Advancement of Colored People.* Cleveland: Cleveland Branch National Association for the Advancement of Colored People, 1973.

————. *The Negro in Cleveland's Political Life.* Cleveland: Western Reserve Historical Society, 1966.

————. *Memorable Negroes in Cleveland's Past.* Cleveland: Western Reserve Historical Society, 1969.

Denes, Thomas A. "Do Small Business Set-Asides Increase the Cost of Government Contracting?" *Public Administration Review* 57, no. 5 (Sept./Oct. 1997): 441–44.

DuBois, W. E. B. *Black Reconstruction in America, 1860–1880.* New York: Simon and Schuster, 1935.

————. *The Souls of Black Folk*. New York: Dover Publications, 1994.

Dymski, Gary A. "Business Strategy and Access to Capital in Inner City Revitalization." *The Review of Black Political Economy* 24, no. 2/3 (Fall 1995/Winter 1996).

Economic Census, 1997. Survey of Minority-Owned Business Enterprises, Company Statistics Series. Washington, D.C.: U.S. Census Bureau, Department of Commerce, Mar. 2001.

Erickcek, George. "The Role of Small Business: A Tale of Two Cities." Kalamazoo, Mich., Employment Research, W. E. Upjohn Institute for Employment Research (Fall 1997): 1–4.

Fainstein, Susan S., and Mia Gray. "Economic Development Strategies for the Inner City: The Need for Governmental Intervention." *The Review of Black Political Economy* 24, no. 2/3 (Fall 1995/Winter 1996): 29–38.

Fairlie, Robert W. *Ethnic and Racial Entrepreneurship: A Study of Historical and Contemporary Differences*. New York: Garland Publishing, 1996.

First Intercity BancCorporation, First Bank National Association, Cleveland. *Annual Report*, 1984.

Flint, Troy. "Ohio Insurance Department Sues Personal Physician Care." *Cleveland Plain Dealer*, Mar. 27, 1999, 2C.

Forbes, George, President of the Cleveland chapter of the NAACP. Interview by author, Nov. 3, 1999.

Fraser, George, CEO of Success Source, Ltd. Interview by author, Jan. 7, 2000.

Fratoe, Frank A. "Rural Minority Business Development." *The Review of Black Political Economy* 22, no. 2 (Fall 1993): 41–72.

————. "Social Capital of Black Business Owners." *The Review of Black Political Economy* 16, nos. 1–2 (Spring 1988): 33–50.

————. "A Sociological Analysis of Minority Business." *The Review of Black Political Economy* 14 (Fall 1986): 5–29.

Freeman, Louise D. "Outlook Bright: Cleveland's Future Outlook League Carried Light into the Dark Days of the Depression with Nonviolent Tactics that Won Jobs for City's Blacks." *Renaissance Magazine* (Feb. 14, 1990): 14–17.

Ganson Rose, William. *Cleveland: The Making of a City*. Kent, Ohio: Kent State University Press, 1990.

Garraty, John A., ed. *The Barber and the Historian: The Correspondence of George A. Meyers and James Ford Rhodes, 1910–1923*. Columbus: Ohio Historical Society, 1956.

Glover, Glenda. "Enterprise Zones: Incentives Are Not Attracting Minority Firms." *The Review of Black Political Economy* (Summer 1993): 73–99.

Garrett Morgan Collection, African American Archives, Microfilm Collection, Western Reserve Historical Society.

The Greater Cleveland Fact Book. Cleveland: Greater Cleveland Growth Association, Research Department, n.d.

Green, Shelley, and Paul Pryde, *Black Entrepreneurship in America*. London: Transaction Publishers, 1990.

Greer, Bart. "Passing the Reins of Power." *Renaissance Magazine* (Feb. 1991): 18–20.

Gunn, Elizabeth M. "The Growth of Enterprise Zones: A Policy Transformation." *Policy Studies Journal* 21, no. 3 (1993): 432–49.

Haber, Louis. *Black Pioneers of Science and Invention*. New York: Harcourt, Brace, 1970.

Hacker, Andrew. *Two Nations, Black and White: Separate, Hostile, Unequal.* New York: Ballantine Books, 1995.

Hall, Brian, CEO of Industrial Transport. Interview by author, Jan. 4, 2000.

Hallett, Joe. "Ohio's Race-Based Contracts 'Unlawful': Need Should Count for More than Ethnicity, Says Magistrate." *Cleveland Plain Dealer,* Oct. 31, 1996.

Handy, John W. *An Analysis of Black Business Enterprises.* New York: Garland Publishing, 1989.

Heywood, John S. "Market Structure and the Pattern of Black-Owned Firms." *The Review of Black Political Economy* (Spring 1988): 65–76.

Holdren, Don P. "Perspectives in Minority Business." *The Review of Black Political Economy* 22, no. 2 (Fall 1993): 11–14.

Hornaday, Robert W., and Bennie H. Nunnally. "Problems Facing Black-Owned Businesses." *Business Forum* (Fall 1987): 34–37.

Hornor, Edith R., ed. *Almanac of the 50 States: Basic Data Profiles with Comparative Tables.* Burlington, Vt.: Information Publications, 1998.

House, Bessie. "African-American Businesses, Economic Development, and the Puzzle of Success: A Pilot Study of Cleveland, Ohio." Executive Summary and Final Report for the Ohio Urban University Program. Kent State University, Oct. 1997.

House, Bessie, and Ilan Alon. "An Exploratory Analysis of Factors Which Promote Black Business Success: A Pilot Study of Cleveland, Ohio." *Ohio Journal of Economics and Politics* no. 1 (1997): 21–27.

House-Midamba, Bessie, and Felix K. Ekechi, eds. *African Market Women and Economic Power: The Role of Women in African Economic Development.* Westport, Conn.: Greenwood Press, 1995.

Jackson, Jesse L., Sr. "Expanding the Market Place: Inclusion, the Key to Economic Growth." Proceedings of the 1998 Wall Street Project Conference. Windows on the World. New York, New York, Jan. 1998, 14–16. Rainbow/Push Coalition, Wall Street Project. <www.rainbowpush.org> Accessed Jan. 11, 2002.

Johnson, Alan. "Rejection of Set-Aside Law Stands: High Court Refuses to Hear Ohio Case." *Columbus Dispatch,* Feb. 21, 2001, 1, A2.

Johnson, Ralph, Executive, Turner Corporation. Interview by author, Apr. 7, 2001.

Jones, Albert C. "Commissioners Shut Out Minority Bidders, Repeal 1993 Equal Opportunity Program." *Cleveland Call and Post,* Jan. 20–26, 2000, 1, 2A.

Keating, W. Dennis, Norman Krumholz, and David C. Perry, eds. *Cleveland: A Metropolitan Reader.* Kent, Ohio: Kent State University Press, 1995.

Kelly, Patricia A. "Glenville Revisited." *Renaissance Magazine* (Feb. 1991): 12–15.

"The Key to Black Wealth: Ownership." *Black Enterprise* 24, no. 12 (July 1994): 24.

King, Gary. "How Not to Lie with Statistics: Avoiding Common Mistakes in Quantitative Political Science." *American Journal of Political Science* 30 (1985): 672.

Kirksey, Ron. "Professor Receives Cleveland Foundation Grant for African-American Entrepreneurs Program." *Cleveland Call and Post,* Dec. 16–22, 1999, 7C.

Kotkin, Joel. *Tribes: How Race, Religion and Identity Determine Success in the New Global Economy.* New York: Random House, 1992.

Kusmer, Kenneth L. *A Ghetto Takes Shape: Black Cleveland, 1870–1930.* Urbana: University of Illinois Press, 1976.

Lewis Mumford Center, University at Albany (State University of New York). "Ethnic Diversity Grows, Neighborhood Integration Lags Behind." <*www.albany.edu.mumford/census*> Accessed Jan. 22, 2002.

Lewis Polk, Anita. "World Class Architect Bob Madison, FAIA. *Crusader: The Voice of the African-American Community* 8, no. 224 (Aug. 31, Sept. 13, 2000): 1, 3.

Light, Ivan. *Business and Welfare Among Chinese, Japanese, and Blacks: Ethnic Enterprise in America*. Berkeley: University of California Press, 1972.

Livingston, Sandra, and Zach Schiller. "Glass Ceiling Cracks but Barely: Few Executives Are Minorities, Survey Shows." *Cleveland Plain Dealer*, Oct. 3, 1999, 1, 15A.

Lowry, H. J. "Vocational Opportunities for Negroes in Cleveland." National Youth Administration of Ohio. No. 1 (Mar. 1938).

Madison, Robert P., CEO, Robert P. Madison, International. Interview by author, Aug. 2, 2000.

McKnight, Keith. "Ohio's Big Cities Losing Residents." *Akron Beacon Journal*, Oct. 21, 2000).

Mann, Philip H. "Nontraditional Business Education for Black Entrepreneurs: Observations from a Successful Program." *Journal of Small Business Management* 28, no. 2 (1990): 30–36.

Marable, Manning. *How Capitalism Underdeveloped Black America: Problems in Race, Political Economy and Society*. Boston: South End Press, 1988.

"Mayor Announces 'Changes' for Minority Business." *Crusader Urban News*, Jan. 7, 1995, 5.

Mehta, Stephanie N. "Affirmative Action Supporters Face Divisive Problem: Many Minority Entrepreneurs Now Question Preferences on Contracts." *Black Entrepreneurship in America: A Selection of Articles from the Pages of the Wall Street Journal*. New York: Dow Jones & Company, *Wall Street Journal*, 1994–95.

Mergenhagen, Paula. "Black-Owned Businesses." *American Demographics* 18, no. 6 (June 1996): 24–33.

Miller, Carol Poh, and Robert A. Wheeler. *Cleveland: A Concise History, 1796–1990*. Bloomington: Indiana University Press, 1990.

Mongkuo, Maurice Y., and William J. Pammer Jr. "The Impact of Targeted Partnership Grants on Minority Employment." *The Review of Black Political Economy* (Winter 1994): 19–29.

Moore, Shelton, partner, The Nelson Group. Interview by author, Dec. 11, 1999.

Morton, Marian J. *Defining Women's Sphere*. Cleveland: Case Western Reserve University, 1995.

Nelson, William E., Jr. "Cleveland: The Evolution of Black Political Power." Unpublished paper.

———. "Cleveland: The Rise and Fall of New Black Politics." In *The New Black Politics: The Search for Political Power*, ed. Michael B. Preston, Lenneal J. Henderson Jr., and Paul Puryear. 2d ed. New York: Longman, 1987.

Nolan, John, "Appeals Court Rejects Ohio's Contract Program for Minorities," *Cleveland Call and Post*, June 8, 2000.

Office of Advocacy. *Minorities in Business*. Washington, D.C.: U.S. Small Business Administration, 1999.

"Ohio Women." Women's Services Division, Ohio Bureau of Employment Services. 1st ed. 1978.

Oldscheider, Calvin, and Francis Cohrin. "Ethnic Continuity and the Process of Self-Employment." *Ethnicity* 7 (Sept. 1980): 256–78.

Oliver, Melvin L., and Thomas M. Shapiro. *Black Wealth/White Wealth: A New Perspective on Racial Inequality*. New York: Routledge, 1997.

Ozanne, Leroy, CEO of Ozanne Construction Company. Interview by author, Aug. 1, 2000.

Peric, T. S. "Overcoming Bad Moves: How A Comeback Is Possible, Even After A Knockdown." *Managing Small Business* 1, no. 2 (1999): 4–5.

Perkins, Olivera. "If the Walls Could Tell Stories." *Cleveland Plain Dealer*, Feb. 22, 2001, 1B, 10B.

Peoples, James. "Potential Welfare Gains from Improving Economic Conditions in the Inner City." *The Review of Black Political Economy* (Fall/Winter 1996): 207–12.

Phillips, Kimberly L. *Alabama North: African-American Migrants, Community, and Working Class Activism in Cleveland, 1915–45*. Urbana: University of Illinois Press, 1999.

"The Photography of Allen E. Cole." Calendar. African American Archives, Western Reserve Historical Society.

Pohlman, Marcus D. *Black Politics in Conservative America*. 2d ed. New York: Longman, 1999.

Porter, Michael E. "The Competitive Advantage of the Inner City." *Harvard Business Review* (May–June 1995): 55–71.

Rice, Mitchell F. "State and Local Government Set-Aside Programs, Disparity Studies, and Minority Business Development in the Post-Croson Era." *Journal of Urban Affairs* 15, no. 6 (1993): 529–53.

Saffold, Oscar, CEO of Metropolitan Dermatology. Interview by author, spring 2000.

Simms, Margaret, ed. *Economic Perspectives on Affirmative Action*. Washington, D.C.: Joint Center for Political and Economic Studies, 1995.

Simms, Margaret C., and Winston J. Allen. "Is the Inner City Competitive?" *The Review of Black Political Economy* (Fall/Winter, 1996): 213–22.

Sonfield, Matthew C. "An Attitudinal Comparison of Black and White Small Businessmen." *American Journal of Small Business* 2 (Jan. 1982): 38–45.

Sowell, Thomas. *The Economics and Politics of Race: An International Perspective*. New York: Quill, 1983.

Stephens, Scott, and Joe Frolik. "Few Want Schools in White's Hands." *Cleveland Plain Dealer*, May 29, 2000, 1, 9A.

Stevens, Robert. "Measuring Minority Business Success and Failure." *The Review of Black Political Economy* 12 (Spring 1984): 71–84.

Stokes, Carl B. *Promises of Power: A Political Autobiography*. New York: Simon and Schuster, 1973.

"The Stokes Story." *Cleveland Plain Dealer*, Sept. 23, 1973, 1–1A.

Tebben, Janet, and Mark Vosburgh. "Cleveland Schools Score Lowest in State." *Cleveland Plain Dealer*, Dec. 23, 1999, 1; 8A.

Thompson, Cliff. *Charles Chesnutt*. New York: Chelsea House Publishers, 1992.

"Tunnel Blast Kills 21, Injures 9, City, County, U.S. Probe Disaster." *Cleveland Plain Dealer*, July 1916.

U.S. Census Bureau. *Statistical Abstract of the United States: 1999*. 119th ed. Washington, D.C., 1999.

———. *Statistical Abstract of the United States: 1997*. Washington, D.C., 1997.

————. *1997 Economic Census: A Survey of Minority-Owned Business Enterprises.* Washington, D.C., 1997.

Van Tassel, David D., and John J. Grabowski, eds. *The Encyclopedia of Cleveland History.* Bloomington: Indiana University Press, in association with Case Western Reserve University and the Western Reserve Historical Society, 1996.

Walker, Juliet E. K. *The History of Black Business in America: Capitalism, Race, Entrepreneurship.* New York: Macmillan, 1998.

Walker, William O. "Down the Road: It Takes More than Money to Run a Business." *Cleveland Call and Post,* Mar. 9, 1974, 2B.

Waller, Deborah Thigpen, President of Thigpen ADsociates. Interview by author, Sept., 15, 2000.

Ward, Alvin. "Black Bank Opens Downtown." *Cleveland Call and Post,* June 29, 1974.

Weems, Robert E., Jr. *Desegregating the Dollar: African American Consumerism in the 20th Century.* New York: New York University Press, 1998.

"Welcome First Bank and Trust, Co." *Cleveland Call and Post,* July 6, 1974, 2B, 14B.

Wells, Sandra J. *Women Entrepreneurs: Developing Leadership for Success.* New York: Garland Publishers, 1988.

"We Won: Call and Post Is One of the Best." *Cleveland Call and Post,* June 29–July 5, 2000, 1, 2A.

Whipple Green, Howard. "Population Characteristics by Census Tracts." *Cleveland, Ohio,* 1930. Cleveland: Plain Dealer Publishing Company, 1931.

White, George, Federal Judge appointed during the Jimmy Carter administration, also founder of First Club of Cleveland, Inc. Interview by author, Apr. 22, 2001.

Wilson, William Julius. *The Declining Significance of Race: Black and Changing American Institutions.* Chicago: University of Chicago Press, 1980.

————. *When Work Disappears: The World of the New Urban Poor.* New York: Alfred A. Knopf, 1997.

Wolff, Carlo. "Madison's Avenue." *Case Western Reserve University Alumni Review* 9, no. 2 (Feb. 1997): 39, 42–45.

Woodard, Michael D. *Black Entrepreneurs in America: Stories of Struggle and Success.* New Brunswick, N.J.: Rutgers University Press, 1997.

Woolf, Arthur G. "Market Structure and Minority Presence: Black-Owned Firms in Manufacturing." *The Review of Black Political Economy* (Spring 1986): 79–89.

Index

Affirmative action, 46, 54, 56. *See also* Business set-aside programs

African Americans: economic detour and, 3, 151–52; economic position of, 2, 15, 17, 149, 152; education and, 6, 14, 16, 71, 149; entrepreneurial success of, 17, 22–23, 75–76, 148; studies of, 3–4, 5–10; great migration of, 32–33, 184n.42; self-employed, 1, 14, 151–52 (*see also* Entrepreneurs); social capital and, 5–6; World War II and, 43. *See also* Black-owned business; Business success, model of; Female-owned business

Ahiarah, Sol, 79

Alon, Ilan, 9

Anderson, Claud, 37

Ando, Faith, 6, 173, 174

Banks. *See* Financial institutions

Barber industry, 14, 18–21

Barker, Lucius J., xvii

Bates, Timothy, xiv, 3–4, 7, 55, 71, 173, 174

Birch, David, xiv

Black, Samuel, xv, 18–19, 29, 40, 41; on minority access to capital, 33; on minority business philanthropy, 38

Black-owned business, xvi, 23, 68, 71, 148, 159–60, 179n.1; business debt and, 74; capital and, 73, 77, 151, 152; customer base for, 79, 156–57; early twentieth century, 23, 25, 33, 41–43; economic development from, 150–51; emerging, 11; failure of, xv, 87, 154–55, 156–57; great migration and, 32; indicator variables for, 85–86; job formation and, 7, 14, 151; majority-owned business contrasted to, 68–71, 72–74, 76–80, 151; methodology for comparative study of, 166–

77; model of success for, 81–92, 152–54; nineteenth century, 14, 17, 18–20; operationalized variables for, 83, 172–77; profits from, 74, 75, 159; revenue from, 151. *See also* Business owners; Entrepreneurs; Funeral homes; Manufacturing; Newspaper business; Real estate

Blue, Welcome T., 22, 23

Brown, John, 14–15

Bryant, Eliza, 36

Business assistance programs, 54–56, 57–58, 65–66, 157–58; proposed initiatives for, 162–64

Business expansion, 156

Business failure, xv, 87, 154–55, 156–57; study methodology for, 170–71

Business location, 4, 78, 87, 172, 173

Business owners, xvi, 68; business debt and, 74; economic success and, 3–4, 6, 9, 71, 80; employment opportunities and, 76–77; family support of, 75, 76–77; manufacturing and, 7–8 (*see also* Manufacturing); mentors and, 75; methodology for comparative study of, 166–69, 170–75, 176, 177; profits for, 74, 75; social capital and, 5–6; years in business of, 70, 74, 153. *See also* Entrepreneurs

Business philanthropy, 37–38, 77, 118, 159; investment fund recommendation for, 163–64. *See also* Social organizations

Business plans, 87, 155, 156; access to capital and, 155

Business set-aside programs, 49, 51, 54–59, 68–69, 154, 158; entrepreneurs experience with, 80, 176–77; research recommendations regarding, 161. *See also* Madison, Robert P.

Business success: business debt and, 74, 84; business maturation and, 3, 6; capital and, 3, 4, 6,